RALPH GRIZZLE'S

ULTIMATE
RIVER CRUISING
HANDBOOK

BY RIVER, BY SEA
Only with Viking

Destination focused.

Award-winning small ships.

Serene Scandinavian spaces.

Cultural enrichment from ship to shore.

The Thinking Person's Cruise.®

Printed/Produced in the United States of America

First Printing/Production, 2018

Avid Travel Media Inc

PO Box 2807

Asheville, North Carolina 28802

www.rivercruiseadvisor.com

Cover photo:

AmaLyra, docked in Bratislava on the Danube,

courtesy of AmaWaterways

TABLE OF CONTENTS

FOREWORD

Though I had written about ocean cruising since the early 1990s, it wasn't until 2006 that I discovered river cruising. It was that year, now more than a decade ago, that I did my first river cruise. During October, I sailed eyes wide open along the Rhine and Moselle rivers on Peter Deilmann's Heidelberg. The ship's classic decor, the gorgeous landscape and the excitement of exploring Europe in such a pleasant way enchanted me to no end.

Peter Deilmann River Cruises went bankrupt during the financial crisis of the last decade, but Heidelberg still operates, and so, of course, do the Rhine and Moselle rivers. What beauties those waterways are, especially the Moselle, a ribbon of river coursing through vineyard-stitched hills dotted with castles.

How can you experience such beauty and the slow pace of river cruising and the cozy confines of the ship and not fall in love with it? The short answer: You can't. And, in fact, a dozen years later my love affair with river cruising continues.

Today, I dedicate a good portion of my waking hours to writing about river cruising. My website rivercruiseadvisor.com has grown so large that even I don't know all that is in it. I do know that there are more than 2,000 posts and pages in addition to dozens of videos and thousands of photographs. The abundance of content, and the challenge of organizing it, is part of the reason for this book.

Launched in 2009, River Cruise Advisor has grown too large for me to manage alone. Thankfully, I have a number of friends and colleagues who have pitched in to help. I'm taking this opportunity to thank them publicly for their work on River Cruise Advisor and this book.

Thanks to my friend and colleague Aaron Saunders for his continuing contributions. Shouts out to Chris Stanley and to Lynne Harty for their excellent work behind their cameras and at their editing desks to produce videos for my sites. Thanks to Tamera Trexler, who spent countless hours compiling the pricing charts that you'll find at the back of this book. Thanks also to researcher and writer Lauri Wakefield for her contributions. A special thanks to Victoria Veilleux for the hours, days and weeks she spent compiling this book, and also to my daughter Britton Frost for curating press releases for your consumption on the site. Thanks to the talented designers, including Marcy McGuire, who made it possible for this book to bridge the gap between digital and print, and to Carolina Loreto for her lovely cover design.

And thanks to all of my friends in the river cruise industry, the owners of river cruise companies who are now profiting from the enormous emotional and financial risks they took. Some weren't altogether sure they would survive the dark days of the financial crisis, and as noted earlier, some did not.

Thanks to those who work on the ships: the hotel managers and cruise managers, the dining room and hotel staffs, and the captains and sailors. Thanks to the ground staff that strives to make our time ashore enjoyable and memorable. Thanks to the more than 15,000 River Cruise Advisor subscribers. You have made it possible for me to run my site and produce this book.

And thanks most of all to the rivers for their timeless and enduring beauty. If you haven't experienced river cruising yet, I urge you to do so. Let the rivers enchant you, as they did for me more than a decade ago and continue to do so even now.

Ralph Grizzle, April 3, 2018, *sailing on the Danube between Vienna and Budapest*

In 2006 on Peter Deilmann's Heidelberg

1

Chapter
ONE

QUESTIONABLE BEHAVIOR?

Ralph Grizzle in Pinhao, Portugal, on a Douro River cruise.

QUESTIONABLE BEHAVIOR?

Choosing a river cruise can be a source of consternation, confusion and frustration. In Europe alone there are more than two dozen navigable rivers and canals. Add the confluence of companies offering seemingly similar experiences and you might just end up feeling as though you're going upriver without a paddle.

That's where I come in. I'm here to help you navigate the ever-changing currents that define river cruising today. As many of you might already know, I produce tons of content for my sites avidcruiser.com and rivercruiseadvisor.com to help travelers make informed cruise vacation decisions. I decided to create a book to streamline this information even further, devising a step-by-step guide to selecting the right river cruise for you. Believe me, it is a process. There are so many personal factors that go into making river cruise vacation decisions. What I think is incredible might be a total miss for you.

But let's face it, sitting down to read one river cruise review after another isn't exactly entertaining. Even I think ship descriptions start to sound exactly the same and I've been on the ships. That's why, in addition to my advice for selecting a cruise vacation, I've included a collection of voyage travelogues, highlighting aspects of a particular vessel, staff encounters, and of course amazing destinations in a more narrative style than your run-of-the mill cruise guide.

My hope is that you'll feel as though you're traveling along with me, all the while learning something about river cruising the waterways of Europe. Throughout this book, we'll admire the mighty castles along the Rhine, marvel at the marquee cities along the Danube, gaze in wonder at the vertical landscapes flanking the Moselle and the Douro, set off on the Seine within sight of the Eiffel Tower, breathe in the fragrance of lavender in Provence while cruising the Rhône, and bundle up for winter during Christmas Markets river cruises. Doesn't it all sound wonderful? It is.

Fans of my websites often tell me how much they appreciate the detailed photos and videos, so this book would be remiss without including a fair share of those too. Hopefully it will further provide you with a sense of traveling vicariously with me. In fact, being able to provide a visual showcase of these experiences is one reason I chose to publish a digital version of my book. Not to mention that a digital format allows for me to quickly deliver information to you about an ever-changing industry on an annual basis, unbound by the time constraints of getting printed books from my computer to your bookshelves. As a concession for those who insist on print, I also have made available a print on demand version of this book, though it will lack the interactive features.

Having focused my travel writing career on the cruise industry for nearly three decades, I've taken hundreds of cruises, and in the past ten-plus years, added more than 50 river cruises to my proverbial travel bucket. Personal preferences aside, what I can tell you is that I have garnered a lot of insights that can help you understand the many options available to you. Within these pages I share with you those that I hold in highest regard.

Clearly, I adore this segment of the travel industry and am grateful for each day that I spend on the rivers in Europe. But more importantly, I can take what I've learned and pass it along to you to ensure your time and money are wisely spent.

But just how does one start to peel back the layers of what seems to be an upstream endeavor at first glance? I decided to apply a journalistic principle that I had to strictly abide in college: "The 5 Ws and one H." I bet that you know where I'm going with this; it's the Why, What, Where, When, Which, Who and How. (Okay, that's 6 Ws, but who's counting? I like to go the extra nautical mile.) If you answer these questions and take into consideration the many aspects that add up to a memorable river cruise, you won't be disappointed.

As someone who has traveled all of my life, I can say without reservation that river cruising is one of the most rewarding ways to experience the heart of Europe.

Before we get started, though, I thought I'd give you a little sense about who I am as a traveler so that you have it as basis of comparison. Perhaps the best way to do this is tell you how I got forever hooked on travel in the first place. Prior to getting a bachelor of arts in journalism from the University of North Carolina at Chapel Hill at the age of 32, I set off on what I like to refer to as my "sabbatical decade." From 1980 through 1990, I bicycled across America, pedaled through Europe and island-hopped the South Pacific. After backpacking through Bali, busing through Java, hopping a boat to Singapore and crossing Malaysia to Thailand, I flew into Burma, tramped to Dhaka and endured a 32-hour train ride from calamitous Calcutta to bustling Bombay. Having my fill of the exotic East, I hopped a plane for Europe, landing in Greece and making my way to Switzerland before returning home to North Carolina. Circumnavigating the globe would take me full-circle, both literally and figuratively, because I would ultimately pursue a career in travel writing, yet still biking, cruising and backpacking across Europe. Only now, those activities are usually followed by fine dining and wine courses back on a ship.

While I still possess a spirit of adventure that craves authentic experiences, staying active is paramount, which is why I enjoy the fact that river cruising offers opportunities to bicycle, walk and hike in nearly every port of call. I'm further fulfilled by encountering new faces and cultures, although my standards have inevitably become much higher as a result of exposure to life's luxuries on cruise ships. As a food and wine lover and proponent of impeccable service, I expect a lot when a hefty price tag is attached—but I'm also laid back enough to forego some of these fineries in the name of budget or when heading off the beaten path.

Sunrise in Appalachia: When not river cruising, I am RV cruising.

Today, I make my home in Asheville, North Carolina (when not on a cruise!), where I enjoy mountain biking, hiking, camping, RV'ing (or land cruising), lingering in coffee shops and frequent trips to the gorgeous Biltmore Estate. I have two grown children, Alex and Britton, who traveled with me often as they were growing up, and still do occasionally.

In addition to my websites, I have done a lot of video work for destinations and for cruise lines such as Seabourn and Silversea Cruises. My work has appeared in USA Today and numerous consumer magazines. One of my articles, "Ship Shape," which appeared in Hemispheres (United Airlines in-flight magazine), even received an award in the category of "Best Cruise Writing," from The North American Travel Journalism Association.

I'm also the author of four books, including Remembering Charles Kuralt, a biography that Publisher's Weekly called "a sweet and lovely homage, a welcome commemoration." But enough about me. My goal is to provide you with content that engages you and compels you to find as much pleasure from river cruising as I do.

If you get stuck or feel lost along the way, please feel free to contact me using the contact form on rivercruiseadvisor.com. Let's go river cruising!

MORE IN VIEW.
MORE TO DO.

IF YOU WANT TO SEE THE WORLD, cruise down its legendary rivers. If you want to see more of the world, look no further than Avalon Waterways. Our Suite Ships feature one-of-a-kind Panorama Suites,℠ with the widest opening windows in river cruising, the industry's only Open-Air Balcony℠ and beds facing the incredible views.

Beyond our wall-to-wall, floor-to-ceiling windows is a world waiting to be explored—your way. Whether you want to enjoy a guided walking tour of one of Europe's great cities, join a cooking class or paddle a canoe, our Avalon Choice® selections of Classic, Discovery and Active excursions offer a wide range of possibilities.

Contact your travel professional for great deals on Avalon Waterways river cruises today!

2

Chapter
TWO

WHY
SHOULD I?

Waterside Restaurant on Crystal River Cruises' Crystal Bach

WHY SHOULD I?

Why should you consider taking a river cruise? For many travelers, the slow chug along the river is just the right pace for getting the lay of the land. Sitting on the top deck of a riverboat under brilliant blue skies, gazing on fabled landscapes dotted with picturesque castles, romantic villages and quiet vineyards are only a few of the pleasures of scenic cruising. Just one flight of stairs down from the sun deck, you have all the amenities of a modern hotel—restaurants, bars, lounges, fitness facilities, spas, Internet access and comfortable staterooms. There would be no reason to leave, if the cities, towns and villages along the way weren't so alluring. In fact, I find river cruising to be one of the most enjoyable travel experiences available to those seeking to get to truly know Europe. Why? Let me count the ways:

① **INTIMATE SIZE.** I love the intimate size of the river ships, most of which carry fewer than 200 passengers, not to mention the coziness of the staterooms and the quietness of the morning. There are few things in life that are better than waking up and stepping out onto your private balcony to feel the cool river air as the morning mist lifts to reveal a landscape that takes the breath away.

② **UNPACK ONLY ONCE.** You've probably heard this many times before, but let me set the scene for you. You embark the ship, follow your escort to your stateroom, unpack and sigh with relief, knowing that you will not need to look at your suitcase again until the end of the cruise. Each day you'll wake up in a different destination, unless, of course, the boat is overnighting. In Lyon, Paris, Bordeaux, Budapest, Vienna and Amsterdam, river cruise ships often remain overnight so that you can enjoy the nightlife of these vibrant and culturally endowed cities. River cruising offers truly hassle-free travel (airlines, take note). Can you imagine trying to visit Europe's marquee cities by motorcoach? Or driving?

③ **VARIETY.** One of the beautiful things about river cruising is that no two voyages are alike. Even if you've cruised the Danube two or three times, you can return and have a new experience. On subsequent trips, maybe you will visit different destinations, or instead of taking the standard city tour, you straddle a saddle and pedal along the river, or sit back and indulge in a coffee or a glass of wine at a local cafe. I've cruised the Danube a dozen times now. I still love it and always look forward to returning. The range of experiences that river cruising offers is vast and no matter what your passion, you can likely find a river cruise that complements your lifestyle and interests.

④ **ACTIVITY.** River cruises can be extremely active. You can pedal along the old river towpaths, many of them now paved for pedestrians and bicycles, or stretch your legs on activities that range from gentle walks to rigorous hikes. Unlike ocean cruising, which has lazy days at sea spent with little to no land in sight, river cruising has no such equivalent. Each day presents its own unique experiences and schedule. A few hours of scenic cruising may be offered during the day, but you'll also stop at destinations where you can stretch your legs during guided walks or hikes, or pedal bicycles (guided or independently on some lines) for a few miles or for many miles. I've pedaled as many as 70 miles in one day on some of my river cruises. Days like those go down as some of my most memorable.

(5) ENGAGEMENT. I'm sure I would love cruising along just about any river (the Mississippi is gorgeous for its broad expanse), but the fact that the majority of river cruising take travelers through the heart of Europe is like the apple in the strudel. It adds an essential flavor to an already delectable experience. During a river cruise, you're engaged not only with the landscape but also with the local life and culture. Often while ocean cruising, you're too far offshore to see much of anything while in transit, but during a river cruise, riverbanks are only yards away. And unlike some shoreside ports, where culture has been compromised by vendors selling their mass-produced wares, river cruises deliver you to European capital cities and country villages alike, where you'll witness the comings and goings of daily life and are able to intermingle with people beyond the confines of the mass-market tourism industry. (Keep in mind that I love ocean-going vessels, too, for a variety of other reasons.)

(6) ACCESSIBILITY. During your river cruise, you often dock just steps away from city centers or major attractions. On most occasions, the only thing that stands between you and the shore is a gangway of no longer than 30 feet. In fact, all you have to do is step out onto your balcony—or open the doors to your French balcony—and you are in Europe. Boarding is a breeze too. You typically fly into a major European city, and with a short transfer you arrive at your floating boutique hotel. There are no long lines at the terminal, no interminable waiting and waiting and waiting to get on board and settled into your stateroom. River cruising is easy and unencumbered from start to finish. Unfortunately, not everyone is able to take a river cruise in Europe. I'm thinking mainly of those with mobility issues who write to me on a weekly basis. It breaks my heart to tell them that river cruis-

IN SOME PORTS OF CALL, GETTING ON AND OFF THE SHIP CAN BE CHALLENGING FOR THOSE WITH MOBILITY ISSUES.

In Budapest, Riviera's Robert Burns had to tie up alongside another ship, so that going ashore required ascending a set of stairs, crossing the top deck of the ship beside ours, descending a set of stairs, then walking the gangway to the riverside landing, where the real work began. In the photo you can see a series of concrete stairs that we had to ascend to get to the motorcoach for our tour of Budapest. Of course, such docking situations are the exception rather than the rule, but those who are mobility challenged should be aware that getting on and off the ship won't always be easy.

where LUXURY

meets AUTHENTICITY

Receive $100 Spa Credit Per Stateroom on 2018 & 2019 Europe Cruises

Contact your Travel Agent or call: 800.626.0126 | www.AmaWaterways.com

The experience of a luxury river cruise should transcend snapshots. It should awaken your senses and envelop your heart in a warm embrace. The ultimate luxury river cruise is the authenticity of sipping a distinctive Wachau Valley Riesling from a Viennese wine tavern visited earlier in the day. It's waking up each morning to another spectacular hilltop castle around the river bend. It's the scent of lavender wafting on the gentle Provence breeze; the beat of traditional African drums. It's the taste of a delicate yet rich crème brulee hand-torched by an expert chef. It's immersive, transformative and unforgettable. It's AmaWaterways.

Immersive, Transformative and Unforgettable

Whether you wish to explore Europe, Southeast Asia or Africa, AmaWaterways offers an incredible array of itineraries in 2019. More than 60 expertly guided wine-themed cruises visit storied cellars and world-renowned vineyards from France's iconic Bordeaux region to Austria's Wachau Valley to the Douro Valley in Portugal and Spain. Get swept up in the magic of timeless traditions and dazzling lights on our holiday cruises, like our new Christmas Markets on the Danube; or play golf at some of Europe's top golf courses during select AmaMagna cruises.

Nourish Your Mind, Body and Soul

Wake up with a sunshine stretch out on deck. Cycle through the French countryside. Leave footprints on storied trails. If you're motivated to lead an active lifestyle, we have a wealth of opportunities for you to nourish your mind, body and soul on board, including fitness classes led by a professional Wellness Host, soothing massages, laps on the sun deck walking track and guided hiking and biking tours ashore.

Bike through quaint villages

AmaMagna–Debuts May 2019

We are passionate about giving our guests the best possible river cruising experience on the highest rated ships in Europe, as recognized by premier travel authority Berlitz. And don't you deserve the best?

Floating Indulgence

AmaWaterways' river ships are the definition of floating indulgence. On board, crew members deliver unparalleled service, while expert chefs masterfully prepare exquisite cuisine. In 2019, AmaWaterways debuts three such luxury ships—the AmaMora, cruising Europe's Rhine River; the AmaDouro, sailing Portugal and Spain's UNESCO-designated Douro River; and the extraordinary AmaMagna, sailing on the Danube in May 2019. AmaMagna is luxury redefined, mostly spacious suites measuring 355-710 sq. ft., with full outside balconies; more unique, alternative dining venues, including al fresco dining and a contemporary wine bar/restaurant; and more enticing activities, including water sports and golf ashore.

Journey One Step Further

With AmaWaterways, you won't just sail legendary waterways—you'll journey one step further. Go off the beaten path with intimate Special Interest Tours that immerse you deeply into local life: truffle hunts in Avignon, an olive farm excursion in Arles, or apricot tastings in Weissenkirchen. Or choose one of our once-in-a-lifetime land extensions, including opportunities to experience the healing waters of the Blue Lagoon and Iceland's Northern Lights, or trek among Rwandan mountain gorillas in Volcanoes National Park.

Blue Lagoon, Iceland

$100 Per Stateroom Spa Credit applies to 2018 or 2019 Europe cruises, so don't delay—contact your travel agent or call AmaWaterways at (800) 626-0126 to book your unforgettable luxury river cruise today!

BEST FOR ACTIVE CRUISERS
2016 & 2017 Cruise Critic, Editor's Pick

BEST RIVER CRUISE LINE
2016 & 2017 Cruise Critic, Editor's Pick

AMAWATERWAYS™
LEADING THE WAY IN RIVER CRUISING

ing may not be the best choice for them. Why not? First, there's the infrastructure in Europe itself. Sharp curbs and cobblestoned streets in many destinations can be rough going for those who rely on walkers and wheelchairs or scooters. While scooters are technically allowed on most river cruisers, they are not recommended and are discouraged as these passengers will find it difficult (if not impossible) to embark/disembark the ships, get on and off the buses, and navigate the cobblestone roads. Complicating the issue is that sometimes ships have to berth next to one another in some of the more popular destinations. That means getting off the ship to go into town—and getting back on the ship—sometimes requires climbing stairs to get to the sundeck of one ship, then back down the stairs to get to the lower level, through the lobby of another ship, etc. To spare you from having to climb too many stairs onboard, nearly all of the modern river cruise ships do have elevators, but these do not always travel to every deck, and not all ships have accessible staterooms. All of that said, I have seen people in wheelchairs touring Europe by river cruise. They usually have good family support and someone, like me and many others, willing to lend a helping pair of hands.

3

Chapter
THREE

WHAT'S WHAT?

AmaCerto on the Rhine from Amsterdam.

WHAT'S WHAT?

As the James Baldwin quote goes, "If you know whence you came, there are absolutely no limitations to where you can go." While I certainly think you can take a river cruise without having a sense of its historical underpinnings, there's no doubt that a little insight into the inception of this form of travel makes it all the more enriching. So before we get into the various modes and approaches to river cruising, let's glimpse its figurative wake.

River cruising as we know it today was an entirely new concept to Europe when it was more widely introduced in the late-1960s. Historically, vessels known as barges were merely used to transport goods along the waterways of Europe. They could carry bulk and other cargo that was difficult to ship by traditional land-based methods, and even after the adoption of the railroad as a method of moving goods and passengers, barging remained an economical and popular way to conduct business. Railroads were limited by their fledgling infrastructure, and fluctuations in the gauge, or track size, used between competing companies often meant that trains could travel no farther than a country's geographical boundaries.

As rail transport improved and became standardized, more and more goods began to be shipped via train instead of by barge. The introduction of delivery trucks and other automobiles in the early 1900s meant that goods could be driven locally between two points, causing a further reduction in the amount of good shipped by barge along Europe's waterways. After World War II, the decline in goods shipped over the waterways of Europe caused some enterprising ship owners to come up with a radical idea: They would convert their barges from cargo ships to passenger ships in order to ferry people on long pleasure cruises up and down the rivers.

One of the earliest innovators of barging as a vacation choice was a young man named Richard Parsons. A newspaper reporter for Reuters, Parsons had purchased an old coal barge that he and his brother John repositioned to Dunkirk and refitted into a passenger ship in 1966. Dubbed the Palinurus, this 20-guest vessel was equipped with just two toilets, two showers and one bath. Parsons didn't really think much of the invention at the time, stating in a 2008 interview with France

From my balcony: September sunset on the Rhine.

Today: "We never thought about luxury then—it was just the idea of a fun holiday, walking and biking and eating and drinking. The most exciting thing for me was that no one else was doing it."

Even though Parsons was at the forefront of barging innovation, there were still drawbacks in those early days. The waterways still catered primarily to cargo traffic, so it wasn't uncommon to be stuck at the back of an extremely long queue of freighters waiting for their turns in one of the many locks along Europe's waterways. Other areas had almost no traffic at all and as a result overgrowth from surrounding trees nearly blocked access to locks and waterways. The experience, on the whole, was an uneven one, only suitable for the adventure traveler who didn't mind a few bumps along the road, or in this case, the river.

Everything began to change in the late 1960s when American writer Emily Kimbrough chartered a barge for herself and some friends. Although nearly 70 years old at the time, Kimbrough published a book in 1968 about her barging adventures that piqued the interest of the American public. Floating Island, as it was called, brought American travelers to France to experience barging for themselves, and it was this influx of North Americans that was largely responsible for the race to outfit ships with better and more luxurious accommodations. What began as a fun diversion by a few dedicated entrepreneurs had suddenly blossomed into an industry that was in high demand.

In attempts to lure even more travelers from North America, barges began to be acquired and refitted at a rapid rate. As competition on the waterways grew for this new lucrative passenger traffic, owners and operators began to think more creatively in terms of both interior fittings and itineraries. Gone were the days of shared bathroom and washroom facilities, replaced instead with staterooms that more closely resembled the finest luxury passenger liners of the day. Exquisite woodworking and lounges that recalled the interiors of the Grand Salons of Paris or the extravagance of the Orient Express instilled these barges with distinctive charm that replaced a once utilitarian persona.

In an age where the internet and other forms of "instant" communication simply did not exist, barging owed its success largely to word-of-mouth. Small groups of friends would often charter a barge for a trip through France, returning to tell friends, family and co-workers about their experiences. Some of these acquaintances would become more intrigued and eventually book passage for themselves.

As airline travel increasingly became more affordable to the masses, the time and expense required to cross the Atlantic by ship, then embark on a multi-week barging experience was mitigated. By the mid 1990s, river cruising as we know it today was slowly beginning to establish itself, though its eventual popularity was far from instantaneous.

By the summer of 1993, there were a number of new, purpose-built river cruise ships plying the waterways of Europe. However, the popularity river cruising enjoys today would remain elusive for another decade. Many of the river cruise ships built in the early 1990s drew heavily on their predecessors for influence—taking

CroisiEurope's Anne-Marie (bottom right) docked in Arles, France

the no-frills barging experience and placing it on a newer ship capable of holding more paying passengers.

While these new ships offered passengers newer hardware and more comfort than the barges of the 1960's, absolutely no attempts were made to lure guests from ocean cruising to river cruising. The ships themselves were generally low and squat, with characteristically narrow staterooms that in many cases didn't even allow for Queen-sized beds, let alone balconies. Instead, staterooms consisted largely of Pullman-style beds that could fold into couches during the day, punctuated by a collapsible end table situated underneath the window. Culinary options were limited (and often not as good as you would find ashore), with little thought given to providing variety—and you'd likely be out of luck if you had special dietary needs.

All of this began to change toward the latter half of the 1990s. Taking a cue from the ocean-cruising industry, many river cruise lines began drawing up plans for ambitious newbuilds that would not only increase their passenger capacities but also offer more space, amenities and services than ever before.

One of the men who was chiefly responsible for this uptick in growth was Torstein Hagen. No stranger to the world of cruising, Hagen had helmed Royal Viking Line during the 1980s—one of the most fondly-remembered cruise lines to ever ply the oceans. Hagen dreamed of bringing the kind of service and amenities that had earned Royal Viking a place in cruisers' hearts to the waterways of Europe. He founded Viking River Cruises in the summer of 1997.

Ever mindful of the competition, Hagen decided Viking River Cruises would initially operate in Russia, using four Russian ships that Viking had purchased outright—a rarity at the time. It was to be a decision that would change the face of river cruising forever.

Viking River Cruises wasn't quite an overnight success, but it certainly came close. Fans of ocean cruising, attracted by Hagen's history at Royal Viking, gave Viking River Cruises a chance. Much of the river cruise industry, even at the dawn of the internet age, was still extremely reliant on word-of-mouth, and Viking's recognition gave Hagen the leverage he needed to announce a series of newbuilds that would enter service in 2001.

In just a few short years, the river cruising industry was experiencing a veritable race to see who could churn out the most luxurious, amenity-laden ships possible. That brings us to another influential figure in river cruising, Rudi Schreiner. If there's one word that can be used to describe Schreiner, "tenacious" would probably suit him best. Along with Kristin Karst and the late Jimmy Murphy, Schreiner co-founded AmaWaterways in 2002. Just 16 years later, the line has grown to encompass a fleet of luxurious ships in Europe, with additional vessels in Asia and Africa and more under construction. To fully appreciate this number it's important to remember the kind of climate in which AmaWaterways was founded. In 2002, much of the tourism industry was still reeling from the effects of the terrorist attacks on September 11, 2001, and the river cruise industry as we know it was still very much in its infancy. Nevertheless, the enterprising trio saw a ray of light in establishing a river cruise line dedicated to providing an exceptional experience both onboard and off, and set to work creating Amadeus Waterways—the forerunner to AmaWaterways.

Villages along the Rhine

Schreiner was no stranger to the river cruise industry; He'd been employed as Vice President of Product Development with Uniworld when the company first launched its river cruise product in 1993. Schreiner was one of the first to recognize the potential that the recently completed Main-Danube Canal, a massive engineering works project to link the Main with the Danube, would have for the industry.

When Schreiner introduced a 14-night voyage from Amsterdam and Budapest using the new canal, it sold out instantly, and Uniworld went from carrying just a few hundred passengers per year to more than 18,000. It is what one would consider a good problem to have, with capacity creating an ever-present need for new ships. Schreiner went about leasing ships wherever he could find them, developing additional programs and itineraries for the line until he joined Viking River Cruises in 2000. But with the experience Schreiner had garnered, he itched to break out on his own and after just two years, he left Viking to partner with Karst and Murphy. AmaWaterways was born. After just a year in business, the company had partnered with travel giant Globus, which provided the capital needed to enter into an agreement to construct its first, purpose-built ships. At the same time, competing lines were also in the process of ordering their own ships, creating the spirit of competitive innovation between the companies vying for passengers on the European runs.

Today, the river cruise landscape is vastly different from that which existed when Schreiner, Karst and Murphy first set up shop. More new, purpose-built ships exist on the waterways of Europe than at any time in history, and river cruising is slowly but steadily gaining in popularity, attracting passengers who have done ocean cruising as well as those who have never set foot aboard a ship.

Now that we've taken a good look back, we can forge boldly ahead. The question is, "aboard what?" There are the longships, rivers cruisers, barges, paddlewheelers … say what? With so many ways to denote "riverboat," selecting the right one for you can become confusing. The next chapters will breakdown the differences between various river-going vessels along with a few examples of tour types you can opt for beyond the traditional river cruise itinerary.

4

Chapter
FOUR

THE MODES

CroisiEurope's Loire Princesse, a paddlewheeler

THE MODES

RIVER CRUISERS, BARGES AND PADDLEWHEELERS

While there are invariably differences between vessels within each classification—some boast indoor pools, spas, multiple restaurants and whatnot—these are the basic categories to help you wade through what's out there.

RIVER CRUISERS

These are the biggies, carrying between 100 and 200 guests. These elongated, flat and sleek vessels make up the majority of the ships within the leisure river cruising industry, appearing somewhat like squashed ocean liners. Their low profiles, no more than four decks high, allow for these riverboats to maneuver under low bridges and maintain a shallower draft in order to compensate for the notoriously-low water levels on some rivers. A few river cruise ships are shorter in length—such as the 103-foot Juno, cruising Sweden's canals—but most hover somewhere around 400 feet in length and approximately 40 feet in width. One exception to this last dimension is Crystal Mozart, Crystal Cruises very first river cruiser, which entered the scene in July of 2016. (Read about my voyage on the inaugural cruise in Chapter 6.) This ship is 75 feet wide; nearly twice the width of most river cruisers, making even more room for public spaces like the four dining venues and staterooms with king-sized beds. This no doubt gives Crystal Cruises boasting rights, but the line will soon have a competitor. AmaWaterways has announced a similarly-sized vessel to launch in 2019, the AmaMagna, carrying 194 guests in staterooms that will measure more than 300 square feet on average.

You may be wondering, if that's a river cruiser, than what exactly is a "longship?" This is simply the term that Viking River Cruises coined (well, and the original Vikings, of course) to be in line with its moniker, but it's simply a "river cruiser." The same goes for Crystal River Cruises' "river yachts," Emerald Waterways "Star Ships," Scenic's "Space Ships," Uniworld's "Super Ships" and Avalon Waterways' "Suite Ships."

River cruisers don't quite match the luxury standards of ocean-going vessels, but most of these newbuilds do come close. As for what's included and what's not on a river cruise, refer to the accompanying comparison chart for a company-by-company comparison. You can also find the comparison chart at rivercruiseadvisor.com/comparisons/

BARGES

The differences between river cruisers and barges are vast but essentially boils down to this: Barges are much smaller, able to navigate canals as well as rivers, and host no more than two dozen people. Typically, you'll travel with friends and family, or like-minded individuals, on quiet waterways through the bucolic countryside. Your means of conveyance, referred to as a "luxury hotel barge," features all-inclusive menus that include tours, bikes, beverages and gourmand-worthy cuisine.

Because of the smaller size of these vessels, barge cruises represent more intimate experiences than those found on river cruises, and you'll often pay handsomely for this autonomy. Luxury barge cruises along the picturesque canals of France are not inexpensive vacation experiences. Rates range from $300 per person per day up to more than $500 per person per day, plus suggested gratuities from 5 percent to 10 percent of the total cost of the cruise, depending on how generous

Bikes and barges. CroisiEurope's Anne-Marie

you're feeling. For a $6,000-a-cabin barge cruise, that can mean paying up to $600 per person in gratuities at the end of the voyage.

On a per-diem basis, barge cruises are certainly among the most expensive river travel experiences offered, but as is often said, you get what you pay for. At these prices, you'd better. What I learned in talking with guests is that for some of them, six days on a barge through a small slice of France was a lifetime aspiration that they had spent years saving for.

There are aspects of barging that seem disparate with the price tag: Staterooms, for example, are typically small but well-configured on the hotel barges. And, while it's not true across the board, barges tend have much more casual and understated decor.

Often these vessels once carried cargo and were gutted to house a "hotel" structure. It's best to refer to them as "luxury hotel barges" to counter the common association of cargo barges. Unless you've been swindled, you won't be traveling with coal or cattle. A few examples of companies offering high-quality barge sailings in Europe include CroisiEurope, European Waterways and French Country Waterways.

Due to their size and relative engine power, barges move at slower pace than river cruisers, allowing for you to step off at locks to walk, run or ride bikes. My typical day aboard barges goes something like this: wake up, have breakfast. Go out on the sun deck and watch the landscape pass by. Step off at a lock to bicycle around my surroundings for a couple of hours. Return to the barge for lunch. Join an afternoon guided tour, and return to the barge in the evening to enjoy the fine dining, convivial atmosphere, and comfortable accommodations.

I created a short video that takes you aboard a barge cruise, and while it was filmed in 2012, it will give you a sense of what a barge vacation is all about: Barging in Alsace France | https://youtu.be/Tp4JM2DbgXo.

Because I enjoy them so much, I host barge cruises each year. In 2019, I'll be offering two trips in Alsace on October 11 and October 25. Learn more here https:// www.rivercruiseadvisor.com/ralph-grizzles-hosted-river-cruise-trips/

PADDLEWHEELERS

This type of vessel is pretty much self explanatory: Attached to the stern (or sides) are telltale paddlewheels that are used to propel the ship. Paddlewheel propulsion, shallow hull draft, low air draft and a ballasting system allows the vessel to navigate notoriously shallow rivers such as the Elbe and Loire—two of the locations where you will find paddlewheelers operating in Europe. Powered only by these wheels, typical cruising speeds will reach up to nearly 10 mph. This technology also makes it possible to sail year-round out of places like Berlin, even during low-water season.

Paddlewheelers in Europe pale in comparison to the size of some of those churning along the Mississippi and are certainly less plentiful. In fact, there are only three paddlewheelers aimed at the river cruise market currently plying European waterways, all owned by CroisiEurope: two cruising the Elbe River and one cruising the Loire River. Loire Princesse, as the name suggests, was designed specifically to sail its namesake river. Dotted with spectacular scenery, beautiful chateaus and UNESCO World Heritage Sites, the Loire is a veritable wealth of cities and regions that, until April of 2015 when this vessel set sail, had never been accessible by river cruisers. Dubbed a "Green Ship" thanks to environmentally-friendly technologies, Loire Princesse is 295 feet long with a beam of 49 feet, capable of accommodating up to 96 guests in a total of 48 staterooms, many with balconies. Onboard amenities include a full-service restaurant, inviting Lounge with a dedicated dance floor and a sun deck that is perfectly suited to outdoor viewing. She became the first ship on the Loire to feature overnight accommodations.

In the spring of 2016, CroisiEurope's Elbe Princesse, a 321-foot-long paddle-wheel-driven river cruise ship, followed suit offering year-round voyages from Berlin to the heart of Prague. Elbe Princesse features 40 staterooms, all of which have river views, spread across two decks. Able to accommodate up to 80 guests, Elbe Princesse has similar amenities to her sister on the Loire and is furnished with fabrics from MissoniHome, an Italian fabrics company headquartered in Rome.

CroisiEurope took delivery of a third paddle-wheel riverboat to operate between Berlin and Prague on the Elbe and Vltava Rivers. Delivered in February 2018, the Elbe Princesse II measures 331 feet in length, with an overall width of 34 feet. The ship's sleek, contemporary design is quite similar to the Elbe Princesse, and features 45 outward-facing cabins measuring 150 square feet, with French balconies featured in cabins on the upper deck. The ship also boasts a restaurant, panoramic lounge, patio and a large sun deck.

Read more details about life aboard a paddlewheeler in my voyage recap found within the Loire river rundown in Chapter 6.

LOCKED AND LOADED

This might be a stretch to be considered a mode of transport, but locks are definitely something you will "ride" on the rivers of Europe. You've probably heard of locks, but may be wondering, "What exactly is a lock?" Much like the Panama

Navigating a lock on the Seine river

Canal—perhaps the world's most famous example—locks are an engineering solution to allow vessels to navigate areas that might not be passable otherwise.

Early canoe-bound explorers would simply pick up their canoes in order to bypass treacherous waterways; an act known as a portage. Of course, large river cruise ships and other vessels can't simply be plucked from the water and carried overland. To mitigate this disparity on rivers, dams and a series of chambers, or "locks," were built. Ships sail into the lock, essentially an enclosed bathtub, move into position and idle their engines. The doors to the lock are shut electronically, and for a period of time, it seems as if nothing will happen. Slowly, the turbulence increases as water is either admitted into or pumped out of the lock chamber so it can be level with the higher or lower waters ahead. Floating guides on tracks run within the concrete walls of the lock, guiding the ship up and down, which usually squeals in protest as the volume of water in the lock changes. Depending on the height and volume of water, ships can spend as much as half an hour in-transit within a lock.

On some itineraries (particularly those traveling the Main-Danube Canal, with its 16 locks), lock-lovers will be in heaven with a full day's worth of transiting these unique, remotely operated structures. Some locks can hold two or more ships at a time, while others are so narrow that simply admitting one ship is a challenge, requiring great skill on the part of the ship's navigation team to enter them safely.

River cruise ships can transit the locks on their own or as part of a larger group of ships, depending on the season and the size of the lock. When water enters the lock, it does so in starts and stops that can result in your ship rising quickly in one motion, then slowly in the second. It was this "elevator movement" that can potentially make one feel "seasick," since the lock walls are literally inches away from the ship. Most passengers are unaffected, but should you find yourself feeling a little woozy, try sitting in the main lounge, which often has 180-degree wrap-around windows and a better overview of the lock itself. I've also heard that you can quit drinking water for the duration of the transit, switching instead to heavier drinks like coffee and soda. I'm not sure if that remedy "holds any water" from a health standpoint, but some travelers swear by it.

CROISIEUROPE'S PADDLEWHEELERS MAKE IT POSSIBLE TO CRUISE SHALLOW RIVERS LIKE THE ELBE AND THE LOIRE

5

Chapter
FIVE

THE MEANS

Passau, Germany: Evening approach on Tauck's ms Savor.

TOURING AND THEME CRUISES

Underscoring my point that river cruising really boils down to personal preferences, the way cruises are packaged might prove just as important to you as the size of the vessel or the ports being visited. Perhaps you have a particular passion that you want to indulge or you want to make a special occasion all the more special. You can take a biking themed adventure, a river cruise hosted by a popular land-based tour operator, or partake in special "themed cruises" designed with a particular topic—like art, history, beer and wine appreciation—in mind. I'll give you a little insight as to what's entailed by showcasing a few of my favorite itineraries—and hopefully instill you with some options to keep in mind when planning your unforgettable river adventure.

TOURING

Some companies like Backroads offer river cruises, expanding the breadth of their offerings. But did you know that they don't typically own their ships? Instead, they lease out blocks of staterooms—and sometimes the entire ship—for their tour package. So if you're choosing a cruise vacation based upon the ship, you may very well discover that you're comparing one and the same vessel. Not to say that the experiences don't warrant separate branding; the itineraries are greatly influenced by a tour company's unique style and approach. It's just that some operators call attention to their elite partnerships, such as Adventures By Disney does with AmaWaterways, while others let the mode of transportation play more of a cameo to the limelight.

Does knowing this matter? Not really. I just thought I'd explain how these partnerships work for those observant travel shoppers who want to know how a "touring" experience might differ from a cruise purchased directly from the affiliate cruise line. Armed with the understanding of how it works, you can decide if it's worth the value proposition.

After recognizing a striking resemblance between a tour company and a river cruise itinerary, travelers are often perplexed by differences in price. Often, it can be chalked up to room categories, with a tour company offering a higher level than the base rates advertised by a cruise line, as well as some additional perks, dedicated excursion guides, and things of that nature. Other times, it's because the tour company is offering something quite specialized. For instance, I like being active. Ten years ago, river cruising would not have been for me as an active traveler, but today river cruises offer bikes and hikes, with varying degrees of difficulty, from gentle hikes through towns to rigorous hikes up mountains, from easy bike rides along the river to epic rides that take the whole day to complete. So there are certainly plenty of ways to increase your heart rate while taking in sights when traveling with river cruise lines. But for die-hard bike lovers like me, there are some added perks when taking a cruise with Backroads, heralded for adventure travel across the globe. From sag wagons carting calorie-rich snacks and energy drinks to the bike-enthusiast guides, tricked-out bikes and personalized jerseys, the details ratchet up your river-cruise-bike adventure a gear or two.

Biking with my son Alex on a Backroads' river cruise.

Read on for a couple specific examples of tour company itineraries as well as some incredible options for family travelers.

BOATS & BIKES:
BACKROADS - VILSHOFEN TO BUDAPEST

All too often, river cruising is portrayed as being a passive experience for old people. That's simply not true. With the right company, river cruising can be an active experience, and cycling is a great way to take in the countryside and life along the river banks—not to mention burn a few calories from the oh-so-delicious-and-irresistible onboard cuisine. One of the things I love about river cruising, in fact, is that it marries two of my favorite forms of travel, bikes and boats—and negates another of my favorite activities: eating.

I have quite a history of bicycling. I crossed America and Canada in my twenties, then cycled New Zealand and part of the east coast of Australia. I spent a few months cycling Europe with a childhood friend, and today, I cycle almost daily, no matter whether I am in Europe or the hills of Appalachia near my home in Asheville, North Carolina. So naturally I wanted to share this affinity with one of my other great loves, my then 19-year-old son, Alex. In August of 2016, we set off on a "bikes and boats" trip with AmaWaterways and Backroads. As regular readers of River Cruise Advisor know, AmaWaterways is a multi-awarded river cruise company. Not as well known as AmaWaterways among River Cruise Advisor readers, Backroads bills itself as the world's #1 active travel company. The combination of cycling and river cruising was a match made in heaven, and a perfect way to travel for this father and son duo.

We used AmaWaterways' AmaSonata as our floating hotel, while Backroads took us bicycling each day along the Danube. "Dad, this may just be our best trip ever," Alex said to me at the start of our trip. We were pedaling at the time under blue skies on a bike path through forests, making our way to the Danube, where Ama-Sonata was waiting for us in Vilshofen, a German city that AmaWaterways uses for turnarounds (where its cruises begin and end).

The ride that day was exhilarating, with more than 20 of us participating in the Backroads program, and it was only a sign of what was to come. Each day, we'd pedal along beautiful stretches of the river, feeling invigorated by the landscape, the fresh air, the activity and group camaraderie. Backroads blocks group space (and sometimes charters the full ship) to layer its program on top of AmaWaterways' river cruise product. There is a premium to be paid for the Backroads program. For example, on the June 1, 2018 departure on AmaSerena, which runs seven nights from Vilshofen, Germany to Budapest, Hungary, Backroads' rates began at $6,098 per person for a category BA stateroom measuring 210 square feet. On the same cruise, AmaWaterways rates started at $4,548 per person for a category BB state-room also measuring 210 square feet. Both rates are based on double occupancy.

Is the Backroads' premium worth it? If you enjoy cycling, then probably yes. Back-roads provided us with an upscale bicycling experience. The team leaders took care of every aspect of our journey, from detailed instructions about our rides to giving us choices (and freedom) to make our own way. We were not shoehorned into a cookie-cutter, one-size-fits-all program. Plus, our lunches were often enjoyed off-ship, in interesting locales and at Backroads' expense. Some lunches would have easily cost $50 or more for Alex and me.

THE RIDE THAT DAY WAS EXHILARATING,
AND IT WAS ONLY A SIGN OF WHAT WAS TO COME.

The condition of the bikes was excellent, and the riding was euphoria-inducing. Our longest day, from Vienna to Bratislava, had us covering nearly 50 miles, under such great conditions and with a stop at a beer garden (though it was only mid-morning, it's beer o'clock somewhere) and lunch at a castle—all taken care of by Backroads. We rode into Bratislava feeling as though we had just finished the Tour de France, victorious and tired but euphoric.

As my son suggested at the outset, this trip certainly ranked among our best ever. The combo of AmaWaterways and Backroads is a good pick for those who want to be active during their vacations and also for those who want to experience Europe at just the right pace and in just the right style—on two wheels and along a river.

ACTIVE OPTIONS ON THE TOP RIVER CRUISE COMPANIES

		AmaWaterways	Avalon Waterways	CroisiEurope	Crystal River Cruises
	Bikes On Board For Independent Rides	✓	✓	On Barges	✓
	Guided Bike Tours	On All Voyages	On Cycling-Themed Voyages	On Cycling-Themed Voyages	
	Gym	✓	✓		✓
	Fitness Instructor	✓			✓
	Yoga	✓	✓		✓
	Pool	Some			✓
	Guided Hikes	✓	✓	On Themed Voyages	
	Gentle Walkers	✓	✓	✓	✓
	Regular Pace Walking Tours	✓	✓	✓	✓
	Active Walking Tours	✓	✓	On Themed Voyages	
	Kayaking		✓		
	Healthy Dining Options	✓	✓		✓
	Walking Track Top Deck	✓	✓		✓
	Putting Green	✓	✓		✓

updated 7/1/2018

That said, AmaWaterways has its own fleet of bicycles for both guided and independent touring, so in the end, you'll need to judge for yourself as to whether the Backroads' premium is worth the difference. Check out Backroads Bike Trips & River Boating: A Winning Combination For Active Travelers | https://www.rivercruiseadvisor.com/2016/08/bicycling-bike-trips-amawaterways/

WANT TO EXPERIENCE BACKROADS BICYCLING & RIVER CRUISING?

In 2018, Backroads offers 53 departures on the Danube, Douro, Rhine and Seine rivers. Prices begin at $5,898 per person for the 8-day Danube Cycling Sensation River Cruise Bike Tour. Backroads will offer 74 Departures in 2019 with rates starting at $6,098.

EMERALD WATERWAYS	RIVIERA TRAVEL	SCENIC	TAUCK	UNIWORLD	VIKING RIVER CRUISES
✓	✓	✓	✓	✓	
✓	✓	✓	✓	On Cycling-Themed Voyages	✓
✓		✓	✓	✓	
✓		✓	✓	✓	
✓		Some		Some	Douro Vessels
✓	✓	✓	✓		✓
✓	✓	✓	✓	✓	✓
✓	✓	✓	✓	✓	✓
✓			✓		✓
✓**				✓	
✓		✓	✓	✓	✓
✓	✓	✓	✓	✓	✓
✓	✓	✓	✓	✓	✓

^Viking added guided hiking, cycling and canoing excursions for 2018 on select river cruise itineraries.
**Selected ports and itineraries.
#New for 2018

A TOUR COMPANY CLASSIC:
TAUCK - PRAGUE TO BUDAPEST

In July of 2015, I landed in Prague and checked into the InterContinental to begin my Danube Reflections cruise tour with the world-renowned tour operator, Tauck. I call it a cruisetour because with Tauck, touring is central to the travel experience. With more than 90 years of leading guided land tours, Tauck's excursions were flawlessly executed, with some of the best local guides I have encountered, and three wonderful Tour Directors who traveled with us from start to finish.

I particularly enjoyed our tour to the UNESCO World Heritage-listed town of Cesky Krumlov and a gala dinner at a Viennese palace where we were hosted by a princess. It was also nice to have time to cycle on my own and with another guest along the banks of the Danube using the complimentary bicycles on Tauck's ms Savor.

On board the 130-guest ship, there was a Tauck Cruise Director in addition to the three Tauck Directors who traveled with us from Prague to Vienna. All excursions, all gratuities, meals at unique dining venues ashore, airport transfers and more were included in Tauck's prices. Likewise, all beverages were included once we were on ms Savor, which is owned and operated by the Swiss-management group, Scylla (the same company that owns and operates Riviera River Cruises' ships).

Aside from the excursions and events, I also enjoyed my Loft cabin. If you haven't seen the video of this extraordinary 225-square-foot stateroom, you can check it out here | https://www.rivercruiseadvisor.com/2015/07/tauck-loft-stateroom/

From my first night in Prague, Tauck had impressed me by exceeding my expectations. Late because of a flight delay, I missed the welcome dinner. Not to worry. Tauck had graciously provided me with a voucher, not just for a standard dinner at the InterContinental Prague, but for a feast on the terrace overlooking the city. In fact, I was unable to spend the entire value of the voucher.

TOURING IS CENTRAL TO ANY TAUCK RIVER CRUISE

Unusual accommodations
on the rivers.
My 225-square foot loft
stateroom and bathroom
on Tauck's ms Savor.

Tauck's gesture was to be a metaphor of things to come. At every turn, Tauck's Tour Directors would go a few steps beyond what was expected (or in the case of dinner, what was totally unexpected but generously given) to offer an unforgettable river "tour" experience. To Tauck I say, "Thanks for the memories."

At the end of our cruise, Tauck put us up for two nights in the Hotel Imperial in Vienna. For an extraordinary gala event, we enjoyed an evening with dinner, dance, opera and classical music performances at the privately-owned Palais Pallavecini in Vienna. The palace, which dates back to 1784, was outstanding, with its opulent and expansive rooms. We felt like royalty as we were welcomed with champagne and music, followed by a grand dinner that began with a greeting from the 14-year-old princess whose family owned the palace. I would imagine that only Tauck could pull off such a spectacular event with a greeting from a princess.

Read a day-by-day report and live voyage reports here | https://www.rivercruisead-visor.com/2015/08/taucks-ms-savor-day-12-vienna-wrap-up/

WANT TO EXPERIENCE TAUCK RIVER CRUISING?

In 2018, Tauck's prices start at $4,990 per person for The Blue Danube 12-day cruise. See our 2019 pricing charts for next year's prices.

FAMILY FIRST:
RIVER CRUISING WITH KIDS

One of the most frequently-asked questions from readers is: Can children go on a river cruise? I'm not talking teenagers or grown adult children here, but specifically, kids under 12 years of age. While I don't have a particularly good example of this segment of family river cruising to share, since both of my kids are now adults—my son Alex is 21 and my daughter Britton is 23—I can attest that traveling with my children has been enormously rewarding. You just read about my unforgettable bike adventure with my son, and later I'll talk about sailing Sweden's Gota Canal with my daughter. So I completely understand the desire to share your river vacation with children or grandchildren and want to discuss the options available—because today, there are many.

Historically, river cruises were never really intended for kids, families or the like. They were targeted (and priced) at a certain segment of the population, typically retired couples with a bit of cash to burn who were tired of the typical bus-around-Europe land vacation. But it turns out that families also are tired of motorcoach and do-it-yourself tours of Europe and want to get in on the river cruise craze, especially during the school holiday months. As a result, the river cruise industry is undergoing some changes.

For those who are seriously considering taking young children on a European river cruise, there are some important things you're going to want to take into account before you book. To start, I recommend only taking a family-friendly river cruise departure. Most of these will be noted on the cruise line's website or in their printed brochure. These family-friendly sailings will offer more for kids to do, with special activities onboard and ashore, not to mention other young families traveling together.

Lines like AmaWaterways, CroisiEurope, Tauck, and Uniworld Boutique River Cruise Collection are among the most family-friendly river cruise lines out there. AmaWaterways partnered with Adventures by Disney to roll out a series of family-friendly river cruises in Europe in 2016, and that program is still going strong. Together families can ride a toboggan during the winter Christmas Market cruises, hike along a waterfall or zipline through the Black Forest, visit the famous sto-

Some of my best river cruises have been with my kids. Here, my daughter Britton is pictured in Rothenburg, Germany, during a Christmas Markets river cruise.

EMERALD
WATERWAYS

2019 EUROPE RIVER CRUISES

cruisecritic
EDITORS' PICKS
2017

Emerald Waterways
Best Value For Money,
River Cruise

2015 EDITORS' PICKS
CRUISE CRITIC
BEST RIVER LINE FOR VALUE

2016 EDITORS' PICKS
CRUISE CRITIC
BEST RIVER LINE FOR VALUE

3 YEARS IN A ROW!

NEW FOR 2019

The Classic Danube
Nuremberg to Vienna

Lower Danube Waltz
Vienna to Belgrade

rybook Heidelberg Castle, and enjoy tubing, snow biking, curling and more at Germany's first indoor ski hall. Whether exploring Alsace on horseback, partaking in a clog-painting demonstration in Holland or taking a macaroon-baking class in France, travel via river cruiser proves to be both educational and fun for everyone.

It is important to note, however, that this isn't Disney Cruise Line that is partnering on these sailings. Adventures by Disney is a completely separate entity that was founded about a decade ago that is jointly managed by both Walt Disney Parks and Resorts and the Walt Disney Travel Company. So while the product will offer the same high quality standards Disney is known for, fans of the massive ships of Disney Cruise Line shouldn't expect the same kind of product transferred over to river cruise ships. Nor will any of Disney's characters be present onboard; instead, Disney-trained guides known as Adventure Guides will introduce families to the wonders of Europe. Approximately half of these guides will be American, while the other half will be locals from countries in and around Europe.

AmaWaterways has also committed physically to having family-friendly river cruises of their own. The line designed its new AmaKristina and AmaViola river cruise ships to feature family-friendly accommodations that include connecting staterooms; still a rarity among European-based river cruise ships. Strasbourg-based CroisiEurope also has staterooms for triples and quads on some of its ships, which is good to note for families traveling together. For those who think that three or four to a

FAMILY FRIENDLY RIVER CRUISES ARE INCREASING IN POPULARITY

room might be too much on a river cruise ship, consider a double stateroom combined with a single-stateroom configuration.

In 2017, CroisiEurope introduced Family Club cruises in which children under 16 to cruise for free and includes a second cabin next door for a family of four (two parents with two children, five years and older) or a child in the same cabin (maximum one child). On some of its ships, Emerald Waterways, Riviera River Cruises, Scenic, Tauck and Uniworld Boutique River Cruise Collection also offer a few single-occupancy staterooms to shore up the numbers without putting two guests in the same room.

Both Uniworld and Tauck also have numerous family-friendly river cruise sailings offered during the summer months, when kids are historically off school; and during December, in the run-up to Christmas and New Year's. Both lines have also designed their programs onboard and ashore to cater specifically to families, but without diluting the onboard experience for adults. CroisiEurope's designated "Family Club" cruises also feature children's activities and fun things ashore in

MINIMUM AGE REQUIREMENTS FOR EUROPEAN RIVER CRUISE LINES

LINE	Kid-friendly sailings?	Special Onboard Programs for Kids on Select Sailings?	Minimum Age Requirement
AmaWaterways	✓ partnership with Adventures by Disney	✓	4 Years
Avalon Waterways	✗	✗	8 Years
CroisiEurope	✓ kids accepted on all sailings. Plus, triple cabins	✗	None
Crystal River Cruises	✗	✗	6 months
Emerald Waterways	✗	✗	12 Years
Riviera Travel	✗	✗	12 Years
Scenic	✗	✗	12 Years
Tauck	✓ Tauck Bridges	✓	3 Years
Uniworld	✓ Family Adventures	✓	4 Years; 8 Years Recommended
Viking River Cruises	✗	✗	12 Years; line reserves the right to limit number of guests under age 18.

updated 6/30/2018

unique destinations, such as Andalucia, Croatia, and Venice, where CroisiEurope offers coastal cruises on specially designed vessels.

So where do the other river cruise lines stand? Most will accept children of a certain age group (see our accompany table), but taking kids aboard a standard, non-family river cruise may not be such a good idea. For one, there will be little to no activities designed for kids, who may find themselves bored with decidedly adult activities like lectures, walking tours and evening entertainment that consists largely of a piano player and adults having cocktails.

The other important consideration before booking your kids on an adult river cruise is that many of your fellow guests have chosen that vacation specifically because it offers an adult experience. That doesn't mean they don't like kids; many guests will have children and grandchildren of their own. But it does mean that the reception you may find onboard from your fellow guests could be, well, chilly if you're not booked on a specially-designated family-friendly cruise.

As river cruising grows in popularity, it's reasonable to expect that other lines will eventually follow suit in offering family-friendly river cruise departures at certain times of the year. Until then, specially-designated sailings aboard the ships of AmaWaterways, CroisiEurope, Tauck and Uniworld may be your best bets.

THEME CRUISING

There are cruises for food lovers, wine lovers, music lovers—and much more. Perhaps you want to take a cruise during Holland's Tulip season or hopscotch from one Christmas market to the next. While specialized cruises might be something offered through tour companies (such as my Backroads' bike-themed sailing), many river cruise lines also designate sailings to delve into a particular pursuit. Certainly, regularly scheduled itineraries offer many ways to explore various interests—be it through a wine tasting or excursion to the farmers' market with the chef. However, a dedicated theme cruise zeros in on an interest with special features, like having master sommeliers on board, attending famed jazz festivals and or in-depth explorations of the art, history and culture of a region. Case in point: Avalon Waterways offers a gamut of options from golf-themed river cruises and Art & Impressionist river cruises to Jewish Heritage and Garden & Nature-themed cruises. To give you a portal into how a theme-centric river cruise plays out, I'm highlighting a few popular topics among river cruisers: wine, culinary, and Christmas market cruises.

WINE CRUISES
AMAWATERWAYS WINE CRUISES

A few years back, AmaWaterways unveiled a series of special wine-themed river cruises. At first, just a handful of itineraries and sailing dates were available for what the line had dubbed In Celebration of Wine theme cruises. That quickly changed: The cruising public booked these voyages faster than the line had anticipated. The following year, more wine-themed voyages were added, with more still the year

after that. That trend continues, with more than three dozen wine-themed departures spanning nearly every European itinerary the line offers, from Bordeaux to Portugal's Douro River to the Danube, Main and the Rhine.

Each voyage is distinguished by having either one or two dedicated wine hosts onboard who discuss wine-making traditions in the region and often bring wines from their personal collection for tastings and lectures. Voyages include notable guests like Paris-based wine expert Preston Mohr, who takes you through Bordeaux; and Bob Morus, owner and vintner of Phelps Creek Vineyards, who shares his insights about Rhine varietals. Think that you don't like Rieslings? You may feel otherwise after you've sampled some in Germany and Austria. The same goes for France, where the sheer selection of wines, champagnes and dessert wines like Sauternes can be overwhelming. Tasting wines within their *terroir* helps one to truly understand the breadth and diversity of certain varietals.

In addition to having onboard guest lecturers who are deeply involved in the wine industry, these voyages also include a host of additional extras that most normal sailings on AmaWaterways do not. Special wine-paired meals and excursions to historic vineyards and wine cellars are tailored to each destination-specific itinerary. You'll have the opportunity to learn about wine's often complex and surprising history. For example, you might not know that every year on the third of November, over a million cases of Beaujolais Nouveau are rushed to Paris. It's a breakneck competition between vintners as they race to see whose Beaujolais Nouveau will be the first to be uncorked at midnight. The event is so popular that in the last few decades that what started as a local annual tradition has morphed into a national celebration in France.

Of course, you don't have to imbibe at all if you don't want to—participation in these tastings is entirely voluntary, and even non-drinkers can appreciate the special excursions to local vineyards to see the production of wine and hear about its historic origins and traditional production methods.

Other highlights on these wine-themed river cruise journeys can include enjoying local music and newly pressed wine at a rustic Austrian tavern; sampling the Alsatian wines in Colmar, the French "Capital of Alsatian Wine"; and a German

"Oktoberfest" experience in the village of Vilshofen, held year-round exclusively for AmaWaterways guests.

I did a wine themed cruise with AmaWaterways aboard the AmaVida, which took me to the heart of the Douro River Valley in Portugal. Port tastings, local pastries paired with Raposeira (sparkling wine), and a wine-paired dinner in a monastery were just a few of the ways that I celebrated the art of wine-making. One thing in particular that I loved about a Douro wine themed cruise is that the fortified wines were well balanced with visits historical sites, like the fortified village of Figueira de Castelo Rodrigo and the UNESCO World Heritage Site of Salamanca, Spain. And, as you'll read about in my voyage recap of my Douro river cruise in Chapter 6, there's nothing quite like the people of Portugal, who made my visit all the more rewarding.

Below I share a cruise with you, not because it was a designated wine-themed sailing, rather because it was in a location that is hands-down one of the most popular for wine cruises: Bordeaux.

AmaDolce docked in Libourne, France

AMAWATERWAYS AMADOLCE – ROUNDTRIP BORDEAUX

When I think back to April in Bordeaux, I think of bicycles and bountiful vineyards. I think of sweet (and dry) white wines and bold and earthy reds. Once you've been to Bordeaux, it is difficult to reflect on the region without feeling some titillation of the palate along with thoughts of uncorked bottles and the scent of crushed grapes fermented to perfection and basking in world acclaim.

That one should think of wine should come as no surprise. Bordeaux has been a center for wine trade for nearly 2,000 years. The Romans, who conquered the region in 60 BC, endowed Bordeaux with vineyards and wine production.

Today, more than 10,000 wine-producing châteaux and 13,000 grape growers produce more than 50 appellations, many of which are world-renown and some of which are among the world's most expensive wines. A fact that will astonish oenophiles: The Bordeaux region produces nearly 1 billion bottles of wine annually.

The French poet and novelist Victor Hugo is said to have found Bordeaux to be so intriguing that he mused: "Take Versailles, add Antwerp, and you have Bordeaux."

To fully appreciate this sentiment, dedicate a few hours to strolling or cycling along the left bank to enjoy Bordeaux's beautiful architecture such as Place de la Bourse with its Miroir d'eau: a stunning courtyard water feature that essentially acts as a mirror image of the palace.

I spent seven nights on AmaDolce, operated by AmaWaterways. This itinerary basically offers Bordeaux wine tours via boat and bike. Built in 2009, AmaDolce features 73 staterooms, and important to this trip, a fleet of bicycles that we could use on a complimentary basis for independent and/or guided tours. We pedaled four days out of the seven we were on board. It's hard to imagine a better way of exploring the wine-producing region surrounding Bordeaux.

AmaWaterways strives to be the most active of all river cruise companies, hence the emphasis on bikes. Guests sailing onboard AmaDolce were also offered walks and hikes as a means of seeing the region. And don't worry: If active tours aren't your thing, you're well covered. A fleet of buses operating panoramic city tours and the offer of "gentle walking" tours will show you all that you need to see in the Bordeaux region.

Evening in Bordeaux

Back on board, we indulged in wonderful meals and regional wines, poured free of charge during lunch and dinner. We enjoyed entertaining lectures and socializing in the lounge before cozying up in our staterooms to sleep away the night. On some days, we relaxed during stretches of scenic cruising.

Along with the Seine and the Rhône/Saône, AmaWaterways' Bordeaux river cruises offer truly immersive experiences. I thoroughly enjoyed exploring this beautiful part of France and its bountiful vineyards.

Bordeaux river cruises are a good pick for those who want to explore France for the first time or for those looking to complete their "portfolio" of river cruises in France. Bordeaux river cruises also rank high for active travelers who appreciate hiking and cycling opportunities, and for those who savor the storied wines produced in the vineyards that give Bordeaux its understated, elegant and timeless beauty.

WANT TO CRUISE BORDEAUX?

In 2018, AmaWaterways' 7-night "Taste of Bordeaux" river cruises are priced from $2,649 per person. That's a per diem of around $378, which isn't bad for all that you get. From March 22 through November 15, AmaDolce operates 23 Bordeaux departures, all with optional packages that include two pre-cruise nights in Paris and two nights in the Loire Valley, followed by one post-cruise night at Charles de Gaulle Airport for approximately $2,000 per person.

CULINARY CRUISES

While there isn't room on most river cruisers to feature huge demo kitchens with double-burner cooking stations, river cruises are definitely adding interesting touches for the globe-trotting epicurean. Most often this is accomplished by adding a thematic twist to existing itineraries, with options to forego city tours in favor of excursions that delve into the region's unique flavors. Avalon Waterways offers several culinary cruises, such as their 9-day voyage from Vienna to Munich in which you can partake in a cooking class with the famous Wrenkh brothers in Vienna, take a city tour focused on culinary traditions of Germany and Austria in Passau and enjoy multiple tastings and dinners with the Master of Wine while in transit.

From Paris and London to Provence, Côte d'Azur, and Barcelona, Avalon Waterways' six culinary themed itineraries in 2018 tap into some of the world's finest flavors.

Adventures by Disney, in conjunction with AmaWaterways, added a new food and wine theme culinary cruise in 2018, which visits four countries: Switzerland, France, Germany and the Netherlands. During this 8-day sailing you can take a patisserie and tart flambé classes in France, sample Riesling in German vineyards and discover the secrets of cheese making in Switzerland.

Tauck features a week long "Savoring France: Paris, Lyon & Provence" Rhône River cruise aboard the MS Emerald that showcases Tauck's time-honored special events ashore. These exclusive experiences include such noteworthy events as a dinner reception at Paris' famed Fouquet's on the Champs Élysées and a pastry class at Le Cordon Bleu, to sampling your way through the striking Les Halles covered food market in Lyon.

Many of the wine-themed cruises are a blend of both food and wine, because in Europe, the two go hand-in-hand. That being said, I was especially fond of the approach that ultra all-inclusive cruise line, Scenic, took in sating the epicurean traveler's appetite for adventure.

SCENIC DIAMOND - ROUNDTRIP BORDEAUX

During my 11-day "Beautiful Bordeaux Culinary River Cruise" aboard Scenic's Scenic Diamond, I got schooled in the culinary arts. A lesson happily learned, of course. On paper, Scenic Culinaire is an onboard cooking school. In practice, it's a lot of fun.

This Bordeaux cruise might visit similar ports to other cruise lines sailing the Garonne, Dordogne and Gironde Estuary: Libourne, with excursions to nearby Saint-Émilion; Pauillac, for outings in the Medoc region; Blaye, flaunting its impressive fortress; Bourg with its Gallo-Roman intrigue; Cadillac, the gateway to the Sauternes wine region and the historic Roquetaillade Castle; and, of course, Bordeaux, the beautiful city that serves as the hub for exploring the region's iconic wine chateaux. However, it's the gourmand-worthy gallivanting that truly distinguishes this journey. I'll simply give you a little taste.

In Bordeaux I was accompanied by Scenic Diamond's French Chef, Jerome, to the city's most popular food market, Marché des Capucins. I've been to markets before but it was fun to go with Chef Jerome to learn more about the local produce, cheeses (oh, the French cheeses), seafood and meat—and to sample and learn what we were going to do with those items back on the ship. After about 45 minutes of shopping, we had a bagful of goodies to take back to Scenic Diamond, where we would prepare special dishes in the dedicated Scenic Culinaire workspace. We learned to make a Fried Camembert with a Compote of Red Onions and Mesclun. It was fresh, light, delicious and something I'd consider serving at home, but the real fun was going to the market and shopping with the chef, then coming back to create beautiful dishes on Scenic Diamond. Scenic Culinaire is free of charge but class sizes are limited.

At the Marche des Capucins in Bordeaux

Scenic is a foodie's paradise. Touting five dining venues may be a little dubious in an industry where something just short of a food cart often constitutes a "venue." However, Scenic Diamond actually has five full-fledged dining venues. If we're splitting hairs, one of them, Table La Rive, is located within the main dining room. Still, Table La Rive, which can comfortably accommodate 10 people, is a multi-course, wine-pairing degustation dinner that is exceptionally well done. Table La Rive is by invitation only for guests on the Diamond Deck.

One deck up, in front of the lounge is L'Amour Restaurant, which serves French-inspired cuisine. L'Amour is open to all guests once per cruise. There's also the River Cafe, which serves light snacks during the day. Then there's the Panorama Bar and Lounge, in the heart of the ship where guests mingle over a cocktail, coffee or tea and peruse the ship's library. Lastly, room service offers a good selection of dishes. Some of the dishes I had on Scenic Diamond were among the best I have ever had on the rivers—the tortellini in L'Amour comes to mind—while the wines were regional and of some acclaim.

Scenic bills its Scenic Enrich activity as "an exclusive and unique experience that takes guests behind the scenes to enjoy moments inaccessible to ordinary travelers." For us, that was an evening in the Medoc countryside at Chateau Giscours, where we dined at an 18th-century farm and enjoyed classical music played by two lovely French musicians. An evening to remember, for sure. Other examples of ways that Scenic savors time ashore during the Bordeaux sailing includes a Grand Cru wine tasting at the exclusive estate of Château Franc Mayne, and sampling foie gras at a local farm in Bergerac. Sip your way through the Sauternes region, enjoy a fabulous Mademoiselle de Margaux chocolate and wine pairing event, and swirl Cognac at the acclaimed property of Rémy Martin.

Cocktail events known as "Scenic Sundowners" are another hallmark of the cruise line that oenophiles and spirit lovers will appreciate. One of my favorites was toward the end of our day in Saint-Emilion; we toasted the evening at nearby Chateau Siaurac, recognized as a National Heritage Site because of the estate's architectural and cultural heritage. I have found these gatherings to be a nice way to end the day and to celebrate the region that I was exploring.

Scenic is for those who welcome refined elegance with a personal touch. I found Scenic Diamond's staff to be professional and personable. While they were always intent on providing the best experience possible, they were easy to laugh with. In fact, I felt like a guest in someone's home, or chateau perhaps given the region where we were cruising. A home complete with your own butler, which may not be a big deal to some, but others will find the butler's services useful. What sort of things does the butler do? Deliver early morning tea or coffee to your stateroom, shoeshine service, make appointments (hairdresser, spa, dinner reservations) and more.

Scenic boasts the most recently updated ship in Bordeaux following a huge refurbishment in spring of 2017. Scenic started by removing six cabins to reduce the passenger count from 167 to 155. Following the refit, the ship now boasts the largest suites on the rivers of Bordeaux, the two super-sized Royal Owner's Suites. I had the opportunity to peek at one of them and my favorite feature was the balcony. Occupying a large space between the living room and bedroom, the balcony was glass-enclosed, featuring Scenic's innovative Sun Lounge system. Behind the balcony was a connecting hallway flanked by a bathroom that featured a shower

Suite balcony on Scenic Diamond

Scenic Diamond docked in Bordeaux

and a huge soaking tub. Measuring 510 square feet, Scenic Diamond's Royal Owner's Suites are for those who desire space to stretch out—and then some.

In addition, the renovation also augmented the ship's amenities with an enlarged gym with four cardio machines and a mini-trampoline. For those who prefer exercising off the ship, Scenic has a fleet of Ebikes, which offer a little assistance when pedaling during guided and independent touring. Then you can return the ship and give your muscles a little TLC in the new Whirlpool on the Sundeck or in the two-bed massage treatment room along with a Salt therapy room. Built in 2009, Scenic Diamond isn't an old ship by any means, but the updates functioned to keep it fresh and relevant to guests. Oh, and lest we not forget, the new Scenic Culinaire cooking school, which brings me back to my original sentiment that this cruise is a wonderful representation of how you can indulge both the palate and your passions during a river cruise.

INTERESTED IN TAKING A CULINARY SOJOURN WITH SCENIC IN BORDEAUX?

Scenic's 2018 departures of the 9-day Bordeaux Sojourn program begins at $4,445 per person.

CHRISTMAS MARKETS CRUISES

For several years since 2006, I've celebrated Christmas with friends and family on the rivers of Europe. It's a tradition that I have very much enjoyed and one that I hope to continue.

I love the cozy feeling of being on a vessel that transports me along the main arteries of Europe during this festive time of year. In wintertime, the rivers are magical. I've cruised through broken sheets of ice, which appeared as pieces of a jigsaw puzzle from the balcony of my stateroom. And although the sky can be brilliant blue, it's often diffused, giving the sky the appearance that reminds me of an Impressionistic painting. Surely, this must be the most romantic time of year to cruise Europe.

A White Christmas in Rothenburg on a Christmas Markets cruise.

If you're lucky, snow will blanket the villages along the rivers. One year, I trudged on powder with my family and friends through the uber-charming Rothenburg ob der Tauber. We felt like we were walking in a fairy tale. Christmas trees were decorated with red ribbons and sparkly white lights. Branches were laden with clumps of snow that had fallen from the rooftops. Icicles appeared like mini-stalactites from awnings, and under them, shop windows presented everything from wurst to gingerbread cookies, baked in Old World tradition.

These sailings typically depart between the last week of November through the year's end, and visit the wooden stalls erected in the town's historic squares of Germany, Austria, France, Hungary and other European countries. Some towns have but one market; I fondly remember visiting tiny Breisach, Germany, with its market that consisted of perhaps a dozen stalls and held plenty of warm, friendly holiday spirit. Big cities, on the other hand, can have more than one. Vienna is one of the most amazing in this regard, with nearly a dozen different markets in any given year—most of which are clustered around the famous Ringstrasse (ring road) that encircles the city's historic core.

Food plays a huge part in these seasonal festivities and varies with each village visit. In Hungary, spicy sausages and goulash soups are the order of the day, while Germany is all about the bratwurst and warm soups like kartoffelsuppe, or potato soup, served in an edible bread bowl. In Slovakia, we indulged in the most amazing shaved potato wedges we've ever had; while in Strasbourg, French and German-influence combined in a bowl of spätzle topped with heavy cream from Alsace. I enjoy bundling up to stroll historic city streets, sampling as I go, and returning to the ship to sip on hot mulled cider or, when the mood strikes, Gluhwein. This is frequently offered as either red or white wine (though red is far more common), and locals will quite often take it mit schuss (a shot of something else).

AmaWaterways offers three distinct winter river cruise itineraries: two weeklong cruises "Christmas Markets on the Rhine" between Amsterdam, Netherlands, and Basel, Switzerland, and "Christmas Markets on the Danube," between Nuremberg, Germany (Vilshofen, Germany in 2019) and Budapest, Hungary. In addition, a special two-week sailing "Magnificent Europe (Christmas Cruise)" is being offered over the official holiday, which encompasses some of the greatest hits from the other two itineraries. In 2018, these same sailings are being offered, but "Christmas on the Danube" gets a name change, called "Iconic Christmas Markets" and "Magical Christmas Markets" when sailing Nuremberg to Vienna or reverse. So same cruise, different wrapping. As the saying goes, "gingerbread by any other name still smells as sweet," or something along those lines.

One particularly fond memory I have was the year that I took my kids on AmaWaterways' "Christmas Markets on the Danube" voyage, which started off with a two-night pre-cruise stay in medieval Prague, including an optional tour to Prague's Christmas Market—an event not to be missed.

IF YOU'RE LUCKY, SNOW WILL BLANKET THE GROUND ON YOUR CHRISTMAS MARKETS CRUISE

All aglow for the holidays in Rothenburg, Germany

After leaving Prague, it was off to the historic city of Nuremberg, where we would board the vessel and rest up in port before a full day of exploration of this town's Gothic churches and ancient ramparts, and of course peruse the Christmas Markets. The following day, we arrived in Regensburg when the medieval city was newly blanketed in snow. It's a day I'll never forget, in part because it's captured in countless photographs that I snapped. During your Christmas Markets journey, you'll be able to visit Passau, Salzburg (by motorcoach), stop in Melk and cruise through the stunning Wachau Valley en route to Vienna, where you can enjoy an evening concert in the City of Music before reaching your final destination of Budapest, Hungary.

AmaWaterways' "Christmas Markets on the Rhine," between Basel and Amsterdam, can commence (or end) with an optional two extra nights in Lucerne and in Zurich. There's nothing like strolling the streets of Switzerland in December to make you feel as if you're on the set of The Nutcracker. Navigating Amsterdam's famed canals, sipping Rüdesheimer coffee while admiring one-of-a-kind stocking stuffers at Christmas Markets, and savoring Alsatian cuisine is the stuff sugar-plum dreams are made of. Dinners aboard AmaWaterways are extra extraordinary events on the Christmas Markets voyages as well, adding up to one unforgettable experience.

Avalon Waterways offers seven different Christmas markets river cruises, ranging in length from five to 17 days, and Crystal River Cruises offers 7 days or longer Christmas markets river cruises. In addition to Uniworld Boutique River Cruise Collection's six different Christmas markets sailings, the company will be offering a "Parisian Royal Holiday" Christmas markets cruise that will operate roundtrip from Paris aboard the new S.S. Joie de Vivre.

Last but not least, Viking River Cruises easily offers the most Christmas markets departure dates this year, thanks largely to its massive fleet of Viking Longships. In fact, the line offers an astonishing 19 different itineraries that operate during the Christmas markets, clustered throughout France, the Netherlands, Switzerland, Germany, Austria, Slovakia, Hungary and other countries.

The ultra all-inclusive cruise line Scenic pulls out all the stops between Budapest and Amsterdam with impressive flair during a 15-day "Christmas Markets" cruise (or 16-day "Christmas Wonderland" cruise in reverse), with options that include a 3-day extension in either Prague or Paris.

CroisiEurope offers 4- and 5-night Christmas market itineraries, as well, including a really unique sailing on the canals through Provence. This tour focuses more on the holiday traditions in places such as Avignon, Tarascon, Arles and Aigues-Mortes.

For instance, in Arles you will witness an impressive nativity scene before heading off to Paradou to visit a museum exhibiting 400 different santons (nativity figurines). From candle making to fougasse hankering, it's an interesting take on tradition in France.

Emerald Waterways also offers a 5-night sailing between Zurich, Switzerland and Weisbaden, Germany. Spice cakes and biscuits and quaint homes that were surely the inspiration behind the gingerbread variety, this cruise covers it all. From Breisach, the gateway to the Black Forest that takes Christmas ham to entirely new levels, to Strasbourg, France, home to one of Europe's oldest Christmas markets, it's a condensed, but rich journey.

As you can see there are choices aplenty, so start making your list and be sure to check it twice.

6

Chapter
SIX

WHERE ON EARTH
(AND WATER)

Illuminated: Hungary's Parliament building in Budapest

WHERE ON EARTH (AND WATER)

Europe has more navigable rivers than any other region in the world, and arguably more diverse cultures along its river banks than almost any other region.

Cruising the entire length of the Rhine, Main and Danube rivers alone—made possible thanks to the Main–Danube Canal—exposes travelers to 10 countries. Along the way are charming villages, fabled cities, fairy-tale castles, vineyards and more—all accessible from your floating hotel. However, this is far from the only inland artery. Germany also boasts the Moselle, Neckar and Elbe rivers, while France showcases the Loire, Seine, Soane and Rhône, and these are but two countries. Then there are rivers that even intrepid travelers may have never heard of: the Marne, the Guadiana, the Guadalquivir, the Dordogne, the Garonne, the Sarre, and Italy's longest river, the Po, largely unnavigable because of low water levels and sediment. And that's just the rivers. There are also many canals, which brings up an issue that those choosing river cruises often confront.

In what follows I attempt to give you a sense of the waterways made available to you through river cruising through geographic description, and highlighting popular ports along the way. In addition, I will include a few voyage recaps of various sailings that I've done within those regions to give you a feel for the ships plying the waters, the overall onboard experience and things to do ashore. Hopefully this will help you set your sights on a river cruise that's right for you. If you're anything like me, every river offers its own intrigue, so even armed with information you might find it difficult to decide. Take a deep breath, and know that this doesn't have to be your only river cruise. Once you do your first river cruise, you'll want to return to do more. Yes, river cruising can be addictive. There are countless other voyage recaps and travel news to peruse on my site, rivercruiseadvisor.com; and as always, I'm reachable via the recommendations form for personal advice.

FAMOUS TRIO:
THE UPPER DANUBE, MAIN AND RHINE

Out of the many famed European waterways, there's a trio that I celebrate as The Three Tenors: the Rhine, Main and Danube rivers. Itineraries incorporating all of these waterways harmonize just as beautifully as the aforementioned singers, with so much of Europe viewable from the railing of a river cruise.

Scenic beauty is the stuff of legends, past fairytale villages and into the epicenters of capital cities alike. From trading posts to water-powered factories, these rivers have long served as the lifeblood of this western continent. That being said, it's important to mention something: River cruising views aren't always that of the Monet and Rembrandt variety. Factory smokestacks often greet your arrival instead of castle turrets and fortress walls. This is something that shouldn't serve to dissuade you by any means, quite the contrary, but understand that given the cultural clout of these destinations, some river cruisers visiting the city must dock in an industrial port more suitable for loading and unloading gravel and grain than river cruise passengers. While that might be contrary to the gloss and glamour of ocean liner terminals, it also encapsulates the essence of river cruising: you are being delivered to culture's doorstep, where locals coexist with visitors and life unfolds before you.

Speaking of industrial influences, the Rhine-Main-Danube Canal is one that changed the face of river cruising on the Rhine, Main and Danube. The man-made canal runs between the German towns of Bamberg and Kelheim via the historic city of Nuremberg, transporting thousands of river cruise ship passengers every year between this famous trio of rivers. While it may go largely unnoticed today, this technological marvel remains a surprisingly recent addition to the German landscape.

Although an early version of the canal existed prior to World War II, heavy damage during the war years destroyed many of the early locks that lined the river. To complicate matters, bridges had been destroyed and waterways were clogged, making resumption of river traffic at the end of World War II anything but easy. By the early 1950s, plans for reconstruction of the canal were no longer a priority, and the idea was shelved.

Just a decade later, it became apparent that a link between the Rhine, Main and Danube rivers was greatly needed after all, thanks to an increase in both passenger and freight traffic on the waterways. The canal would also serve as a sign of German unity in a Europe that rapidly sought to forgive and forget after the horrors of the Second World War. But rather than a simple reconstruction of the locks that existed prior to 1945, plans were drawn up for a system of locks that would unite the rivers once and for all and finally allow ships to travel uninterrupted from Amsterdam to the Black Sea.

By the time the last section was completed in 1992, the canal had grown to span a distance of 106 miles. But this journey is anything but a straight line between two rivers. The canal rises and falls with the surrounding landscape and because of the extreme height differences between the two rivers, a total of 16 locks had to be constructed to alternately lift and lower ships along their journey. At their highest point along the Continental Divide, locks carry ships to a height of more than 1,000 feet above sea level. Now that you know how these rivers are interconnected, let's break them down.

A gorgeous September evening in Bratislava

UPPER DANUBE

If you don't know where to start with your first river cruise, I'll make it easy for you: Choose the Danube. This river is Europe's second longest, touching the banks of ten countries and four capitals. It's my number one choice for people new to river cruising. Why? The Danube features a list of marquee cities—Nuremberg, Passau, Linz, Vienna, Budapest, Bratislava (as well as Bucharest and Belgrade on some itineraries) and it offers something for everyone. I've cruised the Danube more than a dozen times and I love it every time that I go because I see something different every time. Packages on the Danube range from 5 to 23 days, so as you can imagine, there's a vast range of sites that can be experienced during one trip.

The Danube begins in the shaded glory of Germany's Black Forest near the Swiss border, where the Breg and Brigach headstreams converge and stretch all the way to the Black Sea. It flows east to west from Germany to Ukraine, but "the Upper Danube" is technically the eastern side—from Germany to Hungary—and proves to be the most popular with cruise companies. This is the tour for you if you really want to experience a collection of Europe's greatest hits such as visiting the Cesky Krumlov in the Czech Republic, a UNESCO World Heritage Site, or biking Austria's Wachau Valley between Melk and Durnstein. Evening visits to Viennese palaces, lit in their full glory, to witness a waltz or concert, or a stroll from Buda to Pest undoubtedly confirm poets' romantic notions of European charm and grace.

Most seven to ten-night itineraries allow sufficient time to explore the major cities along the river. The most common route extends between Passau, Germany and Budapest, Hungary. Prague is often listed as a starting or ending point of a cruise; however, Prague is not located on the Danube River. It's about 140 miles north of Passau and about 190 northeast of Nuremberg, with guests bussed to and from the ship.

Some vessels operate roundtrip from Passau; some operate one-way between Regensburg and Budapest; and others cruise between Vienna or Budapest to Nuremberg, which requires transiting the section of the Main-Danube Canal over the Franconian Alps. This passage, which I've discussed earlier is known as Europe's Continental Divide. It was the vision of Charlemagne, and the waterway canal only took a mere 1,200 years to come to fruition—reaching completion in 2002. The series of 16 locks is spread over a distance of more than 100 miles, methodically lifting river cruisers nearly 1,400 feet above sea level. The Divide is represented by a concrete monument on the banks, and my first time reaching this iconic milestone, I expected the captain to speak the words reserved for airline pilots, "Ladies and gentlemen, we've reached our cruising altitude." He did not, and crossing the divide passed uneventfully for most guests on the ship, who were having dinner. Not for me. I was out on deck to take in the spectacle.

For the most part the Upper Danube spans more than a mile wide, meandering through fertile plateaus dotted with fairy-tale fortresses, with the only narrow, canyon-like gorges being Hungary's Visegrád north of Budapest and the Iron Gates (see the Lower Danube).

On the pages that follow, I share with you a few of my favorite memories, sneak peeks into new ship interiors, and other river cruising details that have made my encounters with the Danube dynamic.

SCENIC JASPER - BUDAPEST TO VIENNA

Scenic Jasper was one of Scenic's newest "Space Ships" when I cruised her in 2015. The vessel is 443 feet long and carries 169 guests and 53 crew members. Along with her sister Scenic Opal, Scenic Jasper has some of the largest suites in the industry. A couple of suites measure up to 475 square feet.

On a spring day in 2015, I boarded Scenic Jasper in Budapest. I spent six nights sailing from the Hungarian capital to Vienna. Along the way I met the company's owners, Glen Moroney and his wife Karen; key executives; and a slew of North American travel agents and journalists. The consensus among the travel agents was that Scenic serves up a quality experience at a high level.

I had cruised Scenic once, but that was a few years ago, and even though I had read up on how the company sought to differentiate itself, seeing (and experiencing) Scenic Jasper became believing for me. This Australia-based company strives to differentiate itself by being the most-inclusive of all river cruise companies—though Scenic must contend with the likes of Crystal, Tauck and Uniworld. You'd find it hard, if not impossible in fact, to spend for anything on Scenic once your cruise fare has been paid. In addition to a long list of inclusives, Scenic bundles in all gratuities, even those for guides ashore. Scenic isn't skimping either. Champagne is poured, not sparkling (except Prosecco in Jasper's Italian dining venue, Portobello), top shelf spirits are included, single malts, for example. You can belly up to the bar for bottled European beer or a draft, at no extra charge. About the only thing you can dig into your wallet for is a massage.

After a gorgeous night in Budapest, I had a chance to explore Scenic Jasper. Scenic Jasper's ambiance was stunning, from its large aft suites to its beautiful lounges and restaurants. She's a stunning vessel from a company that aspires to be to river cruising what Regent Seven Seas is to ocean cruising, which, as noted earlier, is that Scenic wants to be the most-inclusive luxury player in the river cruise segment.

This is accomplished with elements ranging from pillow and mattress menus to butlers (in addition to room attendants) for all staterooms and suites, Apple technology drives the entertainment systems, and guests have access to incredible electric-assist bicycles that they can pedal in ports of call. There's also a variety of ways to get to know destinations through programs such as "Scenic Enrich," "Scenic FreeChoice," "Scenic Tailormade" and more. These choices allow guests to choose their own way to explore, from self-guided bicycle or walking tours using GPS devices to guided tours with knowledgeable guides. But the most ingenious display of forward-thinking design and decadence is the "Sun Lounge," a mix of open-air balcony/solarium in all but the baker's dozen of standard staterooms. While Uniworld's S.S. Catherine and S.S. Maria Theresa feature retractable windows, Scenic ships feature an actual step-out balcony. A folding glass door (new on Jasper, replacing sliding glass doors on the other vessels) opens the Sun Lounge to the bedroom/living area, creating a feeling of an expansive open space, hence Scenic calling its vessels, "Space-Ships." Within the Sun Lounge are two wicker chairs with cushions and a couple of small tables that complement the chairs. There's enough space for two people to sit comfortably, even with the folding glass door closed.

In addition to the folding glass door, an exterior balcony window spans the width of the stateroom. The window is designed in two pieces, and with the push of a button, the top piece of the window descends so that it is flush with the bottom piece of the window. One particularly nice aspect of this feature is that the window can be opened when sailing so that you can not only admire the passing scenery but also breathe it in. To get a better visual, watch this video | https://www.rivercruiseadvisor.com/2015/05/compared-scenics-sun-lounges-uniworlds-open-air-balconies/.

The Sun Lounge made sitting in my 205-square-foot stateroom enjoyable, which is exactly what Scenic owner Glen Moroney envisioned. He told the story of when Scenic (then Scenic Tours) chartered ships in Europe. He was on board one of the chartered vessels, and after three or four days, he wanted to get away to decompress and relax in his stateroom. The problem: It was 150 square feet with a bed and a single chair, not a room conducive to relaxing while awake. "I thought, why can't we have balconies on river cruises," Moroney told me.

The companies that chartered to Scenic back then would not install balconies, so Scenic began building its own ships in 2007. Scenic was the first, according to Moroney, to put so many balconies on river cruisers. Today, throughout the fleet, 85 percent of Scenic's staterooms and suites feature Sun Lounges.

The ship itself certainly made this river cruise on the Upper Danube a memorable one, but what is travel without the experiences? I didn't miss the opportunity to try to beat the ship to from Durnstein to Melk on a bike. The 20-mile ride between these Austrian cities was anything but slow. We weren't breaking records, but for

A breath of fresh air: Scenic's Sun Lounge

the 20-plus of us who pedaled, the ride was exhilarating and fun. Along the way, we stopped several times for photographs, bathroom breaks and to check out noteworthy sites. Scenic's electric-assist bicycles made the going easy as we pedaled along mostly dedicated bike roads through the beautiful Wachau Valley, a wine-producing region in Austria. During our ride, Scenic Jasper sailed toward Melk. We pedaled alongside her at times and at other times would lose her as we veered away from the river toward charming villages that looked as though they may have been movie sets for the "Sound of Music." In fact, one Scenic tour takes guests to locations where the classic film was produced.

We reached Melk in a little less than three hours after we had left Durnstein. I would highly recommend this tour for anyone who is moderately active and comfortable on a bicycle. Our guides were excellent, a father-daughter pair from the Wachau region, with the daughter leading the way and the father following up at the rear to make sure that no one took an unintended detour.

When we arrived in Melk, we toured the Melk Abbey. The Benedictine Abbey was built between 1702 and 1736 and sits on a rocky outcrop overlooking the town.

The guided bike tour was one of three tours that Scenic Jasper guests could experience that day. The other tours were a visit to the Melk Abbey and afterward a Scenic Sundowner, then a new program that took guests to a special location to toast the end of the day. Our Scenic Sundowner took us to Burgruine Aggstein, 12th-century castle ruins that sit high above the right bank of the Danube and is one of lower Austria's most popular attractions. By coincidence, a Medieval festival was taking place at the castle on the evening we were there.

Thanks to Scenic Freechoice, a program whereby there are three or four choices of guided tours on most days, I felt that I had adequate choices to make the trip my own. One of those choices can always be a self-guided option, using the Tailormade GPS system for directions and commentary. The Tailormade device fits on the bicycles or it can be hand-carried for those doing city tours on foot. It allows for you to get on and off the ship at your leisure to explore while still having the luxury of a "virtual guide." Once or twice per voyage there's also Scenic Enrich, which is an "elevated experience;" a concert at a Viennese palace, for example.

Another gorgeous day was spent in Linz, Austria. Some of the guests headed off for a full-day excursions (complimentary, of course) to the Czech Republic, where they would explore the 13th-century town of Cesky Krumlov, a UNESCO World Heritage Site. Others headed to Salzburg, the setting for "The Sound of Music" and birthplace of Wolfgang Amadeus Mozart. Me? I straddled a saddle for one of the best bike rides yet, but since I've already written extensively about biking, I thought I'd focus on a topic everyone seems to appreciate: food.

First, a little backstory. I was traveling with a group of journalists and top travel sellers on Scenic Jasper to take part in christening ceremonies in Vienna. We were an experienced group of travelers, often a bit skeptical and hyper-critical. But that's because our job is observe the fine details that make or break travel experiences for our readers or the clients of travel sellers who were with us.

I'm not the greatest food critic. I enjoy almost any food that I can lift to my lips. So I'm not your best source for telling you if the food was good, great, or orgasmic. Some of my colleagues have discerning palates, however. What I heard from them and from the travel sellers over and again is that the dining experience on Scenic Jasper was done exceptionally well. The dining outlets were varied (there's the Crystal Dining Room, Portobello, Table Le Rive, the River Café and room service), the cuisine was well presented and tasteful, and the service was outstanding.

There are three options for breakfast: room service, the River Café and the main dining room, called the Crystal Dining Room. Guests on deck three may order a full breakfast delivered to their rooms, as well as those in the Junior Suites on deck two. Those in other categories of staterooms may order coffee or tea delivered to their rooms. After breakfast, 24-hour room service is available for all guests.

The River Café, situated in the Jasper Lounge, also serves up breakfast. I enjoy the tranquil setting, with a table by the window, watching the rippling of the river as Scenic Jasper motors upstream in the mornings. The Crystal Dining Room serves up a little of all that you would expect from a fine hotel breakfast: omelets and eggs cooked to order, cereals, fruits, yogurts, toast, fresh-squeezed orange juice and more. Breakfast is served buffet-style. Like breakfast, there are three options for lunch: room service, the River Café and the Crystal Dining Room.

Table La Rive is situated in a section of the Crystal Dining Room serving a six-course set menu paired with wines; available only to guests on deck three and those in Junior Suites on deck two. The cuisine and service was about as good as I've experienced anywhere. Early in the week, I also enjoyed dinner at Portobello. The Italian-themed restaurant is situated on the main deck, in front of the Jasper Lounge. And, the Wienerschnitzel during an Austrian dinner on board while docked in Vienna was delicious and perfectly complemented my iconic evening: an evening concert in a museum. The concert was presented under a program that Scenic calls "Scenic Enrich." Having done these types of events before, I tempered my expectations. Sometimes the idea is better than the execution. This time, it was the other way around.

The Scenic Enrich concert is normally held in the Lichtenstein Palace, but due to timing issues, our venue was the Arsenal Museum, a beautiful building, but I am told that the acoustics in Liechtenstein Palace are superior. Hard to imagine. The concert, which lasted a little more than an hour with representative works by Strauss, Mozart and Beethoven, was surprisingly good in all respects. The musicians never missed a beat, the dancers flowed like silk in the wind, the emcee/host had a great sense of humor, presenting a serving of warm Apple Strudel to a woman who had shouted the name of the Austrian dessert when asked what Vienna was famous for. There was even a stirring rendition from "The Sound of Music." Some in the audience felt a standing ovation was appropriate at the end of the evening performance. I was among those who stood and applauded.

I returned to Scenic Jasper for a late-night snack, goulash and a Weissbier with my colleagues and newly made friends. It was the perfect ending to a day that started with a long bike ride for me (naturally), followed by a night of Viennese music and waltzing.

The next day I disembarked Scenic Jasper, but I wasn't done yet. After a morning excursion to the Spanish Riding School in Vienna, I checked into the Hilton Waterfront and walked along the dock where Scenic's newest ship was being prepared for its naming event. Tents were set up outside with cooking stations and cakes, bottles of champagne and wine, and all decked out wearing their best duds. There were a few speeches, including one from Scenic Jasper's godmother, Kathy Lette, an Australian novelist and comedienne. Then, a bottle of bubbly broke across the bow, and Scenic Jasper was named. The rest, as they say, is history.

If you're someone who enjoys a luxury river cruise experience with everything included — as well as opportunities to be active—then Scenic's for you.

WANT TO EXPERIENCE SCENIC JASPER ON THE DANUBE?

The 8-day Gems of the Danube sailing between Budapest and Nuremberg is offered between May and October of 2018, starting at $3,895 per person, double occupancy.

The Sun Deck lives up to its name on Scenic Jasper

CRYSTAL MOZART -
A NEW SHIP CHRISTENING IN VIENNA

I was on Crystal Mozart for fewer than 48 hours. Even so I quickly came to appreciate what Crystal Cruises, a leader in luxury blue-water cruising, was attempting to create on the Blue Danube.

I should note that I had no choice but to make a quick study. Two nights on board, and I was to be booted off. I was part of a VIP group in Vienna for Crystal Mozart's christening. After the bottle had broken against the hull, we were expected to start packing to make room for paying guests on Crystal Mozart's inaugural voyage.

To introduce Crystal Mozart, Crystal had to take "The Queen of Europe's Rivers," as the vessel is affectionately known, down to her steel structure and build her back up. It was no easy task, especially with the clock ticking toward the ship's christening date in Vienna.

The restoration was done in Linz, Austria. Transforming the ship took more than 400 shipyard workers going at it around the clock. "We went through every single inch, both technically and from a hotel point of view," said then Crystal Cruises

COO Thomas Mazloum. "We had 14 different contractors, two to three different designers, working the last couple of months in three shifts, 24 hours a day to get it finished in time."

And so it was that in July of 2016, Crystal River Cruises introduced a river cruiser that was as beautiful as it was innovative. It was a remarkable feat. In 2009, I sailed on Mozart when it operated for Peter Deilmann River Cruises (shortly before the company went bankrupt). Touring Crystal Mozart in Vienna, I saw hardly any vestiges of the old vessel. Simply, Crystal Mozart was stunning and appeared to be a new ship.

At 75 feet across, Crystal Mozart is nearly twice the width of the standard river cruiser. That extra width allows for a lot more in terms of public rooms and generally larger staterooms than you might find on the standard river cruiser. Staterooms, in fact, feature king-sized beds.

The double width limits Crystal Mozart's itineraries to the Danube, as it cannot transit the Main-Danube Canal. However the extra width imparts those traveling

Crystal Mozart features king-size beds and luxury throughout

Indoor pool on Crystal Mozart

on Crystal Mozart the feeling of being on a small luxury ocean-going vessel, a Crystal Cruises' ocean-going vessel, in fact. Throughout Crystal Mozart elegant furnishings adorned public areas that would be familiar to those who have sailed Crystal Cruises' two luxury ocean ships, Crystal Symphony and Serenity. Just as on those ships, on Crystal Mozart you'll find the Bistro, the Cove and Palm Court, for example—as well as Crystal's renowned staff. Crystal, in fact, hires and trains its own staff. Most other river cruise companies contract hotel and food and beverage operations.

Staterooms and suites carried familiar amenities: Crystal bathrobes and kimonos, Etro toiletries and even Crystal-logo shopping and laundry bags similar to those that you will find on Crystal Symphony and Serenity.

Complementing Crystal Mozart's elegance were some innovative itineraries and shore programs. Crystal aimed to differentiate itself from the other major players in this region with what it offered ashore.

Consider that Crystal is the only river cruise company currently operating that started as an ocean-cruise company. Crystal has had more than a quarter of a century to perfect its onboard experience. And years of consecutive awards leaves little doubt that Crystal performs about as good as it gets in the hospitality sector.

Crystal Mozart is a beautiful vessel with unique attributes and activities, a good choice for those wanting the style and sophistication of Crystal Cruises, on the Blue Danube.

WANT TO EXPERIENCE CRYSTAL MOZART ON THE DANUBE?

In 2018, Crystal Mozart will offer 27 departures on the Danube with fares beginning at $3,695 per person. The ten-night cruises, roundtrip Vienna, continue through December 20, perfect timing for the Christmas markets along the Danube.

Room service & friendly service on Crystal Mozart

DISCOVER OUR **FIVE-STAR FLEET**

Riviera River Cruises is delighted to introduce you to our award-winning cruises aboard the newest fleet of 5-star ships to grace Europe's waterways. As your floating boutique hotel gracefully glides between towns and cities, maybe unwind on deck with a refreshing drink or savor the finest European cuisine in a choice of restaurants.

LUXURY 5-STAR SHIPS

MS Lord Byron

LARGER CABINS

Deluxe balcony suite, MS Thomas Hardy

CHOICE OF RESTAURANTS

Restaurant on the MS Jane Austen

WHERE WILL OUR RIVER CRUISES **TAKE YOU**?

See the classic sights of Europe and become acquainted with lesser-known places that are often even more intriguing. Our guided tours are conducted in English by insightful experts passionate about bringing to life the places we visit. Our itineraries are thoughtfully balanced so there's time to relax and if you wish, immerse yourself in local culture.

CRUISE THE HEART OF EUROPE

Fifteen days from only **$2,999** per person
DEPARTING MAY THROUGH OCTOBER 2018
AND APRIL THROUGH OCTOBER 2019

RHINE CRUISE TO SWITZERLAND

Eight days from only **$1,799** per person
DEPARTING APRIL THROUGH OCTOBER 2018
AND APRIL THROUGH OCTOBER 2019

THE DOURO, PORTO & SALAMANCA

Eight days from only **$1,909** per person
DEPARTING APRIL THROUGH NOVEMBER 2018
AND APRIL THROUGH NOVEMBER 2019

Riviera River Cruises, 1515 Black Rock Turnpike, Fairfield CT 06825
Prices subject to availability. All rights reserved.

Budapest

Riviera's Robert Burns, docked in Budapest

RIVIERA'S ROBERT BURNS - A SCHOLARLY SOJOURN ON THE DANUBE

In summing up my introductory three-night river cruise on the m/s Robert Burns, two words come to mind: pleasantly surprised. Robert Burns is one of a dozen ships operated by the U.K.'s Riviera Travel, which only recently began marketing Riviera River Cruises to North American travelers.

You're not alone if you find yourself scratching your head about the company's name. Why would a river cruise operator choose a name that brings to mind France's sun-drenched Côte d'Azur? The explanation: Riviera Travel began operating in the U.K. more than three decades ago by offering getaways to the French Riviera, hence the name. One reassuring fact about the name is that Riviera has years of experience in accommodating travelers.

In early April of 2018, I was invited to Austria, along with a couple dozen North American travel agents and company executives, for the christening of Riviera's

Robert Burns. The christening was followed by a cruise from Vienna to Budapest, which gave me time to experience the operational aspects of the new ship.

From the outset, my expectations were that I would step aboard a low-cost river cruise where the company had cut costs to achieve an attractive price point. Riviera's 8-day Blue Danube cruises begin at just $1,399 per person, which is considerably less than similar sailings offered by other river cruise companies.

In part, Riviera achieves its low price point by "unbundling" some features, such as inclusive beer and wine during lunch and dinner. On the other hand, Riviera includes costs that may be hidden, or in the fine print, on competitors, such as port charges. As an example, Uniworld includes beverages of all types (all the time) on its river cruises but does not include port charges in its fares. Port charges for Uniworld's seven-night Delightful Danube cruise total more than $300 per stateroom.

While Riviera includes port charges, a beverage package will cost you $129 per person ($159 in 2019, and $299 for longer voyages). The difference is that everyone must pay port charges whereas on river cruises that include beverages, non-imbibers essentially subsidize their fellow passengers who do drink.

Not so with Riviera's unbundling of beverages. You pay for what you consume. And you need not pay $129 per person. A glass of house wine on Robert Burns will set you back about $3. If you had three glasses of wine a day for seven days (on an eight-day cruise, you disembark early on the eighth day and aren't likely to consume), you'd spend only between $60 and $70.

Two things surprised me, well, three really about Riviera's Robert Burns. The first was the overall ship experience. For most of its ships, Riviera contracts with Scylla, a Swiss river cruise ship owner that also manages the food and beverage, and hotel operations throughout its fleet.

Scylla is the same company that Tauck uses for its European river cruises. It would be a stretch to say that Riviera is like Tauck but at a lower price point (the two are not in the same competitive set and should not be viewed as being so). But as for the ship itself, the similarities were striking. Stepping into the reception area of the

Robert Burns, for example, reminded me of stepping into the reception area on Tauck's m/s Savor.

Likewise, both ships have restaurants situated aft, Arthur's on Savor and The Bistro on Robert Burns. The additional dining venue, in fact, is one of the key points that differentiates Riviera from some of its competitors. The Bistro, a reservations-only, but complimentary, restaurant that serves up specialties such as Black Angus burgers for lunch and lobster tails for dinner, is open for both lunch and dinner. Other river cruise companies that have specialty restaurants typically open them only for dinner.

There are other aspects where Riviera differentiates itself among river cruise companies, and during my all-too-short time on board Robert Burns, I discovered seven ways by which Riviera seeks to stand out.

Lounge on Robert Burns (both photos)

1. Pricing. On several itineraries where I compared pricing, Riviera offered among the lowest lead-in prices. As noted, however, Riviera does not include beverages, even with lunch and dinner. Nor are gratuities of 8 euros to 12 euros per person per day included in the fare, and although tips are at your discretion, most American guests would feel compelled to stuff the envelopes left on their beds on the last night of the cruise. But even with allowances for beverages and gratuities added in, Riviera ranks among the price-leaders on most itineraries.

2. No Discounting. Riviera does not discount. Nor does the company provide booking incentives. No discounting and no booking incentives can actually be viewed as pluses. "It's good to know that you're not going to be sitting beside someone at dinner who paid less than you did," says Jana Tvedt, the company's Vice President, who was on my sailing in April. "Our pricing philosophy is that we don't discount, we don't do promotions."

3. Upgrades Are Reasonably Priced. The cost to upgrade from the bottom deck to the middle deck to the upper deck isn't as costly as it is on some of Riviera's competitors. On Robert Burns' October 28, 2019 Blue Danube eight-day sailing, for example, the lead-in rate is $1,399 per person for entry-level accommodations measuring 172 square feet with fixed, quarter-height riverview windows. Moving

up one deck to 183-square-foot accommodations featuring French balconies adds only $520 per person, for a total of $1,919 per person.

4. No single supplements. Five staterooms on Emerald Deck are made available on nearly all of Riviera's cruises for single travelers (only three cabins are offered for single travelers on the Douro). All are double staterooms that solo travelers can occupy with no single supplements.

5. Stateroom size. The smallest staterooms on Robert Burns and its sister ships measure 172 square feet. That is larger than the smallest staterooms on many other river cruise ships. Moreover, no matter which stateroom you choose, you'll receive many of the same amenities as the occupants do on the upper decks, including bathrobes, coffee and tea maker (as well as an ample supply of coffee and tea) and even room service upon request.

6. Multiple dining venues. Robert Burns features the main dining room, which is open seating (meaning no assigned dining times) as well as The Bistro, situated aft on deck 3 and free of charge. The Bistro cannot be pre-booked, however, so you will need to make reservations when on board. The open-kitchen concept offers dining during lunch and dinner except for embarkation day and is open only for lunch on the day of the Captain's Gala Dinner. I found the setting to be intimate, the service excellent and the food delectable during both lunch and dinner when I dined there.

7. Independence. Generally, Riviera includes a complimentary tour in the morning and free time in the afternoon. "It takes away some of the stress," says Riviera's International Sales & Marketing Manager Thomas Morgan. "We give you an overview type tour in the morning, then the freedom to explore in the afternoon." I enjoyed having the free time in the afternoon to use one of the eight bikes on board Robert Burns without feeling that I was missing a tour.

Quibbles & Brits. I asked travel agents on my sailing what they thought about Riviera River Cruises and Robert Burns. Would it appeal to their American clients? All who I spoke with were unanimously affirmative. They cited the ship's "elegant decor" and "spacious staterooms" among the key selling features. The only real quibble was one that I heard on the last night of our voyage, "We are on a ship

Veranda Stateroom on Robert Burns

operated by a British company," one said. "It could have been even more British." How could any Anglophile argue with that?

I know now why Riviera River Cruises chose its name, but I'm not sure why the company chose to name its ships after famous authors, though I do like it. The company introduces two more ships in 2019. They're to be named the George Elliot and the William Wordsworth. And as Riviera has done with the Robert Burns, the company is poised to do those authors proud.

MOST OF RIVIERA'S SHIPS ARE NAMED FOR FAMOUS ENGLISH AUTHORS

NEW! AMAWATERWAYS UPCOMING SUPER-SIZED SHIP ON THE DANUBE

Construction on AmaMagna started in March of 2017 and while this new ship—almost double the standard width of the company's current ships—won't set sail until 2019, I'd be remiss not to mention it as a Danube option for your future travels. The double-wide vessel appears to be a direct response to Crystal Mozart. I can't wait to see what AmaWaterways brings to the table—or rather, to the Danube. With the expanded space, AmaWaterways can include more features on Ama-Magna than are on its current fleet.

Some of those features that river cruisers may find attractive: an alternative al fresco restaurant; a heated sundeck swimming pool, whirlpool and sky bar; an expanded Zen Wellness Spa as well as AmaWaterways' largest fitness room ever; and an open-water sports platform, the first of its kind for river cruising, where complimentary tours will be offered on the intimate Sundowner vessel.

At roughly 75 feet across, like Crystal Mozart, AmaMagna will be able to cruise upstream only a little beyond Passau, Germany. The new ship will be too wide to transit the narrow locks of the Main-Danube Canal, limiting itineraries to the Danube. Of course, that's hardly a deal-breaker. There's quite a lot of beauty, as well as many marquee cities, along the Danube. And, a special perk for sailing aboard AmaMagna and her skinnier big sisters. AmaWaterways frequently uses Vilshofen, Germany, for christenings, and for its embarkation and disembarkation for Danube cruises. The city appreciates AmaWaterways so much that it puts on a "Miniature Munich Oktoberfest" for guests who are beginning or ending their cruises in Vilshofen. It's little touches like these that differentiate AmaWaterways from its competitors.

MAIN

Sandwiched between the Danube and Rhine, the Main (pronounced mine) River stretches 326 miles through the heart of Germany. Flowing from east to west from its headwaters southwest of Kulmbach to where it converges with the Rhine near Mainz. However, this Rhine tributary is only considered navigable between Bamberg and Mainz. A perfect blend of Roter (red) Main and Weisser (white) Main mountain waters delivers travelers into Franconia wine country, where you can sip Silvaner or stop in for a frothy pint at one of the region's 300 different breweries. But libations aside, the concentration of culture within this region will make you dizzy with excitement. It's no surprise that the hamlets filled with half-timbered homes, dense forests, castles and fortresses served as muse for Brothers Grim tales as well as the melodies in Wagner's Tristan and Isolde. While the UNESCO World Heritage Sites of Würzburg and Bamberg are popular stops for river cruises traversing Main's waters, other prominent cities also visited include Frankfurt, Miltenberg and Wertheim—as well as visits to nearby Bayreuth.

Frankfurt is an ideal embarkation and disembarkation port for river cruises, thanks to its modern amenities and sprawling International airport. While a few cruises begin or end here, in general, most will originate in Amsterdam, Budapest, Vienna or Nuremberg. That's because Main River cruises are always combined with other waterways, unless it's a day or evening cruise. The most common package includes the Main with the Rhine and Danube. (Some cruises also travel along the Moselle and the Dutch and Belgian Waterways.) This is thanks to the Main-Danube Canal that I mentioned earlier, canalizing the river upstream to Bamberg to link the Rhine and Danube and create a 2,200-mile waterway spanning from the North Sea to the Black Sea.

The best river to pair with your exploration of the Main really depends on how much time you have to travel and which direction you would rather go. If you would like to visit the Netherlands, a combination with the Rhine River will provide a chance to visit Amsterdam and a few cities in Germany, such as Cologne, Dusseldorf and Bonn. If your itinerary includes the lower Rhine River to or from Basel, a few of the stops along the way might include Strasbourg and Briesach.

Itineraries taking you from the Main River to the Danube might include some very beautiful and intriguing cities, such as Nuremberg, Salzburg, Vienna, and Budapest. The ultimate combo would be a trip that combines the Main, Rhine, and Danube Rivers. Since most packages are at least 12 days, this is the type of cruise that would be great if you have at least two weeks to spend vacationing. So while Main might not be the river that springs to mind when planning your Danube or Rhine river cruise, it's often the lead understudy that makes your visit the region all the more entertaining.

UNIWORLD BOUTIQUE RIVER CRUISE COLLECTION S.S. MARIA THERESA - WÜRZBURG TO BUDAPEST

In May of 2015, I cruised Uniworld's 150-passenger S.S. Maria Theresa from Würzburg to Budapest. It was a brand-new ship at the time, so in order to check it out I jumped aboard for a half-voyage on the Danube. (Uniworld's 15-day Amsterdam to Budapest sailing, "European Jewels," sails along the Rhine and Main rivers in addition to the Danube.)

I chose to highlight this sailing as an opportunity to let you peek inside a vessel plying the Danube that possesses a decidedly unique river cruise personality. This cruise line offers an upscale experience (think Seabourn on the rivers), with sumptuous surrounds and the impeccable service of crew members. Butlers strut down the hallways in tux and tails, high tea is served in the lounge in the afternoon, and dinner is delivered with ceremonial flair. The stately and palace-like baroque

Uniworld's Maria Theresa docked in Wurzburg, Germany.

interiors hark back to the days of the Austrian empress for whom the 443-foot vessel is named. However, there are also many flashes of modernity, such as the in-room amenities, on-board movie theater, and the popular Leopard Bar. Even more memorable about this particular sailing for me is that I nearly missed it.

I had a great flight on Lufthansa. The disappointment came when I arrived at the train station at the Frankfurt Airport. At 17:20 I made my way down to track 5, but something was odd. The platform was empty and the train directional boards were dimmed. I thought I had arrived at the wrong platform, despite it being printed on my electronic ticket. No, something else was up: Rail strike.

What to do? The ship would be leaving Würzburg at 23:00. The original train schedule would have gotten me there in plenty of time, but I had to scramble to find a new way to Würzburg. Bus? Ugh. Taxi? God forbid; it would cost a few hundred Euro. Wait until the next morning and catch the ship? But where would it be? Fortunately, I discovered that the 19:37 train was running, albeit late. If I could get on that one, I could make the ship, possibly.

That 19:37 train was running late, but at least it was running and late only by about 15 minutes. When it arrived, I boarded, relieved, and found a seat. I wasn't sure

Watching the world pass from my balcony.

Uniworld's bikes are great for exploring.

that it would get me to Würzburg in time, but I was prepared to be flexible, stay in a hotel if necessary and find my way to the ship the next day.

Fortunately, along the way, there were no delays. I made it to Würzburg shortly before 22:00. Outside the station, I asked two rail policemen if they spoke English. "Yes," one of them said. "Can you help me get to the Lion Bridge?" That's where the ship was docked. They said the best way would be a taxi. As I was leaving one said to me with a smile, "Welcome to Würzburg!" Indeed it was good to have arrived.

The taxi driver spoke almost no English, but I made myself understood in German. (Thankfully, I studied it in college.) He put my bags in the trunk and we were off. Even at the late hour, the drive was gorgeous, along the Main River, with castles high on the hills on the other side. It took less than 15 minutes from the station to

Suite on Uniworld's Maria Theresa.

the gangway of the ship. Within minutes I was on board, checked into my room, and savoring a glass of champagne.

I awoke to a glorious morning in Bamberg, Germany. City tours were offered as well as an afternoon tour to a farm, both included in the cost of the cruise.

I opted for neither, needing instead to stretch my legs and breathe in the fresh air of the Bavarian countryside. There was a remedy for what I longed for: Uniworld's fleet of fine bicycles. With 20-inch wheels and fat tires that can roll over cobble-stone streets, Uniworld's bikes were a delight to ride. Eight speeds made it easy to climb steep hills or rip along flat river bank paths. The seats and handlebars could be adjusted so that even someone 6'5" (such as myself) can fit comfortably.

My launchpad for the day's ride was not emblematic of Europe—or of Bamberg. The S.S. Maria Theresa was required to dock in an industrial port, but just a few minutes away were treasures so beautiful that they caused my soul to soar. Bamberg, with its historic architecture and gorgeous countryside along the Main-Danube Canal, appeared before me with cinematic flair. It didn't hurt that cotton-ball clouds were pitched against a royal blue sky. I pedaled past leafy green trees, colorful houses and the ever-present songbirds of spring. I continued out into the countryside past daffodil-hued fields of canola on roads only for pedestrians and bikes. All who I passed were in a cheerful mood. It was a Sunday morning perfect for breathing in life. I pedaled into the city center to see Bamberg's marvelous sights, including the Bamberg Cathedral. While exploring the grounds at Michaelsberg Abbey, overlooking Bamberg, I had a thought that reflected my mood: Travel, and the simple act of setting myself in motion, has time and again provided me with experiences that induce euphoria. Nothing would have made me happier—more money, a leaner waistline, more love, a kiss on the cheek from Julie Andrews (well, perhaps). I was experiencing life not in the past nor in the present, but in that very moment, a moment given to me by a bike in Bamberg, Germany. This would end up being one of my all-time favorite memories on the Upper Danube thanks to my oasis on the rivers, the S.S. Maria Theresa.

My own personal oasis was stateroom 425, a category 1 stateroom measuring 194 square feet. (Suites span up to 410 square feet.) Situated on deck four, port-side aft, I was a few steps away from the Leopard Bar, which was a convenience that I appreciated whenever I was parched for a complimentary glass of champagne or a cocktail—or an afternoon tea. No noise from the corridor or slamming of doors could be heard in my abode while I drifted off in my king-sized Savoir of England bed, sandwiched between high-thread-count Egyptian linens. All state-rooms feature sumptuous fabric-wall coverings combined with rich-handmade carpets, antique furnishings, original art and, behind a mirror, a flat-screen TV with infotainment center. As a River Heritage Club Member, meaning that I had cruised before with Uniworld, I also received a few extra perks in my stateroom, including a complimentary fruit platter upon boarding and free laundry, one bag per week. Should one require more than that, paid laundry service is available as well as a complimentary self-service launderette on deck 2.

ONE OF MY FAVORITE WATERING HOLES ON A SHIP
IS UNIWORLD'S LEOPARD BAR

CRYSTAL
RIVER CRUISES™

THE WORLD OF CRYSTAL®
ILLUMINATES
EVERY JOURNEY

Europe's only all-suite, butler-serviced river ships,
featuring the largest luxury suites,
Michelin-inspired cuisine,
six-star service and all-inclusive luxuries.

CRYSTAL RIVER CRUISES.
Clearly Different.

Moonrise over Rudesheim during our Rhine River cruise on Viking Hlin.

My marble bathroom had a large shower and single sink with L'Occitane en Provence products, lighted magnifying mirror, hair dryer, thick towels and soft robes. Stateroom lighting and electrical features were state-of-the-art, with such features as USB charging outlets built into the receptacles, both European and North American style. My cabin featured a series four small closets, with plenty of drawers and shelves. Even cabins on deck two, in the lowest category, feature small two small closets; one being a wardrobe with a shelf at the top the other with hangers and shelves, as well as a safe.

I mention closet space, because it's something that people ask about frequently, but my favorite feature aboard the S.S. Maria Theresa had nothing to do with con-fined spaces. It was the balconies. Either a French or full balcony can be found in nearly all of the rooms. Elegant sliding glass doors separate the open-air balcony from the bedroom. With the glass doors closed, you have a cozy bedroom. With the glass doors open, the room becomes a large living space with a separate sitting area. Sheer curtains and/or heavy drapes can be drawn across the doors, either closed, or open. Step across the "threshold" onto the balcony where two white antique chairs with blue upholstery awaiting you. A floor-to-ceiling window, divided horizontally, forms the exterior wall. With the push of a button, the upper section lowers so that it is flush with the lower section of glass: Voila! an open-air balcony. Most nights, I left the window open so that the sounds of the river lulled me into slumber. Mosquitoes? With the push of another button, netting lowers so that you can enjoy the breeze without the bugs. The great outdoors is a feature most will enjoy aboard this ship, since most staterooms have either French or full balconies.

There are two main dining venues on the S.S. Maria Theresa. Guests can enjoy snacks in the more casual Viennese Café and dine in a more formal atmosphere in the Baroque Restaurant—both are open seating. But, I really loved frequenting my "neighborhood" haunt a few doors down, The Leopard Bar. Throughout the day here guests may also order from a Bistro Menu, with items ranging from a "Uniworld Club Sandwich" to local specialties such as "Homemade Hungarian Style Goulash Soup" and "Regional Smoked Sausages." On the sweet side, the menu offers choices of "White Chocolate Brownies" and a variety of ice cream desserts. There are also fruit and cheese selections, teas and coffees and more. A "Lite Lunch" is also served in the Leopard Bar and typically includes fresh salads and soups, pasta of the day and assorted sweets. The aft-situated bar transforms into a private-dining restaurant where white-gloved, tuxedoed waiters serve up to 20 guests on select evenings. Dinner in the Leopard Bar is complimentary, though reservations-only. Welcomed with a Kir Royale, we opted for the five-course "Saveur Menu, which included beef that was among the most succulent that I've ever tasted.

The Leopard Bar was absolutely gorgeous, with flowers and greenery, comfortable leather seating, books and games, a bar and open-air deck with four tables and chairs. It also featured one of the most unusual features I've ever seen on a river cruiser—an indoor pool. It's not the only indoor pool I've seen on a river vessel—Uniworld's S.S. Catherine has the same feature in its Leopard Bar, and Crystal Mozart features an indoor pool, but Maria Theresa's pool is unique in that the glass surround turns opaque upon entry (for privacy) and also the pool isn't necessarily what you'd expect to find in a bar.

Perhaps even more unexpected: the name of the bar. It is odd isn't it, particularly given the fact that there are no leopards on the Danube, where we're sailing now, or on the other rivers in Europe? However, there are leopards in South Africa, home of the Tollman family, the founders of Uniworld. The Leopard Bar is a bit of a tribute to the Tollman's homeland. And perhaps their way of saying, "Make yourself at home."

INTERESTED IN TAKING THE 16-DAY "EUROPEAN JEWELS" CRUISE FROM BUDAPEST TO AMSTERDAM?

In 2018, prices start at $7,599 per person for a Category 5 cabin.

RHINE

The second most popular river for cruises in Europe, after the Danube, is the Rhine, with its picturesque castle-lined gorges and storybook villages. It flows 820 miles through four countries—Switzerland, France, Germany and the Netherlands— from the Swiss Alps to the North Sea. You'll get a good dollop of city life and culture on your Rhine River cruises, with cities like Heidelberg, Strasbourg, Cologne, and Amsterdam in the mix. As you should know by now, one of my favorite ways to sightsee is by bike, and in many places along the Rhine, there are good bicycling paths and dedicated bike roads.

Though some cruises operate between Basel, Switzerland, and Amsterdam, in the Netherlands, or Dusseldorf, Germany, the most popular section of the Rhine is between Mainz, at the confluence of the Main and Rhine, and Cologne. Mainz is the birthplace of Johannes Gutenberg and home to the Gutenberg Museum, which presents the history of printing. It's not long before riverboats departing Mainz reach Rüdesheim, perhaps one of the Rhine's most charming villages.

Rüdesheim is situated in the heart of the Rheingau wine-producing region. Taverns and weingartens along the "world's merriest street," a narrow and lively pedestrian street known as Drosselgasse, are packed with locals and tourists enjoying Riesling, sparkling Sekts or local brandies.

Heading north from Rüdesheim, river cruisers pass half a dozen or more castles on both banks as well as the storied Lorelei, immortalized by poet Heinrich Heine, who wrote about a mysterious nymph who distracted sailors and lured their boats onto the rocks to their deaths. In fact, the most-castled section of river lies between Rüdesheim and Koblenz. Some cruises follow the Moselle from Koblenz, as the

Enjoying a 'kolsch" beer in Cologne

Through the locks near Melk, Austria

confluence between the two tributaries is located here. But for cruises that continue along the Rhine, the river takes you on to Germany's capital city of Bonn and Cologne, famed for Cologne Cathedral (a UNESCO World Heritage Site); one of Germany's best-known architectural monuments. (Have a Cologne Kolsch before or after your visit!) These cruises conclude (or begin) farther along the river at Dusseldorf or Amsterdam.

In addition to Moselle, the Rhine has many other tributaries, the most important for cruisers being the Main and Neckar. The Main has 34 locks and becomes navigable at Bamberg, Germany, at the north end of the Main-Danube Canal. It, along with the Main-Danube Canal, connects the North Sea with the Black Sea. Some river cruise companies offer itineraries along the Main between Nürnberg, situated about midway on the Main-Danube Canal, to Trier, on the Moselle. The Necker flows 228 miles from the Black Forest through some of Germany's most beautiful

y

Ivan, picking herbs from atop Viking Hlin

countryside. The primary attraction for many travelers is Heidelberg, Germany's oldest university town and the cradle of the German Romantic movement.

While many sailings aren't exclusive to the waters of the Rhine, on the following pages I share a few of the cruise lines and experiences that I feel truly showcase the region.

AMAWATERWAYS AMASONATA - MAGNIFICENT EUROPE

One sailing that I regularly recommend for travelers hoping to sail the Rhine who have cruised much of the Danube already is "The Enchanting Rhine" aboard AmaWaterways' AmaSerena. This 13-day itinerary from Amsterdam to Basel and reverse, includes a two-night Zurich and two-night Lucerne hotel stays. So in addition to getting to explore places like Heidelberg, Cologne, Strasbourg and Rüdesheim, you get to enjoy a little landlubber fun.

Viking Hlin in Koblenz, Germany

But I think even if you've sailed Danube several times, pairing the Rhine with the Danube is like wine and cheese, it's just better together. Many companies offer an itinerary sailing between Amsterdam and Budapest at least a few times during the season. I enjoyed my experience aboard AmaWaterways' 164-guest AmaSonata. AmaWaterways markets this itinerary as "Magnificent Europe," and that's certainly what it turned out to be.

Leaving Amsterdam, we cruised the Rhine river, the Main River, the Main-Danube Canal and the Danube. How good was this trip? As we approached Bamberg about midway through our trip, I stood out on deck with Steve, an American traveling with his wife. Steve appeared to be about my age, in his late fifties. "I wish we had the time to stay on for the return trip from Budapest," he said to me. "But my wife still works. I'm retired." Indeed, the duration of the cruise, spanning 14 nights/15 days, is perfect for those who have the time for a truly immersive European experience: three rivers, five countries and scenic cruising through the heartland of Europe. And time to absorb and reflect on it all. Of course, with the rise of the digital nomad (requiring that you only have internet connectivity to do your job), mixing work and pleasure is actually feasible considering the availability of blazingly fast internet on AmaWaterways. During our cruise, uploads and downloads nearly mimicked WiFi at home. That's because AmaWaterways invests heavily in its internet infrastructure.

Each day of our cruise we chose from a selection of complimentary tours. Typically two or three tours were offered, and we could always take off on our own using one of the bikes on board. I learned to make pretzels in Miltenberg, rode up hill in a gondola in Rüdesheim for a bird's-eye view over the town and river, sipped wine in one of Germany's oldest wine cellars, pedaled through the Wachau Valley and much more. I visited UNESCO World Heritage Sites such as the Cologne Cathedral and enjoyed scenic journeys through such natural wonders as the Rhine Gorge.

Our two weeks on this sailing ended with an illumination tour in the city of Budapest. AmaSonata cruised for about an hour, with nearly everyone out on the top deck, appreciating Hungary's well-lighted capital city. It was the perfect ending to cap off a magnificent voyage through the heart of Europe.

I'm keeping this write up short and sweet because we've all heard the old adage, "a picture is worth a thousand words." Well, video is more like ten thousand and I actually have video highlights of this very cruise. Take a few moments to get a sneak peak of all of the beautiful landscape you will see during this 14-day voyage, not to mention the interiors of your floating home away from home, AmaSonata. Video https://www.rivercruiseadvisor.com/2016/10/feature-video-amawaterways-magnificent-europe/

WANT TO EXPERIENCE A "MAGNIFICENT EUROPE" RIVER CRUISE FROM AMSTERDAM TO BUDAPEST?

In 2018, AmaWaterways offers only five Magnificent Europe departures aboard different river cruisers. Operating through August 11, 2018 these 14-night cruises are priced from $4,889 per person, based on double occupancy.

VIKING RIVER CRUISES VIKING HLIN - BASEL TO AMSTERDAM

It had been awhile since I was on a Viking Longship, and although I had attended christening events and even did a couple of weeklong cruises on Viking a few years ago, too much time had passed since I'd stepped on a Longship. That changed

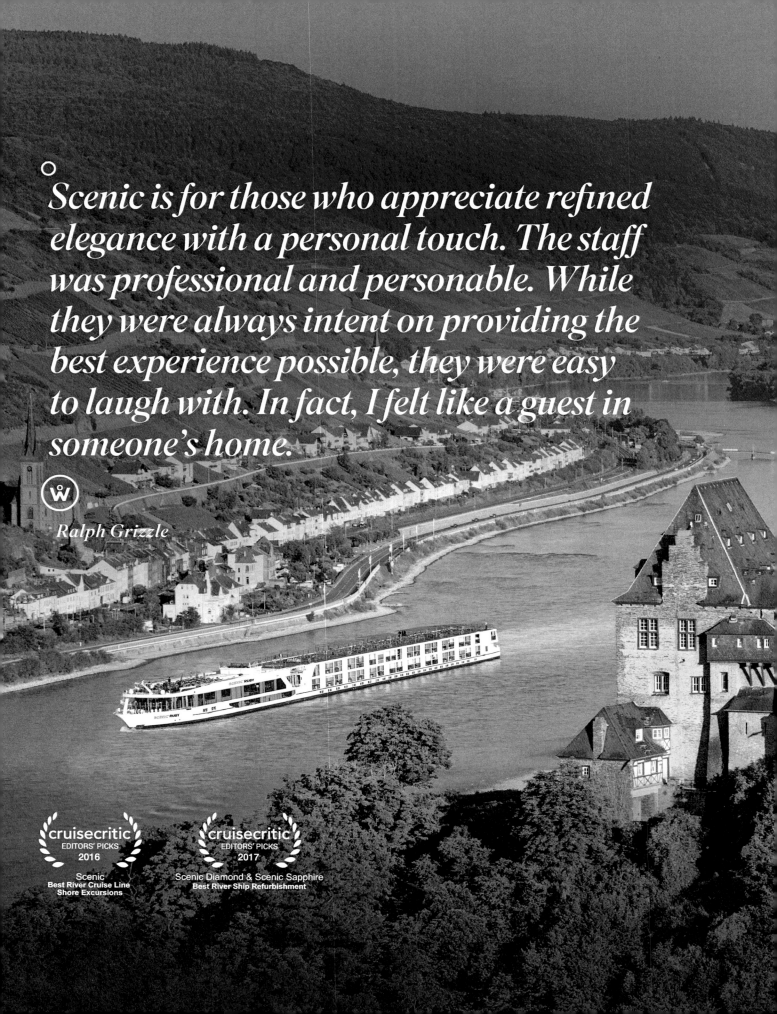

Scenic is for those who appreciate refined elegance with a personal touch. The staff was professional and personable. While they were always intent on providing the best experience possible, they were easy to laugh with. In fact, I felt like a guest in someone's home.

Ralph Grizzle

Table-setting on Viking Hlin

when I boarded Viking Hlin in Basel for a seven-night "Rhine Getaway" voyage to Amsterdam in May of 2017.

After a quick transfer from Basel's airport to the St. Johann docks, I felt good stepping into the familiar light-filled reception area of Viking Hlin (named for the goddess of protection in Norse mythology). All of the Longships showcase virtually the same features, so I was immediately familiar with my surroundings. I checked in, which took all of two minutes, and was escorted to my category A Veranda Stateroom, number 333, situated on the starboard side. After a near-sleepless night across the Atlantic, I was glad to be settled into the cozy confines of my 205-square-foot stateroom (the measurement includes the balcony). Tired but excited about the days ahead on the Rhine, I showered and afterward fell into bed for a quick sleep to refresh myself before awakening for the evening activities.

At 9 p.m. we sailed from Basel for the weeklong voyage that would visit Breisach (Germany), Strasbourg (France), Rüdesheim, Koblenz and Cologne (all in Germany), and Kinderdijk (a village in the Netherlands known for its iconic windmills). Our trip concluded a week later in Amsterdam.

Along the way, there would be many side trips, with diversions in the Black Forest and Colmar, a trip to Heidelberg, visits to castles, and dinners ashore. Complimentary excursions were offered at each stop along the way and about a dozen optional tours were offered, ranging in price from €49 per person to €189, the latter being a full-day excursion called Taste the Best of Alsace (Viking Hlin's program director, Candi Finkelstein, told me that this was the number one rated tour on the Rhine Getaway itinerary).

Fast forward: Midway through the voyage, as I sat in the Aquavit Lounge on a gorgeous day while Viking Hlin was docked alongside the Deutsches Eck ("German Corner" where the Rhine and Moselle converge in Koblenz), I realized something I had nearly forgotten—and that was just how good Viking is. I, and others on this voyage, found much to appreciate about Viking Hlin, the attractive decor of the ship, comfortable environs and an eager-to-please-and-seemingly happy-to-be-there staff.

I could give many shout outs, but here are a few: to our ever-smiling bartenders, Ivan from Macedonia and Krista, whose heritage is a mix of Spanish and Asian; to Armin, our enthusiastic Austrian hotel manager; and to Annie, who kept my stateroom clean and crisp.

Before heaping more praise on the Longships, though, I have a few quibbles that I'll get out of the way. Here they are: Viking would do well to bring bicycles on board and to offer those for complimentary use. Why are there no bikes on Viking's Longships? There's no room to store bicycles. Viking optimized space on the Longships to focus on public spaces and to add more staterooms and suites than you'll find on other river cruisers.

I missed having an on-board gym too. True, the gyms are tiny on river cruisers that have them, but still, I appreciate the option to get the blood pumping for a few minutes by exercising while cruising.

Those are my only quibbles, and with some creativity (such as walking the sundeck track to get your exercise or using the onboard concierge to book bikes ashore for you), active travelers can get past those grumbles to experience what are arguably the most gorgeous ships on the rivers. And in 2018, Viking is adding active excursions, such as biking and hiking, to its roster of offerings.

Because Viking's focus was on public spaces and accommodations, the Longships boast features that few, if any, other river cruisers can claim, notably, two-room suites and my favorite front-of-ship-space, the Aquavit Terrace.

Characterized by classic, minimalistic Nordic decor, the Longships were originally designed by the Norwegian-born chairman of Viking River Cruises, Torstein Hagen, and Oslo-based naval architects Yran and Storbraaten. Imagine the interior of a Volvo S90, all done up with leather seats and birch wood inlays, and you'll have a sense of the interiors of the Longships.

Viking's vessels feature light palettes throughout complemented by a plethora of panes of illuminating glass, lots of wood, herb gardens, marble slabs and mossy stones flanking the attractive wooden staircases, along with leather furniture and beautiful fabrics, including wall linens that appear to be hand-stitched.

Look closely, in fact, and you'll see that Viking paid a lot of attention to detail. Few people who I spoke with noticed until I had mentioned the leather hand-railing along the staircase. The feel of the leather adds to the sense of a stylish, yet simple, elegance, and at a hefty cost to Viking. The leather has to be replaced every two years.

Not one feature on the Longships could be described as over-the-top. Nothing jolts the senses or the eyes. To the contrary, the setting is pleasing, aesthetically and otherwise. The overall sensation that I feel on the Longships is a soothing one. I get something akin to a sense of serenity, particularly during moments when the play of light conspires to create works of art, such as in the reception area, where glass doors and the glass ceiling bathes the interior with sunlight.

Will the pleasing palette make a difference in your river cruise? Hard to say. What may, however, is the Aquavit Terrace. No front-of-ship public space on a European river cruiser comes close to matching the Aquavit Terrace. While on most river cruise vessels, the outdoor space at the front of the lounge is tight and obstructed by anchors and other marine equipment, Viking's Longships are free of such distractions.

The Aquavit Terrace features an enlarged area of indoor/outdoor space that is as gorgeous as it is unobstructed. The bow is nearly squared off with the anchor spindles and other equipment hidden beneath the decking. The result is something like a platform that extends within about two feet of the front edge of the ship. Teak rocking chairs, with cushions, are placed behind a plexiglass barrier that breaks the wind while providing views of the river and the landscape of Europe along the river. It is a seemingly small feature but one that looms large on sunny days on the river. Pull up a chair. The Aquavit Terrace is the perfect place to pitch camp for a morning, afternoon or evening of scenic sailing. It is also used as an optional dining venue to the main restaurant one deck below. In Koblenz, for example, continental breakfast is offered from 6 a.m. until 11 a.m., a light, a buffet-style lunch is offered at noon, and a light dinner, featuring Norwegian salmon, along with salads and other items, is offered at 7 p.m. As in the restaurant, wine and beer are served at no charge during lunch and dinner.

Viking River Cruises (and Viking Oceans) boast a Norwegian heritage. That, and Viking mythology, play a strong role in the fleet's makeup and decor. The Longships emphasize what Viking execs refer to as "affordable luxury." Many of the luxury components are in the details.

On most river cruisers, for example, you'll see soft drinks, sodas and tonics served from fountain dispensers or from plastic bottles. Not so on Viking's Longships. You'll find glass bottles of Coke, Diet Coke, Coke Zero, sodas and tonics. In fact, when it comes to tonic, Viking serves a gourmet brand known as Fever Tree. Cruise Line founder Torstein Hagen is a fan of gin and Fever Tree tonic, and I get the feeling that he would not have anything on his beloved Longships that we would not himself appreciate, which brings me to the Silver Spirit Beverage Package.

At €300 per cabin, double occupancy, the cost of Viking's all-inclusive beverage package seems steep at first glance, but it can be quite a value when you consider the quality of the beverages offered. Are you a Scotch drinker? Then you may know of Highland Park Ragnvald, which goes for more than $500 a bottle on the internet sites I looked at. Yet on Viking, you can enjoy as many glasses as you like of the single malt Scotch whiskey as part of your Silver Spirit Beverage Package. Without the package, a 4 cl shot of Ragnvald goes for €22.

Quai de Grenelle, where most ships dock in Paris

October on the Seine

Let's do the math. My cruise spans eight days. For the purposes of imbibing, let's knock it back to seven days. That is to say that yes, I might belly up to the bar on embarkation day for a premium drink but it's not likely that I will parch my thirst with alcohol on the morning of disembarkation. €150 divided by seven days comes to about €21.50 per day. That's one heck of a bargain when you consider the costs and quality of the beverages on the menu. Add to that Hagen's penchant for quality, which manifests itself throughout the Longships, and Viking's focus to deliver surprising small touches such as heated bathroom floors in the staterooms, and what you have is a match made in, well, Valhalla. And that, as any good Viking would know, is the Norse version of heaven. It couldn't get any better than that.

Check out my video featuring Viking's Affordable Luxury | https://www.rivercrui-seadvisor.com/2017/06/viking-hlin-video/

Want to experience Viking on the Rhine?

Viking's 8-day Rhine Getaway cruise begins at $2,749 per person, with frequent air incentives. But that lead-in price is for a December 28 sailing from Basel to

Amsterdam in the lowest category stateroom, measuring 150 square feet. Category A staterooms like the one I had price out on the same sailing at $3,249 per person with air from $295 per person when I checked prices. Rates during the peak month of September for a Category A are $4,399 per person, based on double occupancy.

QUIET LEADERS:
THE SEINE, MOSELLE, RHÔNE, AND LOIRE RIVERS

This quartet of rivers possess a little less vibrato than The-Three-Tenor types I covered in the Famous Trio section: The Upper Danube, Main and Rhine rivers. Albeit slightly less heralded, the Seine, Moselle, Rhône, and Loire rivers still prove to be popular contenders in the world of cruising inland waters. Given the free-flowing nature of rivers, compartmentalizing them for the sake of highlighting corresponding cruises is next to impossible, with many itineraries combining them with popular bedfellows. Others, like the Loire stand alone, with navigational hurdles such as shallow waters impeding transit by the masses. I think these rivers are the ideal choice for travelers who've already cruised the Danube and are seeking something different, are wine aficionados and/or appreciate unadulterated nature and a slower pace. Read on to find out how each river beautifully bubbles to the surface of travel discussions as effervescent alternatives for discovering Europe's lesser-known charms.

SEINE

While the Seine River is no stranger to European visitors, I categorized it as a Quiet Leader because, to date, much of the travel on this waterway has been limited to boat tours lasting but a few hours—offered as a pre- or post-river-cruise excursion in Paris. Thanks to sleek new ship designs featuring lower profiles, river cruises on the Seine are gaining popularity and making the romantic dream of watching the Eiffel Tower glide by your stateroom window a reality.

Les Andelys, on the Seine

The Seine begins in the Burgundy region of France about 20 miles northwest of Dijon. It flows in a northwesterly direction for 482 miles before emptying into the English Channel at Le Havre and Honfleur in the Normandy region.

During a Seine River cruise, you almost always begin and end your trip in Paris, where ships dock within walking distance (or at least within sight) of the Eiffel Tower. Many itineraries include an overnight in the City of Light, giving you ample time to explore, not only during day but also in the evening. In 1991 UNESCO added "The Banks of the Seine in Paris" to its list of World Heritage Sites. History unfolds immediately before your eyes as you glide along the Seine, from the Louvre and Notre-Dame to the Place de la Concorde and Grand Petit Palais. On the Seine, you can also visit the Normandy landing beaches as well as Giverny where Claude Monet had his home, and Rouen, the city of a thousand spires.

Seine river cruises return back to Paris from Rouen, Caudebec-en-Caux or the beautiful little village of Honfleur. You should note, however, that few vessels can actually make it to the center of Honfleur for docking. Those that can't bus their guests to Honfleur from Rouen or Caudebec-en-Caux.

The Seine is indirectly connected to the Saône River through the Yonne River and Burgundy Canal. Only barge riverboats or other smaller vessels can traverse the waters between the Seine and Saône, though. On the western portion of the river, the Seine is considered navigable for some ocean-going vessels from the English Channel to the city of Rouen.

Adding to the charm, and navigation challenges, many bridges cross the Seine River. The Pont de Normandie Bridge connects Le Havre and Honfleur; and in Paris, the Pont Neuf is one of the city's 37 bridges over the Seine. Pont Neuf was built around the beginning of the 17th century and is the oldest bridge in Paris. Sitting on the top deck as you cruise under these passages (which only the smaller ships can do) serves as a reminder that there's nothing quite like river cruising along the Seine; it offers a peaceful and almost voyeuristic vantage point of the heart of one of the earth's most famed metropolises, all while sipping a Sauterne or Sancerre.

To see what's it like, check out this video | https://www.rivercruiseadvisor.com/2017/09/feature-video-barge-trip-along-frances-petit-seine-yonne-rivers/

AMAWATERWAYS AMALEGRO - PARIS & NORMANDY

AmaWaterways operates in three regions of France: Bordeaux, Provence and Paris/Normandy. One of my favorites is along the romantic Seine, which I did in late October/early November of 2016, during unseasonably warm weather that allowed us to bicycle along the Seine in shorts and t-shirts.

The seven-night voyage began in the "City of Light," where AmaLegro was docked within view of the Eiffel Tower. Once underway, AmaLegro followed the meandering Seine along landscapes that inspired impressionists. In fact, on an included excursion we visited Giverny to see where Claude Monet lived and work for 43 years.

Monet's Gardens in Giverny

An option for getting to Giverny is to grab one of AmaWaterways' bicycles and pedal for not more than 30 minutes to reach Monet's Gardens—there was a dedicated bike road for most of the way there. Upon arrival we found the gardens beautifully dressed in fall color. While the gardens were beautiful, in the days that followed, I discovered that, despite the stereotype, the true beauty of France lies within its people, whose pleasantries sent my spirits soaring into the stratosphere. During our rides we were greeted by locals telling us to have a nice day, *Bonne journée.*

This affinity between the French and the Americans is a natural one. Fred, our tour guide in Rouen, told our group: "There is a very close link that dates back to the two world wars." Underscoring this sentiment, throughout our eight days on the Seine, we would strike up conversations with locals in small bars and cafes in the towns where we docked and were always greeted with nothing but the utmost warmth. I can't help but wonder if our country's shared concerns over acts of terrorism have fostered an even tighter bond. This brings up a topic that I feel is important to address: safety for travel in European destinations such as Paris. Events that have occurred, such as the shooting on Champs Elysees in April of 2017 and the horrific terror attacks in November of 2015 make many travelers give pause before booking air tickets to this dream destination.

While I understand the concerns, I discourage anyone from letting this trepidation derail your travel plans. Terrorism, by design, is unpredictable and aside from putting our lives on hold until world peace is steadily in place, life comes with its share of risks. Quite honestly, I feel that my life is in greater jeopardy behind the wheel of my car on a North Carolina highway than I do a river cruise through Europe. There are other measures that can be taken to help protect you from any financial implications of social unrest. See Deposit Protection Plans in Chapter 8.

So now that we've covered that, let's get back to the fun stuff. Other excursions during AmaWaterways roundtrip Paris sailings visit Honfleur, the charming French harbor town that has been immortalized by generations of artists, and Rouen, the historic capital of Normandy known for its cathedral and Joan of Arc's martyrdom. Those interested in World War II history can visit the Normandy Landing Beaches on included excursions. We sampled Camembert (and other cheeses), cider and Calvados, all staples of the Normandy region. (Back on board we dined on oysters, which AmaWaterways brought back to the ship, fresh from Normandy.)

AmaLegro also stopped for an afternoon in Les Andelys, where one can join a guided bike tour or hike up to the ruins of medieval Château Gaillard, built during the time of Richard the Lionheart.

On any day, passengers can feel free to take bikes out on their own to pedal along the Seine. Return home to AmaLegro, appetites piqued, to enjoy one of the two dining venues, included wine and beer (during lunch and dinner) and cozy staterooms with French balconies and included high-speed internet and WiFi to email loved ones at home photos that will make them green with envy.

View from my pillow on Avalon Visionary

Want To Experience Paris & The Seine On AmaWaterways?

In 2018, AmaWaterways' Paris & Normandy seven-night cruises begin at $2,149 per person, based on double occupancy. AmaLegro was replaced in 2017 with AmaLyra. More than two dozen departures run weekly through November 8, 2018. Two-night post-cruise packages that include hotel nights and tours are available for $760 per person double occupancy.

MOSELLE

A tributary of the Rhine River, the Moselle is regarded as the most beautiful—and perhaps the most romantic—of the navigable European rivers. I wholeheartedly agree. From its headwaters in the Vogesen Mountains to where it joins the Rhine at Koblenz, the Moselle is only about 175 miles as the crow flies. But the actual length of the winding river is a little more than 335 miles, making it the Rhine's longest tributary.

The Moselle weaves its way through the vertical slopes of Germany's Schieferge-birge mountains and into Luxembourg and northeastern France. Cities and towns along the river are of fairy-tale charm: picturesque Cochem, settled by the Celts and later by Romans before being granted a town charter in 1332; Bernkastel-Kues, with its castle ruin overlooking the city center of half-timbered buildings and cob-blestone streets; and the Romanesque city of Trier, Germany's oldest city and also one that claims to be 1,300 years older than Rome itself. Trier's Porta Nigra (Black Gate) dates from the 2nd century, when Trier was a Roman city.

The Moselle is known for its (mostly) white wines, such as Riesling and Piesporter, and indeed much of the pleasure of a Moselle cruise can be found in sampling the wines along the way. Connoisseurs will appreciate that the summer wine festivals fall outside the autumn harvest; sparing you from having to choose what acclaimed wine region to visit when the fruit is bursting from the vine. Or, you can always opt for a mug of glühwein instead at one of the many Christmas markets lining Moselle's banks starting in late November. I've decided to highlight Avalon

Avalon Visionary docked on the Moselle

Waterways' multi-river tour from Amsterdam to Paris because, to this day, it's the views through the ship's floor-to-ceiling windows that springs to mind when I think of the quintessential tour through this delightful region.

AVALON WATERWAYS - AMSTERDAM TO PARIS

What. A. Great. Trip. In April of 2017, I cruised with Avalon Waterways on the Rhine and Moselle rivers. The itinerary, bookended by Amsterdam and Paris, served up some of the same stunning scenery that inspired Dutch landscape painters such as Jacob Isaakszoon van Ruisdael.

But you don't need to be a master to capture its beauty. I could have spent hours out on deck watching the landscape pass. Instead, I drew back the curtains and admired Europe in HD from my Panorama Suite. After only a few days on board Avalon Visionary, I understood what Avalon Waterways has been trying to market: framed postcard-like views from the bedrooms of its so-called "Suite Ships."

Morning on the Moselle in the aft lounge on Avalon Visionary

The top two interior decks on Avalon's Suite Ships feature 200-square-foot and 300-square-foot suites with beds facing banks of sliding glass wall-to-wall and floor-to-ceiling windows.

Though you'll find attractive pricing for the lower deck categories, staterooms in those lower categories are 172 square feet with windows that don't open and smaller bathrooms than in staterooms a deck above. Plus, bathrooms in the staterooms on the upper decks are slightly angled to provide additional room. I appreciated the innovative configuration on my cruise.

But the real bonus is that on the upper decks, you get that wonderful view. I was in a Panorama Suite, number 318, Category P, on the Royal Deck. My room featured those floor-to-ceiling, wall-to-wall windows that spanned 11 feet, with a seven-foot opening. I found myself staying in my room more than I have done on other river cruises, sitting on my queen-sized, pillows propping my back, watching Europe pass in real-life HD.

Along the Rhine, manmade highlights such as the Cologne Cathedral and the storied castles along the river complemented the natural wonder that was the Rhine Gorge. I spent an entire morning marveling at castles perched on rocky outcrops before Avalon Visionary reached Rüdesheim.

The tiny town never fails to charm, luring travelers into its many wine gardens along the Drosselgasse. I skipped the busy street, however, and went for a long hike in the vineyards. The weather was divine, and I enjoyed breathtaking views.

A turn at Koblenz, the Deutsches Eck (German Corner) began the journey along the diminutive Moselle, where vertical vineyards plunged into the river. Along with the Douro, the Moselle competes as the prettiest river in Europe. Both are equally as plentiful in verdant vineyards threading their way up steep hills. The five-year-old Avalon's Visionary appears to have been made for this river, with the 128-guest ship's size matching it perfectly.

After Koblenz came Cochem and Bernkastel, with their half-timbered houses and hilltop castles. I could have spent time wine tasting in both towns, but I was all about

A healthy start on Avalon Visionary.

the view, so at each stop, I hiked up the hills for views of the valley below. Who needed wine? There was plenty of good regional wine back on Avalon Visionary.

The beauty of the Moselle was astounding and villages along the Moselle, in particular, were so perfectly framed by my room's wall of windows that I was continually grabbing my iPhone to snap a photo or capture it on video. And the history here is equally impressive. The Roman city of Trier (Germany) made it seem as though ancient Rome has been transported to the river and plopped down alongside the river's banks, and indeed the Roman Empire had reached this far, with the Romans leaving their legacy in ruins that still stand in what is thought to be the oldest city in all of Germany.

Luxembourg awaited us when Avalon Visionary docked in Remich. There, several complimentary excursions were offered, the highlight being the capital city of Luxembourg and, along the way, a stop at the American cemetery where General George S. Patton is buried.

Complementing the destinations were some wonderful excursions as well as a new breed of excursion, at least for Avalon. Avalon's Active Discovery program serves up a new style of river cruising, targeted at boomers, like me, and younger cruisers. The excursions are designed to provide in-depth experiences and activity and are included free of charge on Avalon's Active Discovery Cruises, a handful of which will be offered on the Rhine and Danube rivers.

Active Discovery cruises kick off in July of 2017 with itineraries on the Danube between Budapest and Linz aboard Avalon Luminary. In 2018, Avalon Felicity offers Active Discovery cruises between Amsterdam and Frankfurt, with ten ports that differ from Avalon's most popular itinerary, "The Romantic Rhine" (which operates between Amsterdam and Zurich). In Xanten, a new port for Avalon, an Active Discovery excursion is offered as a Nightman's watch tour, straight from the Middle Ages. At least three complimentary Active Discovery excursions are offered in each port.

Our cruise was a test run of sorts on Avalon Visionary. I enjoyed the emphasis on immersion and activity. And while Avalon is not alone in offering biking and hiking excursions, the company is seeking to differentiate itself through the active discovery aspects.

On an Active Discovery excursion in Cologne, I pedaled a bicycle with a group for a couple of hours. In Amsterdam, I participated in a local workshop where I learned to paint still-life. See On Avalon Waterways In Amsterdam: Channeling Our Inner Van Gogh | https://www.rivercruiseadvisor.com/2017/04/amsterdam-channeling-inner-van-gogh-avalon-waterways. Both were good diversions from often ho-hum, "let's visit another museum or church" tours.

Avalon has lots of other touches that I also found refreshing, such as Avalon Choice, which allows guests to personalize their vacations online before leaving home. And while Avalon is not all-inclusive, the line does include much of what its competitors do, with a few inclusives that are new to Avalon, such as regional wine and beer served free of charge at lunch and dinner, and bicycles on board for complimentary use.

Another aspect of the on-board experience that I appreciated was Avalon Fresh, a healthy dining option. Vegetarian and vegan dishes were inventive and tasty thanks to a partnership with the Wrenkh Brothers, two rising culinary stars from Austria. The brothers are known for creating great tasting, innovative, vegetarian cuisine, and I ordered Avalon Fresh menu items each of the seven nights of our cruise. I was pleased to learn that the Wrenkh Brothers source their ingredients from small farms and local producers.

I also was impressed with the sheer number of healthy dining options on Avalon Visionary. The breakfast buffet, for example, featured items such as chia seeds, goji berries, pumpkin seeds, puffed wheat, and lots of other healthy items to complement the yogurts and muesli. Of course, going "off course" was easy for those who wanted to do so. The Belgian Waffles may have been the best I have ever had, land, sea, or river.

There's also an alternative dining venue called the Panorama Bistro at the front of the lounge for intimate dinners. The venue, where light lunches are also served, seats 20 on Avalon's 110-meter ships, which includes Avalon Visionary. The dining area's setting is gorgeous, particularly during evening transits along the river.

On our 10-day trip through Holland, Germany, Luxembourg and France, the Moselle, in particular, quickly rose to the ranks of favorites for many of us on board, thanks to the river's meandering through landscapes stitched with vineyards, and villages with castles perched high atop hills. Avalon Visionary visited Amsterdam, Cologne, Rüdesheim, Cochem, Zell, Bernkastel, Grevenmacher and Remich—and also offered excursions to Trier and Luxembourg.

Our overnight in Remich was not the end of the trip, however. Two nights in Paris, which we reached via high-speed train, punctuated the perfect ending to one of the most intriguing itineraries on the rivers of Europe.

Want to experience Avalon Waterways 2018 Canals, Vineyards & Paris cruise?

In 2018, this 10-day sailing from Amsterdam to Paris starts at $2,539 per person, double occupancy.

RHÔNE & SAÔNE

The Rhône River begins in the Swiss Alps in the canton of Valais. The river flows for 505 miles from Switzerland through Lake Geneva and eastern France to Arles where it empties into the Mediterranean Sea. To the east of Lyon, the river is turbulent and is not considered navigable. Rhône River cruises typically are between Lyon and Avignon or Arles in France. (From Lyon to Arles, the Rhône flows in a southerly direction.) In the city of Arles the Rhône divides into two branches—an eastern branch known as the Grand Rhône and a western branch known as the Petit Rhône. These two branches form a delta in the Camargue region just south of Arles.

Many packages also include the Saône River, which joins the Rhône in Lyon. Interconnected waterways are common in France and rivers are joined together by other rivers as well as estuaries and canals. The Rhône and the Rhine rivers are indirectly connected through the Saône River. This is also true for the Rhône and Seine rivers. (The Seine River is connected to the Saône via the Yonne River and Burgundy

Me & Lou in Arles, France.

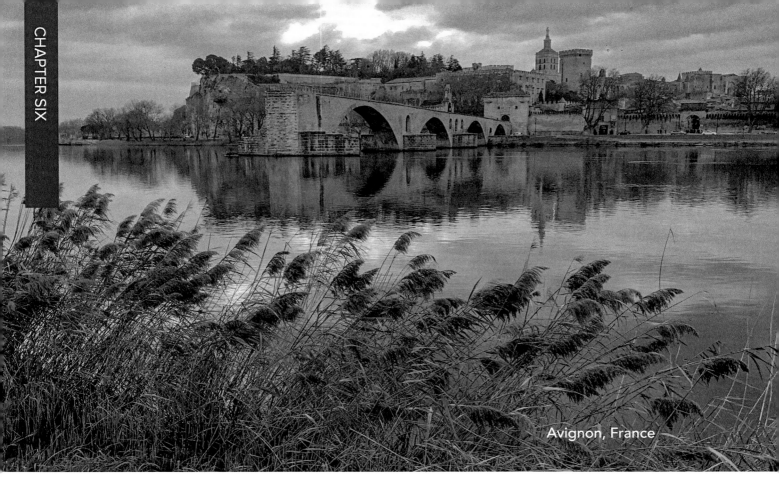

Avignon, France

Canal.) A cruise that combines both the Rhône and the Saône is typically 8 to 14-days in length and allows for you to experience both Burgundy and Provence; it typically begins or ends on the Saône River about 80 miles north of Lyon in the city of Chalon-sur-Saône. In addition to Chalon-sur-Saône, prominent cities often visited on Saône River cruise include: Lyon, Tournus, Beaune and Trevoux.

Complicating this labyrinthian riddle even more, there are also itineraries that combine other waterways that are not directly connected to the Rhône River. For instance, a few companies offer a cruise on the Rhône and Saône rivers and a separate cruise on the Seine River.

Circuitous routes, single-river sailings, you can't go wrong in this region. Who doesn't love Provence and Burgundy? Biking past lavender fields and Bourgogne beauty, the Pope's Palace in Avignon and, nearby, the medieval Pont du Gard, and the constant reminders of Van Gogh's greatness and Roman monuments in Arles: All add up to one fascinating trip. Oh, and then there's the whole most-celebrated (and expensive) wines of the world bit, and the birthplace of gourmet cuisine as we know it today. Need I say more?

CROISIEUROPE MISTRAL – NEW YEAR'S EVE IN PROVENCE

At the end of 2016, I spent the days after Christmas up until New Year's Day in France. Part of my time was spent in Paris, where I visited a friend before heading off to Lyon to spend time with another friend, Lou Le Jacq, nearly three decades ahead of me at 87, an affable and energetic traveling companion who I had met a couple of years earlier on the Loire.

Lou and I are a mix of surrogate father and son combined with a dose of Laurel & Hardy, the early-last-century comedy duo. Lou contacted me and said he was wanting to spend the days after Christmas in France. He spends most of his days

Vienne, France

CroisiEurope's Mistral docked in Vienne

caring for his bed-ridden wife. "I need to re-energize my batteries so as to give quality care to a great lady and my wife for 65 years," Lou told me. (Sadly, his wife passed away in the spring of 2018).

Lou made a successful career in publishing medical journals and has the means to cruise on any river cruise ship he wants, but partly because of his French heritage, he prefers Strasbourg-based CroisiEurope. He told me that he appreciates the French flair along with the cuisine, which is, as might be expected, decidedly French. Over the years, I've come to appreciate CroisiEurope as well for the many reasons that I share both here and on my site.

Unlike many river cruise companies, the only buffet offered on CroisiEurope is at breakfast. Lunch and dinner are served as fixed, sit-down affairs, with typically three-to-four-course menus offering French favorites. That said, don't think you're stuck with only one choice. If you're cruising CroisiEurope, be sure to preview the menus the day before and order something else should you not prefer what's being offered. Lou and I never strayed from the menu, on this trip or the last one. Plate after plate, they were all delicious. And why shouldn't they be? CroisiEurope's chefs have worked alongside such Michelin-starred greats as Paul Bocuse and Marc Haeberlin. The company's head chef, Alain Bohn, was nominated as a member of the Maîtres Cuisiniers de France. This esteemed French association, created 50 years ago, includes only 250 chefs worldwide. So while you might not have the menu selection that you'll find on other river cruisers, rest assured that you're going to have something that approaches gourmet French cuisine along with the ability to order something not on the menu.

The cuisine is complemented by European wines (French on our trips), which come as part of CroisiEurope's all-inclusive beverage package. That package means you can order cocktails, beer, wine, soft drinks and sparkling wine at no charge at any time during your cruise, not just during lunch and dinner.

While CroisiEurope's all-inclusive cruises impress me with their French flair, how does CroisiEurope handle English-speakers when there are only two, Lou and me? I was curious to see how CroisiEurope performed on a cruise that wasn't designated as an English-speaking only cruise. After leaving Gare du Lyon in Paris, I arrived two hours later in Lyon by TGV. Steps from the station, I hopped on a tram, and made my way to the Rhône river, where I wheeled my luggage for about five minutes to reach CroisiEurope's Mistral. In the familiar surroundings (I've been on at least half a dozen CroisiEurope ships), I discovered that we were an "international group" of French, Germans, a few Spaniards and two Americans.

Right from the start, CroisiEurope got it right. As the orientation program was presented in the lounge in French and German, a delightful Hungarian named Monika translated in English to the two Americans and the Spaniards. Throughout the trip, we received programs and menus in English (as noted, the next-day's menus are distributed to staterooms each evening so that you can request changes should you desire). Monika translated to us during every event and was there to answer every question. One thing to note is that the staff comes from throughout Europe. They're not all French, so the staff uses English to communicate with one another. We met staff members from Hungary, Romania, Portugal, and of course, France. So as comments by others visiting my site have confirmed, CroisiEurope handles the English component extremely well.

We boarded our floating hotel at 3 p.m. in Lyon. We set sail an hour later to Arles as we settled into our cabins. After a welcome cocktail in the lounge bar and staff introductions, we headed to dinner. We continued our cruise towards Arles through the night. Following breakfast, we enjoyed a relaxing morning afloat as we cruised gently through the picturesque landscapes of southern France, passing first Valence, dominated by the Saint Apollinaire Cathedral and then Montelimar, famous the world over for its nougat.

After lunch we arrived in Arles around 1 p.m. and set off for our optional guided visit of the town. With many of its ancient buildings still remaining clearly visible today, the city has been justifiably classified as a "Ville d'Art et d'Histoire" in France and its Roman and Romanesque monuments have been listed by UNESCO as World Heritage Sites since 1981. We returned for dinner on board and moored in Arles for the night.

The next day we sailed toward Avignon, arriving at around 8 a.m. We were offered a tour of Avignon and the "Palais des Papes" (Pope's Palace). The latter is a testimony to Avignon's prestigious past as capital of Christianity in the Middle Ages. So wonderful is Avignon's architectural heritage that the old town center was listed by UNESCO as a World Heritage Site. Exceptional monuments include the Saint Bénézet Bridge (the famous "Pont d'Avignon"), the city Ramparts, the petit palais, the cathedral and the impressive walls of the aforementioned "Palais des Papes" flanked by four great towers. We returned to our floating home for lunch and spent the afternoon cruising toward Vienne, resting up for the gala dinner on board.

The next morning after breakfast we set off for a tour of the Roman city of Vienne. Here we visited the temple to Augustus and Livia, built in Corinthian style at the end of the 1st century BC and converted into a church, which has remained virtually intact, the Roman Theatre from the 1st century AD and the Gothic former cathedral of Saint Maurice. Then it was lunch on board as we continued on to Lyon, where we arrived around 2 p.m.

Lyon has also preserved an important architectural heritage from the time of the Romans, through the Renaissance right to the 20th century, and for this reason is listed as a World Heritage Site by UNESCO. On the day of New Year's Eve, it served as an incredible reminder of the beauty of celebrating one's past while

equally bringing forward all you hold true into the future. We were treated to a magical view of Lyon by night as we cruised past Lyon's illuminated old quarters, which looked wonderful seen from the river before mooring for the night. Along the way, we rang in the new year with a celebratory meal. I don't know if Lou returned home re-energized physically, but certainly emotionally and we resolved to try again next year.

Want To Experience CroisiEurope's Provence?

CroisiEurope's New Year's in Provence itinerary has only one departure in 2018, from Lyon, France on December 28. The five-day cruise on CroisiEurope's Camargue starts at $1,607 per person and offers calls on Lyon, Vienne, Avignon and Arles.

THE LOIRE

If you're someone like me who has done the Danube, rode the Rhine, meandered the Moselle, then look to the Loire River for something refreshing and new. Even if you're brand new to river cruising, the Loire would not be a bad choice.

The Loire River begins in the Rhône-Alps region in southern France, flowing about 630 miles until it reaches the Bay of Biscay just west of Nantes. It's the longest river in France, but Loire River cruises on ships offering overnight accommodations were not available until 2015. Only barge cruises on the Upper Loire River between Chatillon-sur-Loire and Montargis and between Rogny-Les-Sept-Ecluses and Marseilles-lès-Aubign have been available. That's because this waterway is notoriously shallow, making it impossible for most ships to navigate the many tributaries along the western portion of the river spanning between Saumur and Nantes, including the Erde, La Maine, Sarthe, Cher and Indre.

The only vessel operating Loire cruises is the Loire Princesse, a paddlewheeler designed just to explore the namesake river. Loire Princesse travels roundtrip from Nantes to Bouchemaine, with motorcoach excursions to Château de Villandry on the Cher River and Château d'Azay-le-Rideau on the Indre River as well as other châteaux.

Nantes offers easy access to the countryside and charming French villages along the rivers, and has an interesting history in its own right, which includes Jules Verne and a link to the slave trade during the 18th century. Itineraries here escort you alongside pastures and through forests leafing springlike. You'll explore tiny villages to delve into fascinating cultural roots like seeing the Apocalypse Tapestry in the Anjou province or the making of Muscadet. The many châteaux in the Loire River Valley are beautiful and worth the trip alone. Even catch a first-hand glimpse of the one that Disney's Sleeping Beauty was modeled after. Speaking of which, while this countryside might be a low-key (and low-water) option, with so much to see and do, it's hardly a sleeper.

CROISIEUROPE, LOIRE PRINCESSE - PADDLE-WHEELIN' ALONG THE LOIRE

No one thought that the Loire River, the shallow waterway where a yardstick can touch the riverbed at times, could be navigated by river cruisers. And yet the Schmitters, the Strasbourg-based family that owns CroisiEurope, designed a ship that could. Loire Princesse is the first of its kind, a paddlewheeler plying the Loire. This 295 foot-long 49-foot wide vessel accommodates up to 96 guests in a total of 48 staterooms. She's a beauty and a technological success, not only for CroisiEurope but also for the region of Nantes and for travelers, like you and me.

Dubbed a "Green Ship" due to the inclusion of environmentally friendly technologies, this vessel features two paddle wheels protruding from each side of the ship. When engaged, they scoop water to propel the Loire Princesse up a river to discover the region's fairy-tale charm. Becoming enamored with this itinerary began even before stepping aboard the ship. I highly recommend participating in some preboarding activity in the city of Nantes. The *joie de vivre* you'll experience will fill unfortunate souls on the other side of the Atlantic with a sense of envy. Sure, the locals are quirky by some standards, they fight hard for their rights (La Liberté, and hence frequent strikes). The French, while not perfect, seem to have perfected seizing the moment to enjoy life, conveyed through their collective appreciation for food, wine, art, and culture.

A little more than two hours by train from Paris, Nantes is as bike-friendly as Copenhagen or Amsterdam, with dedicated bike roads and bike-aware drivers. The weather gods could not have been kinder during my stay here. I pedaled under

sunshine and blue skies on a bike that I rented for 31 euros for three days (actually the nice folks at Detours de Loire threw in an extra afternoon on the day when I picked up the bike.) During my days on the bike, I pedaled to Mauves-sur-Loire, a small village on the river. The countryside was gorgeous and the pedaling easy on dedicated bike roads most of the way. I also made my way to île de Nantes, a small island in the middle of the Loire, where Loire Princesses docks. Among the attractions on the island is Les Machines, an artistic project by François Delarozière and Pierre Orefice's imagination located within the former shipyards. Of the attractions at Les Machines is a giant mechanical elephant, measuring more than 39 feet high and 26 feet wide. Made from 45 tons of wood and steel, the lumbering elephant can take up to 49 passengers for a 45-minute "walk." It was fun enough to simply stand on the sidelines and watch, as I did.

Just upriver is a museum honoring Jules Verne, the imaginative novelist who penned adventure books, including "20,000 Leagues Under The Sea," "Journey To The Center Of The Earth" and "Around The World In 80 Days." Verne was born in Nantes, and Les Machines plays on his wild indulgences. His spirit also is somewhat embodied in Loire Princesse, a ship that took some imagination to able to navigate as little as 27 inches of water.

The Dukes of Brittany had their castle in Nantes. The castle is still a centerpiece of the city, and while Nantes is not within Brittany proper, the city reflects the spirit—and is regarded as the cultural capital—of Brittany. It was in 850 that the region was first conquered by Brittany and with subsequent wars and infighting, the Nantes region remained in flux and changed hands for several centuries. Even the Vikings pitched camp here for a brief period during the 8th century. In 1532, however, the duchy of Brittany became part of the French crown lands, effectively unifying Brittany (and Nantes) with France.

I was particularly intrigued by Nantes' role in the slave trade. I had no idea before coming here. In the early 1700s, ships from Nantes transported nearly 50 percent of the slaves who were taken across the Atlantic to the Americas. Today, a human rights memorial marks the spot where the ships docked at the quays at île Feydeau. The memorial seems to offers up an apology of sorts for the inhumane acts.

Loire Valley Chateau

After my fascinating history lesson, I stepped aboard to commence my six-day cruise from Nantes. Loire Princesse is a comfortable ship, with spacious staterooms, mine featuring a balcony, and large bathrooms by river cruise standards. The ship has a cozy lounge and an elegant dining room. The top deck is a big open space with chairs and umbrellas, an indication that much of our time may be spent up here as we admire the Loire's landscape. The structures on the top deck, mainly awnings and railings, are built to retract so that Loire Princesse can navigate the low bridges along the river. When taken altogether, Loire Princesse truly is a marvel concept. Jules Verne might have imagined such, but CroisiEurope actually set her afloat on the Loire.

Our dinner that evening was delicious, served with a basket of French bread and French wines, including Muscadet, a white wine that is local to the region. (Dining is French-inspired, and local wine, beer, spirits, soft drinks, specialty coffees and bottled water served at no charge 24/7.) The main dish was a filet mignon of pork. My dinner companions were French or French-speaking (one lady was from Quebec). I particularly enjoyed meeting an elderly woman seated to my right, who replied when I asked what city she was from, "Paris. Where else?" When someone offered to fill her water glass, she turned to me and confessed to never drinking water. "Only Chardonnay," she said with a wry smile.

Ah, la joie de vivre. My immersion begins.

We spent the morning cruising along the Loire River to the small town of Ancenis, with its stately castle, built in 984, overlooking the river. Loire Princesse tied up to the dock, and we boarded a motorcoach for an excursion into Muscadet country. Muscadet is a regional wine made from the Melon de Bourgogne grape, and it has been our featured complimentary white wine during dinner each evening on board Loire Princesse.

Our tour took us to the town of Clisson, a medieval city with 15th century vestiges and an Italian feel. We walked the streets, crossing the bridges that spanned over the two rivers that meet here, and admiring the fortifications here on what was the border of Brittany and France as well as visited Château Cassemichère, where we learned about – and tasted — the locally produced wines.

As we approached the dock in Bouchemaine (the furthest we would travel up river), a band greeted us from the shoreline. Trumpets and tubas blared to a steady drumbeat. People alongside the banks snapped photos, as they have done all along the river, and once we were docked, dozens approached the ship to see if they might have a look inside the vessel. The people who live along the Loire had never seen anything like Loire Princesse. This speaks to just how special this vessel is in these waters.

It was a quite the pomp and circumstance kicking off our exploration in Angers, the capital of the historical Anjou province and home to the famous 13th-century Château d'Angers—home of the extraordinary Apocalypse Tapestry. I wanted badly to see it, but I also wanted to go for a long walk along the Loire. The latter won me over. My walk was nothing short of glorious. I followed a path along the river for a couple of miles, passing scenes worthy of postcards—châteaux overlooking the river, beautiful little fishing boats tied up in the tall grass at the shoreline. The river had the feel of an estuary in the south of the United States, except all along its banks, French was being spoken, and I was experiencing the joie de vivre. When I felt I had walked far enough, I journeyed inland to make my way back through the villages, past churches and more châteaux. I had put in more than four miles when my walk came to an end. I felt euphoric and exhilarated, a good day to be alive and in France.

The ability to get out and walk (or bike) is one of the things that I like most about river cruising. While tours are offered every day, you can still tailor your experience to your liking.

For the gala dinner that evening, we men pulled on jackets (some even wore ties) and attended a cocktail reception with a champagne toast, then proceeded downstairs for a delicious dinner. The staff had gone to the trouble of folding the linen napkins to resemble dinner jackets. It was a small touch that added to the sense that we were doing something elegant.

The motorcoach's engine was revving at 8:30 the next morning, gearing up to begin a full-day excursion to visit some of the most beautiful châteaux in the Loire region. Unlike the other excursions on our cruise, which ranged from €37 per person to €71 per person, the Châteaux of the Loire Valley excursion was included for all guests sailing on Loire Princesse.

In my hometown of Asheville, North Carolina, there's a 250-room château on the grounds of the Biltmore Estate. The estate, with its big mansion, is one of my favorite places in the world. Nestled against the backdrop of the Blue Ridge Mountains, George Vanderbilt's Biltmore House was inspired by Château de Blois.

The inspiration is clear not only to me but also to at least one Loire local. During lunch, I pulled up a picture of the Biltmore House on my iPhone and asked our guide if he knew where it was. He studied it and said, "That's the next château we're seeing." The next château we would visit was, in fact, Châteaux de Villandry, but indeed there was a resemblance between it and Biltmore House, even if the two were an ocean apart.

Whereas Western North Carolina can claim only a single château, the Loire Valley is littered with these magnificent mansions. There are few other places in the world where you can see so many palaces in such a concentrated area.

Our first stop was at Château d'Azay-le-Rideau, built on a small island in the middle of the Indre River. The château was undergoing renovation and restoration, and unfortunately, most of the exterior was obscured by scaffolding during our visit. The intent was to restore the French National Monument to the grandeur it reflected under the ownership of Gilles Berthelot, a wealthy financier who wanted to incorporate its medieval past alongside the latest architectural styles of the Italian renaissance. Even with the scaffolding and work going on, the château was beautiful, and its interior and gardens were gorgeous on the day we were there.

We then headed to Villandry, a village with an impressive palace and following lunch visited the gardens of the Château de Villandry. How did all of these palaces come to exist on the Loire? Until about the middle of the 16th century, the Loire had been the center of power for France, when many of the châteaux were built. Then King Francois I shifted power back to Paris. The great architects followed along. In the middle of the 17th century, King Louis XIV built what was arguably the greatest of all châteaux, the Palace of Versailles. At the same time, the wealthy bourgeoisie continued to renovate existing palaces in the Loire region and build new ones as their summer residences. The Loire, with its rollings hills and vine-yards, and its beautiful river, were where many among the French royalty preferred to spend their time.

The last château that we visited had a history that inspired something entirely different from the rest: Charles Perrault's "Sleeping Beauty." Indeed, the fortified towers of Château d'Ussé reminded me of the Disney animation, and along with two friends I made on Loire Princesse, I climbed to the top of one of the towers to see the room where Sleeping Beauty was awakened by a kiss from her handsome prince, at least in the Disney version of the story.

As we made our way back to Ancenis, I couldn't help but think that we had experienced a day when fairy tales took on a degree of plausibility. We had visited three gorgeous châteaux in the Loire region, each a little different from the other. I left thinking I was glad that monuments like this were being cared for. They inspire the imagination as much now as they did back in the day of Charles Perrault.

It was a beautiful evening when we arrived at Loire Princesse. We quickly boarded, and our ship pushed away from the dock to begin its gentle journey downstream. By 10:30 p.m., we would be return full-circle to Nantes, having taken enjoyment to entirely new levels on low waters.

Want to experience the Loire with CroisiEurope?

In 2018, the 8-day sailing "The Royal Loire River" to and from Nantes aboard the MS Loire Princesse starts at $3,170 per person, double occupancy.

THE ELBE

The Elbe River is like the stereotypical socialite: It's shallow and gets around, but no one seems to get to know it all that well. One of the major rivers of Central Europe, it stretches 678 miles, from Czech Republic and all the way across north central Germany before emptying into the North Sea. The Vltava River is a tributary of the Elbe, which passes through Prague before joining the Elbe River in Czech Republic's city of Mělník—the mouth of the river located about 70 miles northwest of Hamburg.

The Iron Gates, on the Danube.

There are a few tributaries that link the Elbe to both Prague and Berlin. The Havel River flows through Berlin and is connected to the Elbe via the Elbe-Havel Canal just north of Magdeburg. Elbe River cruise itineraries are between Berlin and Prague. However, the Elbe River is not located in either city. Embarkation takes place in Magdeburg or Dresden in Germany or in Melník. Although both Prague and Berlin are connected to the Elbe by one or more waterways, transportation to the river cruise ship is usually by motor coach rather than by boat. Berlin is about 90 miles east of Magdeburg, and Prague is about 30 miles south of Melník and 93 miles southeast of Dresden. All Elbe River cruise itineraries include one or more nights in Berlin and Prague.

The Elbe has always been a tricky river to navigate. Many who book Elbe river cruises return home disappointed because their ships were unable to sail due to low water. They end up sleeping on the ships and doing bus tours during the day. The Elbe saw some of its lowest water levels ever in 2015, which prompted AmaWaterways to shuttle its plans to place a new ship on the river. Viking River Cruises has one program for Elbe River cruises. "The Elegant Elbe" itinerary is either from Prague to Berlin or from Berlin to Prague.

To my mind, only one company does the Elbe effectively, CroisiEurope. As on the Loire, CroisiEurope has two paddle-wheelers, Elbe Princesse and Elbe Princesse II that are capable of sailing these exceptionally shallow waters. CroisiEurope's paddlewheelers can cruise right into the center of Prague from Berlin.

UNSUNG HEROES:
THE LOWER DANUBE, GARONNE AND DORDOGNE, DOURO, VOLGA, AND PO RIVERS

This title might not be apropos, because anyone who has sailed the Lower Danube, Garonne and Dordogne, Douro, Volga or the Italy's Po are singing the praises of these incredible waterways. While itineraries here are quickly gaining recognition, they often make only cameo appearances in glossy river cruise brochures donning cover shots of ships sailing past the capital cities flanking the Danube and Rhine's cornucopia of castles. These rivers (along with a litany of others like the Guadalquivir, Marne, Sarre, Oder, Sava and Tiza--just to name a few!) make their way onto the bucket lists of intrepid travelers who have cruised the major rivers and are looking for clandestine river ports. Or for those who prefer a more pioneering approach to travel.

Don't get me wrong, not all of the places cruises frequent on these rivers are obscure locales. Quite the contrary. For instance, the Lower Danube delivers you to ancient Eastern European empires in Romania; Garonne and Dordogne itineraries take you to the heart of Bordeaux and France's most popular vineyards; the Douro is the lifeblood of Portugal; and the Po trickles past Venice. The Volga also happens to be the longest river in all of Europe, by far. However, the rivers cruises here are far and few between and veer off the trodden river cruise course—and as a result slightly less in demand.

For this reason, I haven't sailed as extensively in these regions as others. So I share with you a couple of my experiences as well hit the high notes on sailings that I have yet to embark upon so that you can choose one that will make your heart skip a beat.

LOWER DANUBE

One river I did get the opportunity to experience is the Lower Danube. While the upper portion of the Danube River is hardly foreign to river cruisers, with many cruise companies anchoring itineraries in Budapest. Heading down river from this Hungarian capital one starts to see the disparity between West and East.

The lower Danube technically starts at the Iron Gates, with the section between Devin Gate (at the border of Austria and Slovakia) and Iron Gate considered the middle Danube. (The watery intersection for the Danube's major tributaries, such as the Drava, the Tisza, and the Sava.) But for all intents and purposes, anything south of Budapest is off the beaten path for the traditional river cruiser—and is what I'm referring to when discussing itineraries on the lower Danube.

The Danube is full of locks, 70 of them to be exact, and you'll transit 18 on the popular stretch between Passau and Budapest alone. While these locks are certainly interesting engineering feats, I love the freedom you feel sailing open and unadulterated waters. That's exactly the sense that you'll get on the lower Danube, where nature and even architecture feels decidedly untouched. Sailing through only two locks feels uninhibiting, despite the name of the most popular: Iron Gates. In this gorge you'll cruise through the European Alps and Carpathian Mountains along the watery border between Serbia and Romania. Ensconced by rocky curtains for 80 miles, it feels as though the earth has parted just wide enough for you to pass. It's stunning.

But what really makes this final stretch leading to the Black Sea so memorable are the destinations ashore, including ports such as Osijek, Croatia; Belgrade, Serbia; Vindin and Belogradchik, Bulgaria; and Bucharest, Romania, to name a few. I think river cruising is the ideal way to experience locations where you might not book a weeklong land vacation, per se, but prove to be incredibly fascinating stops, with the river leading you to the doorstep of the nation's most iconic locales.

While itineraries here aren't as plentiful as those offered on the Upper Danube, you do have some options. CroisiEurope has several itineraries and has announced

On Emerald Sky, the pool area transforms to a cinema in the evenings, with complimentary popcorn.

a new 11-day journey between Central Europe and the Balkans on the Danube and Sava river in 2018. It includes a lot of stops in Croatia, which is more uncommon among itineraries typically offered on the lower Danube. Avalon Waterways features a sailing through the Balkans and one between Bucharest and the Black Sea while Viking River Cruises has an 11-day Passage to Eastern Europe Sailing and longer 22-day European Sojourn from Amsterdam to Bucharest. On the other end of the spectrum, AmaWaterways offers a shorter 7-day itinerary that commences in Budapest but stops short of the Black Sea in Romania in addition to a two week itinerary that starts from Vilshofen (near Passau) Germany. Read on to get a peek of my Emerald Waterways' trip from Budapest to Bucharest.

The 'Paprika Lady' in Hungary

EMERALD WATERWAYS' EMERALD SKY - BUCHAREST TO BUDAPEST

I'm intentionally keeping my overview of my voyage with Emerald Waterways on the lower Danube abridged. This 10-night "Enchantment of Eastern Europe" sailing, starting in Bucharest and ending in Budapest, proved so extraordinary that I actually wrote an entire ebook on my experience. For those who are truly contemplating a river cruise on the lower Danube, peruse the pages of my ebook | https://www.rivercruiseadvisor.com/e-books/eastern-europe-river-cruise-guide/ and I can assure you that you'll know exactly if travel here is your cup of proverbial tea. For now, I'll give you a little taste.

It was April of 2016 and I felt like a true adventurer, in part because Emerald Sky took me to developing countries I had not been to before—namely Romania and Bulgaria. Budapest and Bucharest were perfect bookends for exploring this beautiful and fascinating region of the world. The start of the journey was not unlike those undertaken by the younger me; one who spent his 20s bicycling and back-

Orthodox church in Bulgaria

packing around the world. On both trips, I visited villages where a globalized economy falls short, and I witnessed people living traditional lifestyles and maintaining many of their old customs.

The experiences felt authentic and genuine, and though this region is beginning to see its share of tourists, I felt as though I was exploring a frontier of sorts, places far removed from the busiest parts of the Danube and the major tourist attractions. While Eastern Europe may appear familiar to those who have traveled Western Europe (you'll find H&M and Starbucks in the big cities, for example) it can also be as exotic as the East. The fruit brandy *rakia*, for example, originated from *Raki*, the unsweetened, anise-flavored Turkish alcoholic drink introduced to Bulgaria and elsewhere during the Ottoman rule. You'll have plenty of opportunities to try rakia in Romania and Bulgaria should you wish. Just be careful: It can be deceptively strong. A sip will do.

EMERALD SKY TOOK US TO THE DEVELOPING COUNTRIES OF ROMANIA AND BULGARIA.

The familiarity of this region combined with the foreign is, in part, what made Emerald Waterways' Enchantment of Eastern Europe itinerary so appealing to me. My 10-night voyage started with two nights in Bucharest, followed by a one-week cruise that ended in Budapest. I've detailed each day of my journey in my ebook, from our start in Bucharest before sailing away to Bulgaria and then through the Iron Gates all the way up to Budapest.

There were two big differences in my travel during in my twenties and my travel on Emerald Sky. For starters, I am now three decades older. And Emerald Sky was a far cry above any hotel that I stayed in during my travels back then. Built in 2014, Emerald Sky is bright, contemporary and inviting. The 182-guest river cruiser featured roomy staterooms with lots of storage, large flat-panel televisions, and in some categories, "indoor" balconies that with the touch of a button opened stateroom floor-to-ceiling windows to the outside air. Emerald Sky also featured something I'd never seen on a riverboat—an indoor pool that doubled as an evening cinema (I've seen indoor pools on both Crystal Mozart and on some Uniworld ships, but not a pool that converted to an evening cinema).

Emerald Sky provided the perfect platform for seeing this enchanting region of Europe, with its war-ravaged history and cultural intrigue. And it ended with a bang: the "Illumination Cruise" in Budapest. We sailed for close to an hour past the well-lit buildings of beautiful Budapest, making our last night a night to remember.

Read more in my Guide to Eastern European Rivers Cruises ebook. | https://www.rivercruiseadvisor.com/e-books/eastern-europe-river-cruise-guide

Want To Experience the Enchantment of Eastern Europe?

In 2018, Emerald Waterways offers 10-night Enchantment of Eastern Europe cruises from $3,270 per person. Operating through October 8, eight departures are offered on Emerald Dawn, Emerald Destiny, Emerald Sky, Emerald Star, and Emerald Sun.

GARONNE AND DORDOGNE

Those interested in cruising the Garonne and Dordogne usually share one thing in common: the love of wine. While you don't have to be a total oenophile to appreciate the beauty of hills striated with vineyards or delectable French cuisine accompanying local varietals, wine is definitely the topic du jour when sailing these waters. (And if you want to know more, be sure to read about wine themed river cruises in Chapter 5.)

River cruises begin in Bordeaux, which is located on the Garonne River and flows for 374 miles from northern Spain into France. (The Dordogne River is north of the Garonne.) These two rivers meet northwest of Bordeaux and form the Gironde Estuary, which divides the Bordeaux region into Left and Right banks. This estuary stretches for 50 miles, offering portals into historic Blaye and pastoral Pauillac before emptying into the Bay of Biscay, which is part of the Atlantic Ocean.

The Dordogne is located entirely in France and flows for 300 miles in a westerly direction from Auvergne to its mouth—the Garonne River. A few cities on or near the Dordogne, include Libourne, Saint-Emilion and Bergerac.

Once overlooked by river cruise companies, the wine-producing region of Bordeaux, attracts river cruisers who are wine aficionados as well as history lovers, thanks to the region's intoxicating mix of culinary delights and old-world charm. It's one of the few destinations where river cruisers and ocean cruisers can access the city. I've visited Bordeaux on Silversea Cruises and on river cruisers operated by AmaWaterways, CroisiEurope, Viking River Cruises and Scenic (see my culinary cruise in Chapter 5). Access to the Atlantic for ocean cruisers is through the Gironde estuary, and in fact, river cruisers also transit the estuary along with the Garonne and Dordogne rivers.

A tidal phenomena called the Mascaret gives Bordeaux another distinction. The Mascaret is a tidal bore that creates waves powerful enough for surfing. River cruise ships must take precautions to avoid the brunt of these tidal fluctuations, which also dictate timetables and itineraries. To give you a sense, take a peek of

My stateroom on CroisiEurope's Cyrano de Bergerac.

this video I filmed of kids surfing the Mascaret in Bordeaux | https://www.rivercrui-seadvisor.com/2017/06/bordeaux-scenic-differently/

Roundtrip voyages from Bordeaux are usually about 8 days in length. CroisiEurope, Viking River Cruises, AmaWaterways are all great weeklong options. In 2017, Scenic began offering 11- and 12-day Bordeaux itineraries, peppered with some interesting extras like excursions to the oyster hotbed, and Europe's longest coastal beach of Arcachon, and nearby, Europe's tallest sand dune.

Some river cruise packages on the Garonne and Dordogne include pre-and-post land excursions to Paris or the Loire Valley and are 12 to 13 days in length. A handful of cruise lines combine multiple river cruises together on back-to-back itineraries that are connected either by direct TGV high-speed train or by overland motorcoach travel. If you have the time and the budget, Uniworld Boutique River Cruise Collection's 22-day Ultimate France cruise will provide you with a chance to take three river cruises on one trip to France.

I'd be remiss to talk about cruising in these two rivers without sharing an experience that is très French, a voyage aboard Cyrano de Bergerac.

CROISIEUROPE CYRANO DE BERGERAC - ROUNDTRIP BORDEAUX

CroisiEurope is the only company that I know of that offers Bordeaux cruises of four different durations. The company operates two ships in Bordeaux, Cyrano de Bergerac and Princesse d'Aquitaine, on 5-, 6-, 7- and 8-day cruises.

My four-night/five-day sampler cruise provided only a taste of Bordeaux on Cyrano de Bergerac. That is too short of a cruise for those who endure a trip across the Atlantic but perfect for pairing with overnight stays in Bordeaux.

My recommendation? Book a night or two at the Intercontinental Bordeaux—Le Grand Hôtel, a five-star hotel in the heart of Bordeaux, and also a night or two (post-cruise) at Les Sources De Caudalie, a five-star hotel surrounded by the vineyards of Château Smith Haut Lafitte, about eight miles from Bordeaux. The hotel also features a spa with treatments and therapies using products from grapes and grape seeds.

River cruises begin in the city of Bordeaux, where ships dock along the waterfront, typically overnighting, and depart the following morning to visit a handful of ports of call during the next several days. Our first stop was Libourne, where we set out for Saint-Émilion, just a few miles away. Here we toured the largest Monolithic church in Europe, located mostly underground, carved into the limestone cliffs before doing a wine tasting at one of Saint-Émilion's celebrated vineyards.

After a late afternoon of scenic sailing, we made it back to Bordeaux for the evening. The next morning we cruised to Cadillac to visit the impressive Roquetaillade Castle, set on a stunning hilltop about 30 minutes away by motorcoach. The castle excursion included guided tours around the grounds and inside the castle. After lunch back on the ship, we visited a vineyard producing Sauternes for tastings of the renowned sweet wine.

As we were sipping Sauternes, the ship returned to Bordeaux to overnight again before disembarkation. We would catch up with Cyrano de Bergerac by motorcoach. It was a short but sweet cruise, adequate enough for a burgeoning Francophile to be convinced to start planning a return visit to Bordeaux.

Want To Experience CroisiEurope's Bordeaux?

CroisiEurope's Bordeaux cruises operate through October 24, 2018. There are 5-day Bordeaux cruises priced from $1,276; 6-day sailings begin at $1,469; 7-day sailings starting at $1,812; and 8-day sailings begin at $2,297. Three, 8-day Biking Along The Gironde sailings are offered in April and May and again in July with prices beginning at $2,738.

DOURO RIVER

The Douro is one of my absolute favorite cruising regions. Its translation is "river of gold," and I agree that it's indeed precious. The third longest river on the Iberian Peninsula, the Douro wells up in Spain's Sierra de Urbión, crosses the country's Numantian Plateau, and heads westward across northern Portugal before releasing into the great Atlantic Ocean.

DOURO

Emerald Radiance docked in Porto.

The Douro River didn't merely act a conduit between the ocean and the inner reaches of Portugal, it was a transportation system that enabled the region's famous port wine production to flourish. In fact, Alto Douro, or the Upper Douro, is the world's oldest demarcated wine region. Aptly deriving its name from the city of Porto, Port wine is produced exclusively in the Douro River Valley—named a UNESCO World Heritage Site in 2001. Flat-bottom boats called rabelos used to deliver casks to the cellars directly across the river from Porto to a town called Gaia, which serves as the official point of embarkation for several river cruise lines today.

The pastoral countrysides, rural villages, and pocket-sized towns lining the Douro provide a unique river cruise panorama. Steeply terraced, verdant vineyards surrounding Porto give way to rock faces carved by nature and etched by ancient men; traces of some our ancestors' earliest illustrations are harbored within this region. As you wend your way closer to Spain, the arid landscape points to its constant companion, the sun, which also makes the Douro glimmer in the 18-karat hue so fitting of its moniker. However, the float down history's memory lane will stop shortly after reaching Spain, with river traffic from Spain's upper regions halted by dams built along the river in the 50s and 60s.

While its distinctive beauty and rich history make the Douro a destination unto itself, it's the Portuguese people that make me want to return again and again. They are among Europe's friendliest. You also get a mix of ports in Portugal and Spain on Douro River Cruises. That means good Port wines from Portugal and paella from Spain, along with Flamenco dancers and Portuguese pingo (similar to espresso). Several companies offer weeklong cruises on the Douro roundtrip from Porto, typically heading south to Spain's Vega de Terron and back, including pre- or post-hotel stays in Lisbon. In Porto, stroll Rua Diogo Leite where popular wine cellars, like the famed Sandeman's, wait for you to duck inside. You'll likely feel torn, because outdoors the colorful buildings on the hillside of the opposite bank and small local bands singing with spirited bravado beacon, suspending you beautifully in Porto's present. At Porto's Cais da Ribeira, diners enjoy the fish restaurants and tascas (tavernas) situated in the charming old buildings along the pier. From the halfway point of your journey, Vega de Terron, your cruise may have you heading out on a day trip to Spain's Roman city of Salamanca, dating back to medieval times. Here, even those oblivious to architecture can't help but notice the amazing blend of Renaissance and Gothic, old and new. The same can be said of the itineraries being offered here, with time-honored routes being plied by several new vessels—many constructed specifically to content with the unique size requirements of the five locks you'll transit.

Late May and June as well as the autumn harvest season proves to be the most idyllic time to visit the Douro. If you can take the heat, August is still a great time to visit and can be a little cheaper. The same goes for November on the opposite end of the spectrum, with chillier temperatures and rain requiring a few extra layers, although I have had beautiful weather on the Douro in November, notably in 2017. Viking River Cruises even offers departures in December, but don't expect to find Christmas Markets here.

Just in time for the start of the 2017 sailings on Portugal's Douro River, Scenic opened a new dock for exclusive use of Scenic and its sister company, Emerald Waterways. Unlike other river ship docks that tie up across the Douro in Gaia, this is conveniently located in Cais de Miragaia, a historic area of the World Heritage city of Porto and only a five-minute walk to the Ribiera, one of Porto's most popular

Suite on Emerald Radiance.

riverfront promenades known for its distinctive small alleyways and pastel-hued buildings.

Scenic launched the custom-built luxury Scenic Azure in April 2016 as one of the only owner-operated river cruise ships on the Douro with sailings that both begin and end in Porto. At 260 feet long and only 48 cabins, this is the next-generation of river ships designed with only one purpose: to navigate the calm waters of the Douro and its short and narrow locks, vineyard-covered gorges and abundance of incredible scenery. The vessel boasts the same all-inclusive luxury experience synonymous with the all Scenic Space-Ships—a 1:2 staff-to-guest ratio; private butler service and unlimited complimentary beverages and spirits; full-size private balcony staterooms, which come equipped with Scenic's Sun Lounge technology.

Douro itineraries range from eight to 17 days sailing roundtrip—with no overnight sailing—from the World Heritage city of Porto to Vega de Terron over the Spanish border. Highlights include many of the region's best sites and activities: sparkling wine tasting at the fairytale property of Quinta Aveleda; exploring the restored Monastery of Saint John of Tarouca; a sumptuous lunch and Flamenco dance in the architecturally-rich city of Salamanca. You can also opt for a canoeing adventure on the Sabor River and learn about life in the port wine town of Pinhao from residents. Enriching this journey even further, itineraries can be combined with Bordeaux and Seine river cruises plus extensions in Lisbon and a land tour from Porto to Madrid.

Emerald Waterways added another "Secrets of the Douro" eight-day voyage, aboard the company's new Emerald Radiance. The ship carries carry 112 guests in 56 suites and staterooms, including the Riverview Suites, a new category of stateroom with 300 square feet of living space and panoramic floor-to ceiling windows on two sides. Emerald Radiance also boasts a serenity pool on the sun deck, a choice of two restaurants, an onboard hairdresser, massage therapy room and fitness area, not to mention a three-to-one guest-crew ratio.

The cruise sails round trip from Porto, where guests will get a feel for the quaint villages and working vineyards and farms that typify the area as well as a day trip to Salamanca. During an excursion to the Coa Valley Prehistoric Museum in Pocinho you can view stone carvings made by early inhabitants of the Douro followed by dinner at a traditional local wine estate. A visit to the historic icon of Mateus Palace, depicted on the labels of Portugal's famous rose wine and the numerous wine caves of Vila Nova de Gaia bring the region's wine culture to life.

Yet another newcomer to the Douro is U.K.-based Riviera River Cruises' MS Douro Elegance, christened in March of 2017. It is one of the four new ships built in 2017. Fitted with polished marble and hardwoods, the 63 cabins and suites span a minimum of 161 square feet. The upper and middle deck cabins and suites feature floor-to-ceiling windows that slide down halfway to create an impromptu balcony, while the Deluxe and Superior Suites feature Juliet balconies. The eight-day sailings travel roundtrip Porto, with visits to the medieval village of Castelo Rodrigo, Lamego, home of Portugal's sparkling Raposeira wine, a visit to Mateus Palace, and a dinner at Quinta da Pacheca, a 18th-century manor house and home to the first wine in Portugal to carry the owner's name. The 11-day option extends your exploration of Portugal heading south by land, visiting the Roman aqueducts in ancient Coimbra, the olive groves of Fatima and the bustling capital of Lisbon, where your journey ends. Launching in the fall of 2018, the Douro Splendour joins her identical sister-ship Douro Elegance in operating river cruises along the Douro.

Viking River Cruises' 106-passenger Viking Osfrid joined sister ships Viking Hemming and Viking Torgil on the Douro in 2016. All feature the 10-day "Portugal's Rivers of Gold" itinerary, from Lisbon to Porto (sailing roundtrip from Porto), but also offer an interesting post-extension tour in Santiago, Spain, as well as a pre-extension tour in Madrid.

I took a wine-themed voyage with AmaWaterways along the Douro in 2014 and again on with Emerald Waterways in 2017. Catch a glimpse of some of the stunning landscapes and fascinating sights you'll see by viewing the video series I filmed during my trip on Emerald Waterways | https://www.rivercruiseadvisor.com/2017/12/cruise-along-portugals-douro-river/

VOLGA RIVER

It's one of the most historic waterways in the world, but river cruises on Russia's Volga River are becoming a rare commodity. Geopolitical issues have seen the reduction of these voyages in recent years, though there are still cruise lines that continue to be committed to the region. For the adventurous traveler, now could be the best time to go to Russia, as demand is lower and ships don't frequently sell out. Like any kind of travel, it is an opportunity to glean a real understanding of the issues facing a culture different from that of our own.

As I already mentioned, the Volga is Europe's pride and joy when it comes to going the distance. It stretches 2,294 miles, which is more than 500 miles longer than the Danube. If one took into account all of the arteries branching off from this lifeblood, that number is closer to 350,000 miles. A testament to this waterway's significance, only two-fifths of the river basin lies within Europe's borders, yet it is home to half of Russia's population. Cities and villages cluster at its banks from the marshy forests to the semi-desert lowlands before the Volga empties into the Caspian Sea.

The vast majority of river cruises through Russia operate between Moscow to St. Petersburg. Itineraries tend to be just shy of two weeks in duration, with no week-long options. This makes these voyages ideal for "port collectors" who want to see something different and don't mind committing the time and financial resources to do so.

Despite the recent controversy surrounding some of the decisions that Russia has made politically, the country remains one of the most fascinating destinations for river cruisers. Visits to multiple UNESCO World Heritage sites, including the city of Yaroslavl, which is recognized for its historic town center and numerous 17th century churches, make for a historical and culturally enriching journey. For instance, in Uglich, guests can visit the church of St. Dmitry on the Blood, which commemorates the murder of 10 year old Dmirty Ivanovich, youngest son of Ivan the Terrible, in 1591. In addition, most itineraries are structured to provide guests with ample time in both St. Petersburg and Moscow without the need for costly pre-and-post hotel stays. Viking River Cruises' 13-day "Waterways of the Tsars" itinerary, for example, includes four days in both St. Petersburg and Moscow.

So who offers river cruises through Russia? At the moment, there are four major lines that all feature departures in the region: Scenic, Uniworld Boutique River Cruise Collection, Viking River Cruises, and CroisiEurope. It comes as no surprise that Viking offers sailings along the Volga, since the company got its start in Russia back in 1997, and is in the unique position to own its ships outright (other companies tend to charter their ships due to Russia's myriad of rules and regulations). Scenic, however, offers the biggest variety of itineraries, with six different options, some mixed with visits to Baltic countries and Berlin. CroisiEurope's 8-day sailings from St. Petersburg to Moscow includes a visit to the artisan epicenter of Mandrogi, a stop in Kizhi where an open-air historic museum showcases Russia's historic architecture, as well as Uglich where you can delve into Ivan the Terrible's tale of destruction.

It's also interesting to note that some lines—like AmaWaterways used to offer river cruises through Russia, but stopped following Russia's involvement with the Ukraine. AmaWaterways in particular had put a lot of time, energy and resources into upgrading its ship AmaKatarina just before the current crisis, and could certainly be ready to re-start Volga River cruises should the opportunity arise. For the 2018 season, though, AmaWaterways has no current plans to do so.

PO RIVER

The Po River is the longest river in Italy. It flows for more than 400 miles in an easterly direction through cities, such as Piacenza, Mantua and Ferrara. Your cruise here, however, will only cover about 100 miles of it. Itineraries typically sail from Venice to Polesella, though smaller barge cruises allow travel farther west to Mantua, about 60 miles west of Polesella. To give you a geographic touchstone, the city of Turin is about 178 miles west of Mantua and while it's on the Po River, Turin is not visited on a Po River cruise.

Italy is one of the world's most beloved travel destinations. Land tours and ocean cruises regularly visit this mecca of wine and culinary delights, but river cruises tend to bypass Italy altogether. It's not because Italy isn't a river cruise destination—it is. Rather, it's because the Po River is tricky to navigate.

Once used by the ancient Romans for trade between the Mediterranean Sea and areas further inland, the Po River's fast-flowing waters and constantly shifting sandbanks make it a lot less popular today among leisure travelers. And sadly, Strauss never penned a waltz after the poor Po like he did the Danube.

Perhaps it's just as well, given the river's shaky environmental past: Milan dumped its raw sewage into the river between 2002 and 2005 because the city couldn't be bothered to develop a proper waste-management plan, and officials taking samples of the Po in 2005 were shocked to find that the water was full of benzoylecgonine—an ingredient secreted in the urine of cocaine users.

But don't let that scare you off: Po River cruises offer a unique way to see some of Italy's most historic sites without the need for grueling overland bus tours or a do-it-yourself road trip in a dinged-up Fiat. Plus, it grants you passage to sites you might otherwise miss, like the flamingo-stippled wetlands, quaint islands, and fishing villages. For the true voyage and port collector, a sailing through the heart of Italy on the Po is hard to beat.

Po River Cruises typically begin on the canals in Venice—a city that needs little introduction, but interestingly is made up of 150 canals. So needless to say, a cruise on the Po River is always combined with the canals of Venice and the Venetian Lagoon; the body of water that leads to the Po River. A few destinations that are often part of the itinerary are reached from Venice or the Venetian Lagoon and include the glass-capital of Murano, the quaint island of Burano and Shakespearean-favorite Verona. In addition, cities like Polesella, Bologna, Ravenna and Ferrara are often visited. Transportation to and from most of these cities is by motor coach.

There are several opportunities for day and evening canal cruises in Venice. However, for overnight cruises, there are only a few companies that travel along the Po River: European Waterways (barges), Uniworld Boutique River Cruise Collection, and CroisiEurope.

Perhaps this is a good time to mention that these are not the only river cruises visiting Italy. Technically a Rhine river cruise, Tauck will be offering a tour that spends three nights exploring Italy's fashion capital and the Italian Lake District—the only European river cruise company to do so—before sailing on to its final destination of Amsterdam.

While Po is still on my bucket list, I highlight the staple of Uniworld's Po River lineup below: the magnificent 10-day Gems of Northern Italy itinerary to give you a sense which crown jewels bedazzling the top of the Boot that you'll visit while aboard the magnificent River Baroness. CroisiEurope's offerings come in more digestible chunks, with departures spanning five, six, and seven days in length. This may seem odd to North American travelers faced with a massive transatlantic air journey ahead of them, but remember: CroisiEurope draws a substantial portion of its passenger base from Europeans who are fortunate enough to be roughly two hours' flying time away from Italy.

With the slew of travelers hoping to see Venice before it sinks, not to mention Italy still topping traveler bucket lists, should we expect to see more river cruise companies Po-ward bound? It depends. With limited port of call options and relatively short distances to sail between them, many river cruise lines have understandably chosen to focus on more diverse rivers like the Danube and the Rhine.

UNIWORLD BOUTIQUE RIVER CRUISE COLLECTION

RIVER BARONESS - MILAN TO VENICE

This all-inclusive luxury line leads the pack when it comes to Po River cruises. It was among the first of the North American-based river cruise lines to set up shop in Italy, and it has crafted some truly impressive itineraries in this historic region.

This voyage kicks off in the fashion capital of Milan. A two-night pre-cruise stay awaits guests here, complete with free time and a guided tour of Milan and the chance to see Da Vinci's historic Last Supper mural that was painted by the master between 1495 and 1498.

From Milan, guests travel to Venice to embark River Baroness. Along the way, a stop in romantic Verona—the city of Romeo and Juliet—is included as well as a wine tasting and lunch at Serego Alighieri estate, owned by the descendants of Italy's most beloved poet. In Venice, the River Baroness acts as your hotel while you explore famous sights like the Bridge of Sighs, Piazza San Marco, the Doge's Palace, or maybe just a stroll across the Rialto Bridge and into the labyrinth of waterfront passages. Uniworld even provides an after-hours tour of St. Mark's Basilica, provided no prior religious festivities are taking place in the evening.

On the fifth day of your journey, River Baroness departs Venice, bound for Chioggia, a Venice-in-miniature seaside town and fish monger's delight. Next, picturesque Padua, with its medieval ramparts and fresco-lined chapels. In Polesella, guests can elect to either visit the food capital of Bologna for a pasta-making workshop or sift through Renaissance treasure during a half-day tour of UNESCO World Heritage site Ferrara, which has been rated as a major center of the arts for generations.

After that, it's back to Venice on Day 7 for more complimentary guided excursions, including offerings that explore local markets, the surrounding islands (like Murano, with its famed Murano Glass), and even Lido, home to both the gorgeous Lido Beach and the Venice Film Festival.

Want to experience the Po River with Uniworld Boutique River Cruise Collection?

The 10-day Gems of Northern Italy between Milan and Venice start at $4,339 per person, double occupancy for a Category 5 stateroom. Or, opt for the 15-day "Splendors of Italy" tour that extends your journey by land to Rome, visiting Tuscan treasures like Florence and the Chianti region, starting at $6449 per person, double occupancy for a Category 5 room. Both are offered through November 2, 2018.

CROISIEUROPE MS MICHELANGELO - ROUNDTRIP VENICE

This affordable cruise line offers three separate river cruise journeys along the Po, ranging 5 to 7 days in length, aboard the nimble MS Michelangelo; a vessel perfectly suited to the river thanks to its shallow draft and accommodations for 158 guests.

Even the shortest of these itineraries—the five-day "Short Break In Venice"—includes visits to Venice, Burano, and Chioggia. It's not a great sailing for those who value lazy days of scenic cruising, but it is a terrific sailing for those who are okay with essentially using the MS Michelangelo as their very own floating hotel with meals and beverages included. In cities like Venice where the sky's the limit in terms of traditional incidental charges at hotels, these river cruise journeys not only offer the quintessential room with a view; they're also the most economical way to see this part of Italy.

CroisiEurope recently added 6-day Family Club sailings in which kids under the age of 16 cruise for free and you still get to enjoy the same iconic locales. See where Romeo was said to have professed his love for Juliet in Verona (port of Polesella), tour Doge's palaces in Venice, and visit the lagoon islands of Murano and Burano. The holidays are also a special time of year to travel with CroisiEurope in Italy, with 5-day roundtrip Venice sailing that gracefully glides into the New Year.

My daughter and me cruising Sweden's Gota Canal.

Want to experience Italy with CroisiEurope?

In 2018, the 5-day "Short Break Venice" itinerary aboard MS Michelangelo through June 30, 2018 and then August 31-October 14, 2018 starts at $1,193 per person, double occupancy; the 6-day "Venice, the Lagoon and the Po Delta" aboard MS Michelangelo July 10 - August 19, 2018 and starts at $1,530; the 7-day sailing adds the lagoon islands and increases the starting price to $1,935. "Family Club: Venice and Lagoon" sailings depart from July 10-August 19, 2018, starting at $1,243 with kids under the age of 16 sailing for free. Holiday sailings aboard MS Michelangelo escort us into 2018 with the 5-night "Italian New Year in Venice" sailing on December 28 from $1,777.

COVETED CANALS

While river cruising is the more common type of experience that travelers seek, canal cruising represents some of the best travel experiences available on the European continent. These watery inroads are often no more than 40 feet wide and take you to quiet villages and small towns. You'll feel as though Europe has opened its closely guarded vest to reveal its most cherished possessions. Plus, that intimacy translates to the onboard experience, too, with barges being the only means of transit, capable of carrying no more than 25 people on average—sometimes as few as three couples!

Foregoing on the need for spacious interiors opens up a world of new possibilities, too—with more than 5,000 miles of canals in France alone.

The most popular canals for barging are the Canal de la Marne au Rhin, which links the Rhine with the Marne, and between Canal Latéral a la Marne, a canal that follows the course of the Marne river, passing through the heart of Champagne; and Canal Latéral a la Loire, which follows the course of the upper Loire. (Latéral indicates that the waterway parallels the course of the river. Some rivers, like the upper Loire, are not navigable, hence the latéral.)

Transiting these canals takes lots of time, as you pass through many locks that can takes as long as 20 minutes to transit. But barge cruising is meant to be relaxing, and if you get bored, just hop on a bike or walk to meet the barge at another lock upstream.

Out of all types of cruises, I find canal cruising to be the most foreign to North American travelers. I've included more extensive recaps of my voyages to better provide insight into these unique river cruises. My fondness for this type of travel is undeniable, but I understand that this much more discreet form of cruise travel isn't everyone's idea of the perfect vacation.

If it is, you can always join me! I actually host my own canal and barge river cruises. See Cruise With Me for details | rivercruiseadvisor.com/ ralph-grizzles-hosted-river-cruise-trips

Juno transiting the Carl Johan staircase, with its 7 connected locks.

GOTA CANAL CRUISING JUNO - SWEDEN

When you think of European river cruising or canal cruising, you normally think of Central Europe. But it is possible to take a canal cruise across Sweden, between Stockholm and Gothenburg. I've done it. The four-day journey was remarkable and beautiful—and a bit quirky too.

After an early morning breakfast at Radisson Blu Strand Hotel, my daughter and I rolled our luggage for about five minutes to our ship, Juno, docked on the waterfront at Stockholm's Royal Palace. Greeted by the captain and crew, we were on board within three minutes. We set off around 9 a.m. under cloudy skies, past Stockholm's Old Town (Gamla Stan). Within 15 minutes, our guide, a retired journalist from Goteborg, announced: "Ladies and gentlemen, in a few minutes we will transit our first lock. After that, we have only 65 more to go."

The traditional route between Gothenburg and Stockholm has been operated since the Gota Canal Company was founded in 1869. The ship Juno is the world's oldest passenger ship still in operation, built soon after in 1874. Operated by The Gota Canal Company, Juno is capable of carrying 54 guests, but for comfort, the company limits capacity to 48.

The three categories of staterooms are on three decks, and even the top categories are small, similar to a sleeping compartment on a train, as the pre-cruise documentation explains it. My stateroom was so small that exiting the lower bunk bed was a bit like doing the limbo, because of the lack of headspace above me. And, in order for my daughter to get out of the top bunk bed, I had to leave the room. Standing room only took on a literal meaning all throughout the ship.

Passengers are advised to pack lightly, although luggage can be stored—and retrieved on a regular basis. My daughter and I kept our two, 24-inch bags in our room, along with a few smaller bags. That left us with little floor space, and sometimes maneuvering, when we were both in the room, became a matter or acrobatics—or awkward dancing. Still, the stateroom experience was exceptionally charming, and I began to call our way of getting around in the confined space, the Gota Canal dance.

Klara, a crew member on Juno.

Though small, the room is designed smartly. There is a closet that allows for hanging six to eight items. A sink basin with running water is situated in a cabinet that also has storage underneath for small bags, such as purses and camera bags. The cabinet opens and closes to expose or hide the sink basin. Closing it creates extra space on top, which is where we found our complimentary bottle of champagne and strawberries upon boarding (included only in the top-deck categories).

During our four-day transit, we would cover about 500 nautical miles, navigate 66 locks, lifting Juno 301 feet above sea level. Starting Wednesday in Stockholm we would end our cruise in Goteborg on Saturday at around 2:30 in the afternoon. There would be lots for us to see and do along the way, including guided tours, as well as opportunities to get off the ship to bicycle or walk.

Juno's timetable is more of an aspiration than a rigid schedule. The reason: the canal's shallow draft, maximum 2.8 meters. Juno's draft, 2.82 meters. The captain assured us that we would drag the bottom at times during our transit. Not be alarmed, though. "They can't afford to build ships with steel this thick any longer," he told us during the welcome. Juno may be old and small, but she's sturdy.

The captain also told us that the pitch propeller sucked up everything, such as "bicycles," he said jokingly, but which was probably true. Stolen bikes are sometimes thrown into the canal. The captain said we would see divers from the ship now and then clearing the propeller. Dragging bottom, clearing the propeller, transiting 66 locks, all the reasons why the timetable is only an aspiration.

Our fellow passengers were from Sweden and other parts of Europe—as well as North America. One woman from Lulea, in Sweden's north, is traveling with her cousin, a Swede from the United States. They had another cousin who lived along the canal, and as we passed, we all waved to him from the ship. We also are meeting a friend for ice cream on Thursday. He lives within a few minutes of the canal.

Breakfast, lunch and dinner are served in two smallish but attractive rooms, the main dining room on the second level, and a lounge on the top level. All meals are included in the fare, but beverages, with the exception of tap water, cost extra. There is an Honesty Bar, where you retrieve and account for self-service beverages, on the top deck.

Dining is pleasant, and the food good, beginning with a starter and followed by a main course and dessert. Fresh breads are served tableside. Seating is assigned, but guests can request to change tables. We are seated with a couple from Stockholm and a woman from Germany. English is our common language, but we three non-Swedes are eager to learn a few Swedish words and phrases.

Our first stop and chance to go ashore was in Trosa, a charming town with a canal running through the center. It was Sweden's National Day, so most of the shops were closed. We watched a parade and explored the town, stopping for coffee, before heading back to Juno. On the dock beside Juno, an 87-year-old man sere-

CRUISING THE HEART OF SWEDEN ON THE
GOTA CANAL, A PRICELESS EXPERIENCE.

Welcome aboard CroisiEurope's Anne-Marie.

naded us with his accordion and Swedish songs. It was a sweet moment, someone who appeared to enjoy giving people the gift of song and a wonderful send off.

The next day we transited the staircase of seven locks at Berg, situated near the town of Linköping. It was fascinating to watch for an hour or so as Juno worked her way up the staircase from Lake Roxen, at 33 meters above sea level, to eventually arrive at Lake Boren, 73 meters above sea level.

Sweden's long summer days imbue our cruise with an aesthetic element that is hard to convey in words. The sunlight, and the canvas on which it displays its rich colors, makes it hard to go to sleep at night. Sure, our ship has blinds that darken the room, but who wants to miss the spectacle of nature happening through the threshold of our stateroom door? Idyllic days were marked by brilliant blue skies, cotton-ball clouds and fields of wildflowers on either side of the ship as we made our way along the canal, through forests and past charming Swedish villages.

One evening we had quite the show. Juno's belly ran aground while transiting a bend of the canal as we were having dinner. The captain explained our predicament and said that we needed more water to lift the ship, so he phoned someone, a lock-keeper presumably, to release water from the locks upstream. His phone call worked, and we were soon under way.

At the next lock, however, the captain thought it prudent to have a diver check the propeller, which had been eating mud as Juno struggled to loosen herself from the canal bottom. One of the crew members dove in to remove a few items that had wrapped around the propeller, nothing significant, but enough to keep us entertained for 15 minutes or so. We all applauded when the young man once again stood ashore and toweled himself dry.

We had an early breakfast the next day and joined an included guided tour of Karlsborg Fortress, built nearly 200 years ago but made obsolete for defense shortly

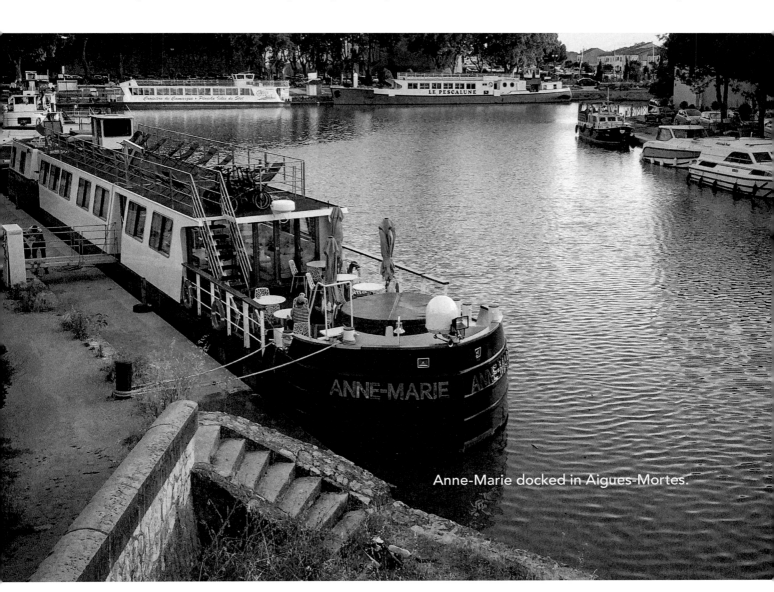

Anne-Marie docked in Aigues-Mortes.

Arles, France

after becoming operational. The tour was well-done, with the use of multimedia and special effects, and knowledgeable English-speaking guides. After sailing from Karlsborg, Ingemar, our cruise director, told us to be on deck for something we would not want to miss at the next lock. There, at Forsvik, a Swedish spiritual group greeted our ship with flowers and song. It was a sweet gesture, and the greeting is extended each time a ship passes. We were at the lock for a good 10 minutes, the captain intent on safely maneuvering Juno through, while we enjoyed the show and warm hospitality from our serenaders ashore.

We arrived in Gothenburg, Sweden, about four hours late according to the published schedule.

Despite the speed bumps along the way, or perhaps because of them, our Gota Canal cruise certainly was a memorable one, as charming as Sweden itself. It's difficult to find fault with the cruise, particularly when you consider you are cruising on a museum piece. I recommend it for any avid cruiser wanting to cruise on a piece of history itself, our ship Juno, and for those desiring an immersion in Sweden. The thought of it still makes me want to do a little Gota Canal jig.

Want to experience the Gota Canal aboard the MS Juno?

Rates for a 4-day cruise between Gothenburg and Stockholm (May through August) range from $3,000 per couple to about $5,000 per couple.

CROISIEUROPE'S ANNE-MARIE - ARLES TO SETE, SOUTH OF FRANCE

A few years ago, Strasbourg-based CroisiEurope began building a fleet of barges designed specifically to cruise the canals in Europe. I chartered CroisiEurope's barge (in 2015 and in 2018) for a group trip exploring the Languedoc-Roussillon region, where the Camargue is situated—extending from Provence to the Pyrenees Mountains.

The journey began in Arles at the Hôtel Jules Cesar, a five-star property housed in a former convent dating back to the 17th century. Our group would be here for two nights before boarding our barge SS Anne-Marie. I welcomed the members of

Zoltan, our cruise manager.

our group in a lovely courtyard where we toasted with glasses of French wine and introduced ourselves. We were comprised of seven Americans, two Australians, and one Swede. We talked about the days ahead and all that we would see, beginning with a full-day tour Friday when we'd explore Avignon, Châteauneuf-du-Pape and Pont du Gard, followed by our voyage along the Canal du Rhône-à-Sète on the barge, and then a post-barge night in Montpelier.

Though the first day was technically a free day to explore Arles, I had a surprise in store. I had rented a van for anyone who wanted to make an excursion. We had many choices but two came to mind. We could go to Aix-en-Provence (an all-time favorite of mine), or to Uzes, a gorgeous town that lies at the source a river where a Roman aqueduct was built in the 1st century BC to supply water to Nîmes about 30 miles away. The unanimous vote was to go to Uzes before heading our separate ways for dinner. I dined near the walls of the ancient Roman arena in Arles. We could have mistaken it for Rome that lovely summer night as we dined within sight of a coliseum on risotto with mushrooms and steak-frites.

The next morning, after a hearty breakfast at Hôtel Jules Cesar, we prepared for our trip to Uzes, where we'd get to know one another and enjoy a lunch we'd long rave about. As we were leaving Uzes, we decided to stop at the UNESCO World Heritage Site Pont du Gard. What a good decision. The Romans were known for their incredible mastery of architecture and engineering. This impressive sample of this mastery is absolutely gorgeous. It's no wonder this bridge, crossing over the Gardon River, is considered one of the most-well preserved legacies of ancient Roman architecture in all of Europe. During the Roman Empire, the bridge was built as an aqueduct to provide water to the town of Nîmes, which, because of its geographical location, formerly had complications getting a steady water supply. As water was used for bath houses (which were popular in the Roman Empire) and in the residences of the wealthy, it was a lauded accomplishment.

Luckily, the bridge did not suffer the fate of most Roman structures, which is to say that Pont du Gard was not left abandoned and in ruins. Though Romans used it mainly as an aqueduct, after the Roman Empire fell, Pont du Gard continued to be used as a bridge, which ensured its preservation. The bridge's incredible beauty

Lounge on Anne-Marie.

and awe-inspiring architecture also played a role in its preservation, as it became the object of visits by the French court, including several kings. Paintings of it can be found in palaces, such as Fontainebleau.

It is not surprising, then, that the picturesque qualities of the bridge have also inspired writers such as Jean-Jacques Rousseau and Henry James. Nor is it a surprise that it has been named a UNESCO World Heritage Site, and that it is now one of the most popular sites in the entire county of France.

Luckily, we managed to squeeze in a visit Pont du Gard, because it may have been too much to do Avignon and Châteauneuf-du-Pape and Pont du Gard in one day. Our pace was relaxed the next day as we visited Avignon and Châteauneuf-du-Pape with our guide Catherine.

A UNESCO World Heritage Site, Avignon's medieval walled city has a fascinating story to tell, from its impressive Pope's Palace that was once the seat of Catholicism to a bridge that has captured the imagination of millions of people over the ages. Spanning the Rhône river (well, almost) is the Pont d'Avignon, the bridge that inspired the French song, Sur le Pont d'Avignon.

Part of the UNESCO World Heritage Site, the Pont d'Avignon is one of the world's most famous bridges. Hundreds, perhaps thousands, of people come to walk on this bridge every day. The odd thing is, the bridge doesn't go anywhere. That's because it was built back in the 1100s, destroyed many times, and what you see now is all that remains of the bridge. Still, there's something magical about the ancient bridge, and indeed it has captured the imagination of millions of children throughout the world. In the happy song Sur le Pont d'Avignon various members of French society—ladies, gentlemen, soldiers and musicians—meet on the bridge and do a little dance.

We also visited The Pope's Palace, one of the largest and most important medieval Gothic buildings in all of Europe. It was once a fortress and a palace, and in 1309 became the home to six successive popes. Our 90-minute tour included a visit to the Grand Chapel, where the Avignon popes worshiped, which I found to be impressive and humbling.

Anne-Marie stateroom.

The Pope's Palace wasn't the only thing the popes left behind in Avignon. They also left behind a legacy of an internationally acclaimed wine, and no trip to Avignon would be complete without a taste, or two, of Chateauneuf du Pape, or basically, the Pope's wine. For that, we headed to Chateauneuf du Pape for lunch and a wine tasting.

Our lunch venue, La Table des Fines Roches, was outstanding, on the grounds of an impressive palace overlooking the vineyards of Chateauneuf du Pape from a terrace punctuated by cypress trees. It was a gorgeous setting on a gorgeous day. The lunch was one of those that went down in the books as "must return here one day." Afterward, the group headed with our guide Catherine into Chateauneuf du Pape for a wine-tasting.

We were told that Van Gogh, who lived in Arles (pronounced Arl) from 1888-1889, painted his masterpiece, The Starry Night, near the very dock where our tiny, yet elegant, SS Anne-Marie awaited: Quai Max Dormoy in Arles. As it turns out, that's not true. The painting depicts the view from his asylum room at Saint-Rémy-de-Provence. Following a breakdown in 1888 that resulted in the self-mutilation of his left ear, Van Gogh had voluntarily admitted himself to the Saint-Paul-de-Mausole lunatic asylum. Nonetheless, Van Gogh probably did walk along the docks here in Arles—he'd be crazy not to—and I couldn't help but hum the tune of Don McLean's "Vincent" as we boarded Anne-Marie.

The group returning from the wine tasting in Chateauneuf du Pape gave the tasting, and the wines, high marks. In fact, one traveler from our group bought a case of wine and had it shipped back to the U.S.

The entire crew welcomed us aboard. We enjoyed a champagne toast and an orientation talk. CroisiEurope's barges are custom-built for hotel barging, as opposed to being modified from cargo barges. Anne-Marie featured bicycles, included excursions, a jacuzzi, and complimentary WiFi that actually worked well—and the all-important open bar.

The staterooms are down one deck from the living room and bar, cozy, measuring 110-square-feet, but exceptionally well-configured, with plenty of space for storage. Knowing that the staterooms were small before boarding Anne-Marie, I found that the cabin exceeded my expectations.

The staterooms featured smartly designed storage in the headboards of the twin-bed configured staterooms, as well as a small closet for hanging clothes and storage of suitcases underneath the beds. I was pleased to see the bathroom offered plenty of storage in a drawer beneath the sink and that the shower was large enough to accommodate all of my 6'5" body, even with the glass doors closed and elbows extended when washing my hair. For the mobility challenged, there is something very close to an ADA-compliant stateroom with a wider door and other features for those who find getting around difficult. This stateroom is the only stateroom on the same level as the living room and dining room.

Unpacked and cleaned up, we were ready for dinner. There is a single dining room that will seat up to 22, but as there were only 10 of us, we enjoyed sharing one large table. Dinner was served course-by-course, beginning with an amuse-bouche, followed by a starter, then the main course, then cheese, then dessert—all complemented by wines from the region, which just so happens to be the largest wine-producing region in France. We enjoyed Côte du Rhône, Provençal Rosé as

Evening on the canal in the Camargue region.

Flamingos in the Camargue.

well as Chablis and Chardonnay, along with other wines on our voyage. For those with food allergies or food preferences, the galley can be flexible, serving alternative dishes. Bottled water was at our table, both sparkling and still. Specialty coffees and soft drinks, as well as spirits and beer, were all available at no extra charge.

We enjoyed a restful overnight on board, and following breakfast headed out to the countryside to learn about olive oil production in Provence. Once we got to the farm, we sat atop bales of hay for a 15-minute tractor-pulled ride through olive groves. Through our guide Peggy, we learned that the olive groves benefited from the mistral, the strong northwesterly wind that blows through the Rhône valley. The mistral keeps insects from damaging the olives..

Our tour of Arles showcased the city's impressive Roman monuments, of which the earliest—the arena, the Roman theatre and the cryptoporticus (subterranean galleries)—date back to the 1st century B.C. During the 4th century, Arles experienced a second golden age, as attested by the baths of Constantine and the necropolis of Alyscamps. Then the city experienced another resurgence when in the 11th and 12th centuries, Arles once again became one of the most attractive cities in the Mediterranean.

Arles was also home to the famous impressionist painter Van Gogh from 1888 to 1889. During his stay here, he managed to paint more than 300 works before his increasingly unstable mental health took hold. Peggy told us that some people have said that his friend, the artist Paul Gauguin, cut Van Gogh's ear and to spare the former embarrassment, Van Gogh was said to have claimed to have done it himself. Not true, of course.

Unfortunately, there are no Van Gogh paintings in the museums in Arles, but we visited one of the sites that inspired the artist's works, Le Jardin de La Maison de Santé. We snapped a few photos and admired the beautiful garden. Peggy told us that Van Gogh's Yellow House, where he lived and which he painted, is gone. The building was severely damaged in a bombing raid by the Allies on June 25, 1944, and demolished. Van Gogh's works from this period are richly draped in yellow, because, Peggy told us, yellow was the cheapest of paints. Still, there can be little doubt that Van Gogh was enchanted by the local landscape and light.

At the arena, we learned about the highly controversial bullfights that take place in Arles every year. Arles practices both Provençal, and Spanish bullfighting. In the camarguaises (bull fights in which the bull is not killed), a team of men attempt to remove a tassel from the bull without injury. On Easter and the first weekend in September, however, Spanish-style bullfights are held here, where the bull is killed at the end.

We enjoyed our short tour in Arles. Though small, Arles has an interesting history, beautiful sights and a rich cultural heritage that intrigued us. It was a good place to begin a cruise along the Rhône à Sète Canal, and that is exactly what we were about to begin next.

We returned to Anne-Marie, where we sat down for lunch as we started cruising toward Galician. It is difficult to imagine a better moment. We had enjoyed a morning of touring, learned a few things about Arles and about olive oil (as well as about Van Gogh and bullfighting), then sat down for a beautiful lunch, with complimentary French wines, and now, here we were, motoring away from Arles on a sunny afternoon. Life could not have been better.

Certainly, there is a magic in motion, particularly on water. The afternoon was relaxed (read napping). We arrived in Galician in the late afternoon. It was a small, small town. Some from our group walked in to explore the few houses and buildings that made up the town center. My friend Monica and I pedaled bicycles, available at no charge on the barge. The pedaling along the canal was easy and enjoyable. And of course, it was gorgeous. We passed fishermen along the banks of the canal and, in broad expanses of pastures, the grazing "wild" horses that are common to the region. With the breeze at our backs and the sun in our faces, we were pedaling through moments that we would never forget.

We returned to Anne-Marie, having ridden for 45 minutes or so. A glass of champagne was never beyond our arm's reach, so why not celebrate the moment before getting washed up before dinner? Like last night, dinner was exceptional, with those beautiful French wines and cheeses complementing the cuisine.

As sunset approached, I stepped out on the top deck to admire the beauty of the region. It seemed that we were the only ones on earth, here in our little Anne-Marie, tied up alongside the banks in this small place. I could hear the song of the cicadas. At the risk of repeating myself, this too was a moment to remember.

The next morning aboard Anne-Marie started with breakfast, followed by an included excursion to the Camargue. As the largest river delta within the entire continent of Europe, the Camargue is wrapped within both arms of the Rhône river and hugged by the Mediterranean sea in the south. So abundant is the nature here that UNESCO named the Camargue a World Heritage Site, as well as a biosphere reserve, in the hopes of protecting its incredibly delicate ecosystem, especially within its natural park, the Parc Naturel Régional de Camargue.

THE CAMARGUE HAS AN EPONYMOUS HORSE BREED, THE FAMOUS WHITE CAMARGUAIS.

One of France's most beautiful natural landmarks, the Camargue is dotted with rich marshland, lakes, ocean coastline, sandbars and gorgeous lagoons that make for some of the country's most incredible natural fluvial landscapes. We traveled through the Camargue for about 45 minutes in the direction of Sainte-Marie-la-Mer. Along the way we passed pastures where we saw the majestic white Camargue horses grazing. The region also is known for its hundreds of species of birds, which include the beautiful flamingo species only found in certain areas in Europe. At one point during our drive, Peggy instructed the driver to pull over so that we could photograph storks, their nests up above us.

We arrived in Sainte-Marie-la-Mer, a quaint little beach town that is popular for tourists on summer holiday. For most of the year, Sainte-Marie-la-Mer is fairly quiet. The majority of the inhabitants are farmers, fishermen, and ranchers. In the summer months, however, the town's population swells from 4,000 to 20,000. The summer residents love to spend their time at the beautiful beaches, often in small wooden cabins on the sandy landscapes.

Cowboys in the Camargue.

Each evening, a treat: Here, pre-dinner hors d'oeuvres are served.

We visited the Church of Notre-Dame-de-la-Mer, a fine example of Medieval architecture, and one of the most iconic landmarks in Sainte-Marie-la-Mer. Popularized by the legend of the landing of the "Three Marys" on the Camargue coast, the church is thought to have been built on the site where the Phoenicians erected a temple to Artemis.

Back on board Anne-Marie, our excellent chef Romain Chassignet surprised us with a barbecue. We'd be dining outdoors as we made our way along the canal to Aigues-Mortes (pronounced eggmon).

After a couple hours of sailing, we reached the stunning fortified city with a large salt factory just steps outside the town walls. The name of the Medieval town translates to "dead waters." Aigues-Mortes is surrounded by salt marshes, and having once been on the Mediterranean coast (a position that has changed over time), the town has been a salt-mining commune for thousands of years. In fact, when visiting the salt ponds and factory the next day we learned what a big role the salt industry played in the town's history—dating back to the Benedictine monks who settled nearby in the 8th century to exploit this valuable commodity found in the pink-hued Peccais Ponds.

This town has largely preserved its Medieval structure and architecture. From outside, we admired the well-preserved walls that surround the town. Aigues-Mortes was also one of the few places in France where Protestants could live in safety after the Edict of Nantes. Aigues-Mortes' historical importance is evidenced in the structures it has kept intact. The Tower of Constance, for example, was built during the 13th century in the same place that Charlemagne himself had built a guarding tower. The tower stands above the city as a beacon of power and safety and is probably one of the most iconic historical landmarks in the entire Languedoc-Roussillon region. The Carbonnière Tower and the Église Notre-Dame des Sablons are also some of the town's most important landmarks. The entire commune, however, is a historical landmark that no history, architecture or culture lover should miss.

Anne-Marie had docked overnight in Aigues-Mortes; in the morning I peeked outside my stateroom window to reveal a basin of water so flat that it appeared glass-like. The houses on the shoreline reflected in the canal. The canal's beauty and its gentle rhythm make for easy starts to our days. Here, there was no rush, no pressure. One of our group gave a toast on the first night of our trip that essentially said, "Let's live in this moment, in the now, together," and we all seem to be embracing that, enjoying the stillness of time and sense of togetherness on our little Anne-Marie.

This notion was further cemented after our tour of the salt ponds and factory the next day. The crew has the option of serving lunch indoors or outdoors, and all of us were pleased when we saw that the outer deck was set for lunch. Zoltan, our friendly cruise director, welcomed us aboard with a cold fruity cocktail and explained that we would enjoy a regional specialty, similar to Beef Bourguignon (but made with bull) served on quinoa. We could not have asked for a more beautiful day as wine was poured and the captain began to maneuver Anne-Marie away from the dock and Aigues-Mortes. Chef Romain's dish was delicious, and as usual, it was followed by a two-cheese presentation by Zoltan and dessert.

After a pleasant sailing that lasted a few hours, we reached our next docking place on the canal just outside of Palavas-Les-Flots. Once a fishing village that earned its living from nearby Montpellier, Palavas-Les-Flots is now a popular beach resort. I pedaled to the town center and its beach, a 15-minute ride at most. While tempted to head up to the Phare Bar, a revolving restaurant constructed in a former water tower, I skipped it and continued my ride along the beach. It was too nice to be inside, even for a view like the Phare Bar offered. After a few hours of pedaling, I headed back to Anne-Marie, where once again, we had a wonderful dinner.

The night was still and peaceful on the canal, with Anne-Marie docked between the sea on one side and the lagoons on the other. Montpelier twinkled in the distance as we took a long after-dinner walk along the canal.

The next day, back in the Camargue not far from Aigues-Mortes, we set out to learn more about the cattle here and to watch cowboys at work. I never knew there were cowboys in the south of France, but indeed there are. They may not wear the broad-brimmed Stetsons that top the heads of North American cowboys and the French cowboys (known as guardians) don't amble along bow-legged from hours in the saddle, but they do have a kinship with their brethren in the American West: They both herd cattle. A hay ride rambled past vineyards and pastures where the cattle grazed before returning to a roundup demonstration and, of course, a wine-tasting.

When we returned to Anne-Marie at noon, the tables were once again set up outside for lunch. We had a beautiful afternoon of cruising ahead to reach Sete (pronounced Set).

Ready Sete? Here we go. Our transit along the canal was heavenly, with Romain's good food and glasses of rosé being poured. It would be hard to imagine a better day. If only real life were like this.

The following morning we partook in a Gourmet Walking Tour I personally organized, which allowed us to explore Sete's colorful markets and a few of the food outlets that serve up regional specialties. An expert guide accompanied us: Owner of Absolutely Southern France, Nancy McGhee has been running her top-rated tour for years. A Canadian living in Sete, Nancy consistently gets rave reviews, as it's much more than the typical "walk-through-the-markets tour." It's an educational visit, where we learned such things as how to eat an oyster properly. Funny, I thought I knew. I did not. Chew a little to release the flavor and wash it down with a glass of PicPoul de Pinet wine. Best oyster I've ever had.

Over the years, Nancy has made many friends at the markets in Sete, which added a personal element to her tour. After a morning of sampling, it was a light lunch onboard before our afternoon excursion to sample fresh oysters along the Étang de Thau, the second largest lake in France. The basin is composed of several lagoons, and connects to the Canal du Rhône, Bordeaux, Sète, and the Mediterranean.

The Étang de Thau is dotted with harbors, villages, and beautiful landscapes. The northern part of the basin is mostly occupied by fishing villages. These villages not only produce delicious fish, but also a large supply of fresh shellfish, especially oysters. Because of the high quality of the water in the basin, the product doesn't have to be processed, and can be eaten as soon as it is harvested. We visited an oyster museum and later sampled fresh oysters, with a local wine—of course.

We returned to Anne-Marie for our last night on board and the "Gala" dinner. The crew bid us farewell. I think they enjoyed the trip almost as much as we did. It was not over yet, however. We still had one more full day to enjoy a cooking class, visit a mansion in Montpelier, and overnight in a hotel before heading home.

Because one of Seabourn's vessels needed to docked in Sete, Anne-Marie moved to Frontignan, only about 10 kilometers away from Sete's city center. After dinner, I walked into the center of this small village, which appeared to be dead asleep until I turned a corner and discovered karaoke being performed outdoors in the town square.

It was a lovely night among French families and couples who were enjoying the performance put on by some talented—and not-so-talented—crooners. One more glass of wine? Why not? I was caught up the joie de vivre and loving every minute of our trip in this beautiful region. As I finished my wine, a young girl performed "La Vie En Rose," the signature song of Edith Piaf that roughly translates to "Life Through Rose-Colored Glasses." That seemed like an appropriate ending to our day in Sete and our time on CroisiEurope's Anne-Marie.

The next morning we said our farewells to the crew of Anne-Marie. I can't praise them enough for all that they did for us. They were present and engaged, and, as often happens, among us there was some discussion about gratuities. How could we show our appreciation of the crew? We agreed on 10 euros per day per person, which we placed in individual envelopes at left at the bar. Zoltan had told us the evening before that the gratuities are shared evenly among the crew.

We headed back into Sete for a Mediterranean Lunch Workshop. We stepped into a small shop and restaurant known as L'Épicerie. In the well-equipped kitchen, we'd learn to make a starter, main course and dessert with master chef Sebastien Terron. After lunch, we headed to Montpelier for a visit to a private mansion rarely open to the public. The owner gave us a tour, and afterward, we enjoyed a glass of champagne to toast the end of our trip.

During each of our ten days traveling in the Languedoc-Roussillon region, I knew there would be moments I would remember long after I returned home, and I was right. What an amazing experience aboard a beautiful barge with a capable chef and crew. Undoubtedly, barging on Anne-Marie is an all-inclusive, intimate experience that will create a lifetime of memories—for prices that won't leave you questioning the value.

Want to Experience the Canals of France with CroisiEurope aboard Anne-Marie?

In 2018, CroisiEurope features several itineraries on the Canals of France. My 2018 trip is sold out but you can barge cruise with me in Alsace in 2019. See Cruise With Me for details | rivercruiseadvisor.com/ralph-grizzles-hosted-river-cruise-trips

7

Chapter
SEVEN

WHEN SHOULD I GO?

Misty morning on the Seine.

WHEN SHOULD I GO?

The main river-cruising season begins in March and continues through the end of December, beginning with Tulip Time" cruises in Belgium and the Netherlands and ending with "Christmas market" cruises in Hungary, Austria and Germany.

The summer months are decidedly high season in Europe and along with the bright and sunny days you'll find longer lines and often crowded attractions. Yes, the shoulder months during the "off-season"—October, November, December, and mid-to-late March—are cooler, and yes, you'll probably need an umbrella, but I find Europe in the fall and spring to be a wonderful, relaxing place. If you are heading to Europe in the spring, you'll enjoy longer days than in fall and late March-early-April is a wonderful time to tiptoe through the tulips in Holland.

The months of September and October can still be plenty warm in Europe, the fall foliage is stunning, and there's a lot of festivity in the air: farmer's markets and wine festivals crop up in September and October. There are also several wine-themed cruises in November, when vintners are unwinding from a busy harvest and ready to kick back enjoy the fruits of their labor with you.

After that, much of Europe switches into festive Holiday mode as the Christmas Markets get set up across much of France, Germany, Austria, Slovakia, Hungary and other countries.

It also stays warmer a bit later in the season on the southern European rivers such as the lower Danube, touching on Croatia, Italy's Po River, and the Douro, which wends its way through Portugal.

When the conversation about the best time to take a river cruise arises, it typically has nothing to do with how many layers of outerwear you need to don or throngs of crowds you need to contend with; it has to do with water levels. That's why I dedicated a chapter of this book to discuss this topic in greater detail. However, I put it at toward the end of the book because while it's an important factor to keep abreast of by signing up for ongoing updates on water levels on my website, rivercruiseadvisor.com, it shouldn't be something that impedes planning your next vacation. Mother nature is unpredictable and if you wait to have clear signs that water levels won't fluctuate, there likely won't be any staterooms available. You'll miss the figurative, and literal, boat.

On The Seine River

8

Chapter
EIGHT

HOW MUCH?

Sunset on the Seine.

HOW MUCH?

A 7-day ocean cruise costs as little $900. A 7-day river cruise? $2,500. So there's no doubt that river cruising, in general, will set you back a little more than sailing the seven seas.

Thankfully, the industry has streamlined pricing with all-inclusive pricing. But what exactly does "all-inclusive" mean? It depends on the river cruise company. In general, the higher the base price of the cruise, the more likely it is to be all-inclusive. This can make comparing cruise packages more complex, and it's one of the reasons why seeking the advice of a travel professional can be helpful.

Generally speaking, river cruises in Europe tend to be more inclusive than they are in the United States. This could be due to the fact that there are more river cruise suppliers operating in Europe, and each company has its own policies about what's included in the cruise fare.

What are some of the things that could be part of an "all-inclusive" package? The list is somewhat arbitrary, as each company can decide for itself. However, there are some industry standards by which you can gauge just how inclusive a package really is—nearly all river cruise companies operating in Europe including wine and beer with lunch and dinner, for example, yet some include complimentary beverages period, at any time of day or night.

What are some of the items that could be bundled in the cruise fare? There are quite a few. And even within each, there are varying degrees of how much. For instance, one cruise might include premium drinks while another only includes house options, charging extra beyond the bar rail. You might not care about having all of the bells and whistles included, and not having them factored into the bottom line is a good way to save you money.

But don't just make your decision by comparing brochure rates. When figuring out the value of a river cruise you'll want to calculate the total cost, derived by factoring in all the inclusions and special offers. For example, are there air incentives? The cost of air can have a huge impact to the bottom-line price of a river cruise.

Let me give you an example: On one particular 2017 sailing, Scenic's per diems for eight-day Bordeaux itineraries were considerably higher than AmaWaterways (by 28 percent), CroisiEurope (by 90 percent) and Viking (by 45 percent). On some sailings, Scenic's per diems in Bordeaux approached $700 per person, compared to Viking at $481 per day. At first, I thought, "Wow, Scenic is over-the-top," even though Uniworld came in higher (nearly $750 per day in staterooms that are a third smaller). A closer look at the numbers, however, revealed a much different picture than what I saw at first glance.

On its website, Viking prices round trip economy air at $1,595 between select North American gateways and Bordeaux. That fare seems consistent with what I was able to find by searching Google Flights for May and June 2018 airfares between Atlanta and Bordeaux. Tacking on air at $1,595 per person adds an effective daily cost of nearly $200 per person for an eight-day Bordeaux cruise.

What happens to per diems when the current air offers are included? As of this writing, Viking was offering air for $695 per person. That's a savings of $900 per person, or about $112 per day for an eight-day cruise. Scenic and Uniworld had similar offers. Scenic was extending free air for June, July and August 2018 sailings. Uniworld had the same offer but with an earlier deadline. That's a savings of $1,595 per person, or about $200 per day. Though these offers won't be available by the time you are reading this, it gives you a good example of what incentives to keep a lookout for so that you can grab them when they do crop up.

You'll also want to calculate other incentives. Keeping with this specific example, those who paid their Scenic sailings in full by October 31, 2017, saved an additional $500 per couple on 8 to 10 day sailings and $1,000 per couple on 11+ day sailings. Uniworld was offering a 10 percent savings for those who book before September 30, 2017. AmaWaterways offered savings of up to $750 per person on select Bordeaux departures in 2018. These too have an impact on the bottom-line per diem.

As you can see, it all becomes a bit of a math problem, that's why I include so many charts like the price comparisons at the back of this book and on rivercruiseadvisor.com.

All to illustrate that it's important to look at what holds most value for you and best aligns with your travel style. The higher rate just might end up being a bargain for you. Here are a few line items to factor into your river cruise formula.

Airport Transfer Fees

Transfer fees are not usually included in the fare. Some companies include transfers if air travel is booked together with the river cruise. Emerald Waterways, Scenic and Uniworld do not charge for transfers no matter how you book your air.

BEVERAGE POLICIES ACROSS MAJOR RIVER CRUISE OPERATORS

		AmaWaterways	Avalon Waterways	CroisiEurope	Crystal River Cruises
	All-Inclusive Beverages			Select Voyages	✓
	Bottled Water	✓	✓	✓	✓
	Tea and Coffee	✓	✓	✓	✓
	Beer, Wine and Soft Drinks with Lunch and Dinner	✓	✓	✓	✓
	Happy Hour	✓		✓	✓
	After Dinner Drinks			✓	✓
	Optional Beverage Package?				
	"Premium" brands at additional cost?			✓	

updated 5/10/2018

Beverages

Another added feature that many lines include in the cruise fare is complimentary beverages. There are the non-alcoholic variety, such as soft drinks, coffee, tea and bottled water. There are also those drinks that contain alcohol—beer, wine and spirits. Some river cruise lines include some or all of these with lunch and dinner. At least one company charges a fee regardless of when they are served, Riviera River Cruises. Some companies allow you to drink whatever you want whenever you want—all are on the house. These include beer, wine and soda. Spirits (like whiskey, vodka or Aquavit) are typically not included, but can be on ships operated by Crystal, CroisiEurope, Scenic, Tauck and Uniworld. AmaWaterways introduced Happy Hour in 2018, offering up free drinks before dinner.

Your location on the ship also plays a crucial role in the complimentary beverages: A glass of wine at dinner is complimentary, but a glass of wine in the lounge after dinner could cost you.

So who offers what? Here's our rundown of current beverage policies on a few of the major river cruise lines.

EMERALD WATERWAYS	RIVIERA TRAVEL	SCENIC LUXURY CRUISES & TOURS	TAUCK	UNIWORLD	VIKING RIVER CRUISES
		✓	✓	✓	
✓		✓	✓	✓	✓
✓	✓	✓	✓	✓	✓
✓		✓	✓	✓	✓
		✓	✓	✓	
		✓	✓	✓	
✓	✓				✓
					✓

While this chart will give you a sense of who offers what, it's still important to clarify details for your particular sailing. That's because there isn't just a standard, fleetwide policy that governs what is and isn't provided on a complimentary basis. Much of it depends on where you are cruising, either in Europe or elsewhere.

Part of the issue relates to who owns the ships. Most river cruise lines, but not all, own their European ships outright. They're generally designed and built specifically for a particular river cruise line. But outside of the core European waterways like the Danube, Rhine, and the Main, things get complicated.

In areas like Russia and Portugal, ships are generally chartered by river cruise lines. Sometimes these ships are for one company's exclusive use, while other times different cruise lines may "share" the ship on a rotating basis. The exceptions are Viking River Cruises, which owns its fleet of Russian river cruise ships outright, and CroisiEurope, Emerald and Scenic, which own their Douro ships.

Because cruise lines charter—or lease—vessels, they have less input into the hotel operations. There are certain standards the river cruise line expects its partners to maintain, and usually these are met. Some lines, like Uniworld, take great strides to mention in brochures and marketing that while these ships are some of the best operating in particular regions, some amenities and features found on the European vessels may not be available.

So why do river cruise lines not own ships outright in other areas of the world? In some cases—like Russia—it comes down to bureaucratic restrictions and technicalities that prevent the construction of new vessels. In other areas of the world, it simply wouldn't be cost-effective to operate company-owned vessels. Instead, river cruise lines charter them from existing companies and tour operators. Tauck, for example, charters its ships from Scylla, which also charters ships to Riviera River Cruises.

Fitness Center and Equipment

For those who keep fitness in mind, is there a fitness center or a pool onboard? Are bicycles available during your time onshore? This varies by ship more than by supplier.

Port Charges

Some river cruise lines roll the port charges and other taxes into the package, so you won't see an additional charge for these items. Again, keep in mind that this can change from year-to-year.

Prepaid Gratuities

Gratuities are not necessarily mandatory, but they are often expected. They are paid to both cruise ship staff and to tour guides and motorcoach drivers ashore. Some companies, such as Scenic and Tauck, include gratuities in their cruise fares. If gratuities aren't included, a good rule of thumb to follow is approximately 10 Euros per person per day, or 10 percent of your overall cruise fare. Gratuities can be added to your onboard account and paid in cash or by credit card if they are not already included in your fare.

Private Butler Service

Which river cruise lines offer private butler service as part of the package? Are there different levels of private butler service if it is provided at no additional cost?

Shore Excursions

Shore excursions are usually included in river cruise packages, but not always. Some companies also offer premium packages that can be purchased in addition to or in lieu of shore excursions that might be part of the package.

Wi-Fi Internet

Is Wi-Fi available free of charge on the ship? Is it available in your stateroom? This seems to vary more by region than supplier. Note that, in almost all cases, connectivity will be free but slower than broadband, except when docked in cities where the ships have direct linkups to fast internet.

Consider the Category

Now that you have a sense of what kind of amenities comprise the rate, let's look at the general categories the major players fall into. To learn more about the individual cruise lines, see the company overviews in Chapter 9.

FULLY ALL-INCLUSIVE - Everything included in one upfront price, from pre-paid gratuities and drinks to shore excursions—even laundry on many cruise lines. Uniworld, however, does not include port charges.

- **Crystal River Cruises**
- **Scenic**
- **Tauck**
- **Uniworld Boutique River Cruise Collection**

NEARLY ALL-INCLUSIVE - Itineraries with these cruise companies generally price out a little less than the All-Inclusives above, but don't include prepaid gratuities or port charges.

- **AmaWaterways**
- **Avalon Waterways**
- **Emerald Waterways**
- **Viking River Cruises**

LOW-COST LEADERS - While one doesn't typically consider river travel to be a value proposition, some companies price out lower than their competitors.

- **CroisiEurope**
- **Riviera River Cruises**

TAKE IT DAY-BY-DAY

Though there are no hard and fast guidelines, I recommend thinking about how much you would be comfortable spending on a daily basis. Knowing what you're comfortable spending can help you match the ship to your budget.

Below, I provide a range of per diems, from less than $400 per day to more than $400 per day. Pricing is a moving target, however, and there are many special offers that are not reflected in my pricing guidelines. It is possible, for example, to find cruises that cost less than $200 per person per day.

For the most current pricing, click here to Get My Recommendations.

SKY'S THE LIMIT, MORE THAN $400 PER PERSON PER DAY.

If the sky's the limit, you'll find a good fit with Crystal, Scenic, Tauck or Uniworld. All are truly all-inclusive (except for Uniworld, which does not include port charges) whereas on the other river cruises you'll typically need to pay gratuities, and you'll need to dole out extra for drinks outside of lunch and dinner and some excursions. For truly all-inclusive cruises, expect to spend more than $400 per day per person.

As an example, Scenic's 12-day Bordeaux sailings from May through September, 2017, started at $6,230 per person, double, and include free or reduced airfare. That's $519 per person per day. But keep in mind that air is included or reduced. French Country Waterways is the most luxe choice when it comes to barge cruising, averaging around $1,000 per person, which doesn't include gratuities or air, but proves to be a priceless experience for gourmands. European Waterways is close behind averaging around $800 per person, per night for 6-night packages depending upon the vessel—with suite category rooms reaching upwards of $1,300 per person per night.

DOWN TO EARTH, UP TO $400 PER PERSON PER DAY.

If your budget is up to $400 per day per person, AmaWaterways, Avalon Waterways, Emerald Waterways, Riviera River Cruises and Viking River Cruises will usually fall within your budget. Example, in 2017, AmaWaterways' 8-day Enticing Douro river cruises, one of its higher priced river cruises, started at $3,099. That's $387 per person, per day.

BUDGET FRIENDLY, $300 PER PERSON PER DAY OR LESS.

CroisiEurope is a good example of a quality cruise line that falls into a cost-conscious category. The quality surpasses what one would expect for less than $300 per person per day. While the line is better known among the European crowd, it's far from uncomfortable for North Americans; the 5-day itinerary NYE Provence starts at $1,530.

LANDING GREAT AIRFARE

We already looked at how included airfares can impact the overall cruise value, but what about when airfare needs to be purchased separately? For many of us, airfare can be a struggle, both in terms of cost and availability. But when it comes to planning your river cruise vacation, there are some simple research precautions you can take early on in the process to ensure you don't end up on the wrong side of the airfare game. The first step starts with doing some research on your hometown airport.

For the sake of convenience, we'd all like to live near a major hub like New York or Toronto, but the fact is that river cruisers come from different parts of the world—and chances are your hometown airport doesn't have direct service to places like Budapest or Prague. But it's equally likely that you have more options than you realize. Wikipedia can be a great resource for researching your airport, as most have a complete listing of airlines that serve each airport along with their respective destinations.

Once you know where you can go from your own airport, you can better plan how you want to get to Europe, and that brings us to a few tips and tricks for making air travel easier.

EMBRACE CONNECTIONS. Unless you're lucky, chances are you'll have at least one connection on your way to Europe or Asia, but there's good news here too: Connecting flights can be cheaper than direct flights.

CONSIDER ANOTHER DEPARTURE AIRPORT. If you live near more than one airport, make sure you look at all available flights from each airport. Chances are one will be much cheaper than the other, or offer better times and aircraft. A good example of this is the New York area, which plays host to three major international airports: John F. Kennedy (JFK), LaGuardia (LGA) and Newark (EWR).

USE POINTS. If you belong to frequent flier programs from airlines in the Star Alliance, Oneworld and Skyteam networks, you can use your frequent flyer points to book tickets to Europe, provided you have enough.

PRICE ISN'T ALWAYS EVERYTHING. It's all about what matters to you that determines whether airfare is truly "great" or not. Do you value price over schedule, or schedule over price? Usually, there's a trade-off. After all, you may get a great deal by doing a three-connection flight littered with red-eyes, but unless you really love to fly it may be worth spending the extra money to get yourself there comfortably.

Being in control of your airfare instead of surprised by it can make all the difference in planning a successful river cruise vacation.

FLY BUSINESS CLASS FOR LESS. For tips on how to fly business class for about $1,000 each way between North America and Europe, see First Class Flying Tips on MY sister site, avidcruiser.com.

NEIGHBORLY ADVICE

As you can imagine, where you're going in Europe can greatly impact the price tag too. One wouldn't expect to pay the same at a three-star Michelin restaurant in Paris as they do a for a croque monsieur from an outdoor vendor near the Metro.

But what if you were trying to pick between two gourmet restaurants in the same arrondissement? That's where it can get tricky. The same goes for quite similar itineraries on European waterways. For this reason, I offer region-specific cost comparisons on my site and also at the back of this book. If you are largely determining your cruise by where you want to travel, this is just the tool to help you know how the different cruise lines stack up when it comes to price.

SEEK OUT ADDITIONAL WAYS TO SAVE

Incentives range from included air to two-for-ones and free stateroom upgrades to dollar-amount discounts to spur bookings. But unlike airfares, which might suddenly drop prices to fill planes, booking your river cruise early tends to garner the greatest deals. Inventory, once abundant, is disappearing, and soon there will not be a lot left to choose from, particularly if you're set on a sail date and stateroom category.

The fact that there's such a demand ends up keeping prices fairly predictable. There are deals every now and again, but low pricing will hardly be the norm because the pace for bookings has been on an upward trend from the relatively soft 2016. In talking with river cruise companies, the demand for 2018 sailings is roughly on-par with the successful 2017 river cruise seasons. There is still a chance to get exceptional value on some sailings. Current incentives range from included air to two-for-ones to other special offers that are spurring bookings. So be sure to ask your travel agent or river cruise specialists about what incentives are floating around.

OFF-PEAK TRAVEL

Traveling to Europe during off-peak months can seem like you're saving a bundle—because you are. Firstly, your airfare will typically cost less than during the high-season summer months. That goes for hotels as well, which regularly offer discounts to lure travelers during the off-season. Museums are less crowded, bike paths are less busy, and the experience on the whole is generally more pleasant. And you're saving money at the same time; who doesn't love that?

Finding that perfect stateroom or suite on your cruise is a lot easier in the off-season too, which doesn't always book up as quickly as the prime-time summer months. While this is less of an issue if you're just after the run-of-the-mill French balcony stateroom, it can be a huge issue if you're thinking of booking one of two suites on a particular ship. Even the basic (but highly economical) riverview staterooms can sell out quickly during the summer months because most ships have so few of them. In the off-season, it's easy to take advantage of these value-priced accommodations.

SINGLE SUPPLEMENTS

If you want to get onboard for a reduced cost, a Single Supplement sale or waiver may be just the answer. Possibly the best invention for the solo traveler, Single Occupancy Staterooms are just that: smaller rooms designed for one. Sure, you're trading off some space for a lower fare, but isn't that the point? And let's be frank: While small, these rooms offer everything their larger counterparts do in terms of amenities.

Many newer river cruise ships feature at least a handful of solo occupancy staterooms, although their sizes and availability will vary from line to line. It's best to take a look at some brochures and deck plans to see which lines offer what. If your river cruise line of choice doesn't offer Single Occupancy Staterooms, look to see if the company is offering something called a Single Supplement Sale, or waiver.

Essentially, this makes certain stateroom categories (typically lower-level accommodations) more palatable to the solo cruiser. The cruise companies either reduce—or altogether eliminate—the onerous Solo Supplement fare.

Now, that's not to say that if you're traveling solo that you have to book one of these staterooms; you can go ahead and book the biggest suite on the ship, if you'd like. Just be forewarned that nearly all upper-level accommodations will have a single supplement fare pegged at 200 percent, so you're essentially doling out the equivalent of two full-paying guests. An exception is Riviera River Cruises, which makes available five double cabins (three on the Douro) for single travelers with no single supplement.

It is possible to avoid the single supplement altogether. However, the waivers often apply only to select itineraries for select dates, so you may need to be flexible.

Keep in mind that it's best to book early if you're a single traveler, especially if you are looking for a single stateroom since there's usually a limited supply.

GROUP TRAVEL DEALS

Cruises prove to be a convenient solution for group travel and this is especially true of river cruising. While ocean-going vessels can design activities tailored to your group of friends, family, or coworkers, river cruises are already more relaxed and intimate affairs. There's less orchestrating involved to be able to rendezvous with one another on the pool deck or set out on an impromptu excursion.

That being said, since a group can end up comprising a large percentage of a river cruise passenger list, planning well in advance is necessary. What you might not know is that traveling with fellow buddies in tow can also save you a lot of money.

This savings might come to you by way of a free stateroom with a certain number of staterooms booked, a dedicated private guide and vehicle for excursions, or a discounted fare for everyone within your group. Often the magic number is 10 passengers before you can expect to receive free staterooms and discounts of that nature, but this often varies by cruise line and the length of your journey. Scenic extends a free cruise to the eleventh passenger, meaning you need to book at least five staterooms, for sailings 12 days or less, but for itineraries longer than 13 days you have to find five more friends to get a free stateroom. Avalon Waterways offers group cruise pricing and some extra perks after only eight passengers and CroisiEurope requires a group of 20; 80 will actually land you a privately chartered vessel, or 22, your own barge.

AmaWaterways extends group benefits after booking five cabins (a maximum of 20 cabins) as well as a really unique opportunity to host your own theme cruises—be it wine, botanical tours, music, you name it. For this, ideally you should be able to recruit a group of 30. That's the optimal size for private tastings in the Chef's Table, a specialty restaurant situated aft on deck three on AmaWaterways' vessels. With a minimum of 35 full-paying guests, the group also gets an exclusive bus and English-speaking guide for shore excursions during cruises on the Danube, Rhine, Moselle, Rhône and Seine rivers. If you have a favorite winemaker or lecturer who you would love to have accompany your travels, you can also work with a travel agent to help you put together your very own themed sailing.

Almost all of the cruise lines have a dedicated group travel account specialist, who will be your go-to person for organizing any private dinners, excursions, and securing deposits from individuals within your group. This makes it much easier for the person spearheading travel plans. Some cruise lines, such as Tauck, will also organize the air travel, and pre- and post-cruise hotel stays.

Luckily, there are typically no penalties for cancellations prior to the group's official booking, giving you a little time to get all of the moving parts into place. So if group travel is something you are contemplating, start the process first and figure out the details later. (Verifying first, of course, that this is the policy with the cruise line that you are considering.)

Sometimes you don't even have to travel with a group to receive group travel discounts and perks. Say what? It's true. Travel agents and consortia such as Signature Travel Network, Virtuoso and travel agencies affiliated with those and other networks award their clients with exclusive benefits that you wouldn't be able to receive booking directly with the cruise line. This can range from cruise discounts and complimentary stateroom upgrades to onboard credits, free excursions or welcome amenities. And, even if the cruise line has a group travel representative, it can be much easier to use an experienced travel agent to ensure that you've covered all of the bases as well as wrangle all of the people within your group. They can streamline everything, from booking contracted international airfares (when available) and coordinating airport arrival times and transfers to making special menu requests. Plus, travel agents well-versed in group cruise travel can often garner VIP perks for you that you didn't even know were available.

DEPOSIT REQUIREMENTS FOR MAJOR RIVER CRUISE LINES

LINE	DEPOSIT	DEPOSIT EXCEPTIONS	FINAL PAYMENT DUE	REFUNDABLE DEPOSIT?
AmaWaterways	$400 per person	$2,400 per person (Africa) $350 per person (Economy Airfare) $600 per person (Business Airfare)	90 Days Prior to Departure	✓ Half of the cruise deposit is refundable prior to 121 days
Avalon Waterways	$250 per person	Delfin III: $500 per person Obergammau: $600 per person	90 Days Prior to Departure	✗
CroisiEurope	25% of total fare	None	90 Days Prior to Departure	✓ $100 per person penalty if canceled prior to 90 days.
Crystal River Cruises	20% of total fare	None	90 Days Prior to Departure	✓ If canceled 91 + days before your cruise, you receive a full refund
Emerald Waterways	Varies depending on itinerary	$1500 per person required prior to ticketed airfare if purchased through Emerald Waterways.	90 Days Prior to Departure	✗
Riviera Travel	Varies depending on itinerary	None	13 weeks prior to the departure	✓ If canceled 91+ days before your cruise, you lose your deposit (2019 policy)
Scenic	$500 per person	$1500 per person required prior to ticketed airfare if purchased through Scenic. Bookings less than 21 days prior to departure incur a $50 "Late Booking" fee.	90 Days Prior to Departure	✗
Tauck	Varies depending on itinerary; must be paid within 10 days of booking.	None	90 Days Prior to Departure	✓ Only within 10 days of initial reservation.
Uniworld	10% of the total cruise fare due within 72 hours of booking.	$450 per person deposit required for all Uniworld-booked airfare.	120 Days Prior to Departure	✓ $200 per person penalty for canceling prior to 120 days out.
Viking River Cruises	$500 per person	$1500 per person nonrefundable for air ticketed through Viking	Six Months Prior to Departure	✓ $100 penalty per person applies if canceled prior to 121 days out.

updated 6/30/2018

Even better than the savings that you'll receive, I find all-inclusive cruising with groups helps to manage expectations in terms of out-of-pocket expenditures, mitigating potential misunderstandings, and family squabbles, when it comes to paying the tab. Having the cost of excursions, meals, and accommodations outlined upfront helps everyone know out-of-the gate if their participation is feasible; instead of discovering halfway through the journey that dining and excursions proved more expensive than anticipated, drying up vacation funds.

DEPOSIT PROTECTION PLANS

Deposit protection plans allow guests who need to cancel or change a cruise for any reason to reallocate their non-refundable deposit for use toward an alternative future sailing. The plan must be purchased at the time the deposit is due, and with most programs, guests must rebook within 24 months of cancellation. Deposit protection plans are non-transferable and cover cruise and tour deposits only, not air deposits.

This type of protection hasn't been the norm, but with travelers expressing growing concern over events in Europe, we are witnessing more cruise lines making efforts to mitigate concerns that might prevent them from booking their dream river cruise.

Scenic and Emerald Waterways, both part of the Scenic family of brands, are offering cruise travelers some peace of mind with their newly launched Deposit Protection Plan. Working in conjunction with the brands' River Cruise Travel Guarantee, guests know that they are well protected against many of the elements that can make vacation planning difficult. Deposit protection can be purchased for $125 per person for river cruises.

Both brands also offer the River Cruise Travel Guarantee, which automatically covers every guest on the commencement of their cruise for any delays or cancellations due to weather, natural disasters, mechanical breakdowns or labor strikes. This guarantee is offered at no cost to guests and, unlike other cruise lines that offer credit toward future trips, Scenic and Emerald offer approved claimants direct monetary refunds, up to $750 per day with a maximum of seven days or $5,250 per guest.

AmaWaterways offers a trip protection of sorts as well when it comes to deviations from planned itineraries. For each day that does not go according to what's outlined in the company's brochures or on its website, guests will receive a 100 percent future cruise credit for that day. This is almost as good as deposit protection when one considers that most people don't take just one river cruise.

Most cruise lines extend optional travel protection through an outside insurance provider to help guard your investment from the unexpected for an additional fee. Consider purchasing travel insurance for Trip Cancellation, Trip Interruption, Emergency Medical Expenses, and Emergency Evacuation/Repatriation, Trip Delay and Baggage Delay. It's moderately priced and goes a long way in protecting your vacation investment (because really, that's what it is) if anything unexpected should arise.

Also check with your credit card company about travel benefits. Some credit cards, particularly those with high annual fees, offer trip delay and trip protection insurance. I heard from one reader who, because of a sudden illness, needed to cancel an ocean cruise for which he'd paid $35,000. The cruise company said tough luck and would do nothing. His credit card company, however, reimbursed him every penny. Priceless, as they say.

9

Chapter
NINE

WHICH CRUISE LINE?

Misty morning on the Danube

WHICH CRUISE LINE?

Once you've chosen your river and decided on your budget, you'll have likely narrowed your choices to a limited few. Now it's time to delve into the ethos of each cruise line to see which one best resonates with your style. Below I provide an overview of my preferred river cruise lines, highlighting their history, onboard ambiance, and distinctive flair.

AMAWATERWAYS - ACTIVE INNOVATORS
RIVERS: DANUBE, RHINE, SEINE, MOSELLE, MAIN, RHÔNE, SAÔNE, DORDOGNE, GARONNE, DOURO, DUTCH AND BELGIAN WATERWAYS (CHOBE AND MEKONG)

Family-owned and operated, AmaWaterways has been a passion project for its founders since its start in 2002. President Rudi Schreiner designed his first ship back in 1975 while sailing the Amazon for seven months. Since the completion of the Rhine-Main-Danube Canal in 1992, Rudi has been a driving force for river cruise travel—and for these efforts has been recognized as the "Most Innovative Cruise Executive" and has been presented the prestigious "Lifetime Achievement Award" by Cruise Lines International Association (CLIA). Making up the rest of the executive team that now runs AmaWaterways is Kristin Karst, Executive Vice President, Co-Founder and Co-Owner, and Gary Murphy, Co-Owner and Vice President of Sales.

AmaWaterways features a fleet of 23 modern river cruise ships, all but two operating in Europe. The only exception being AmaDara, which visits Cambodia and Vietnam and Zambezi Queen, a 28-passenger ship that offers five different itineraries exploring Africa's wildlife and wine. In 2019, AmaWaterways will unveil its biggest ship to date, the 196-passenger AmaMagna. She'll be almost twice as wide as the line's current ships, with bigger staterooms, more dining options and even a water sports platform. Ensuring that an active pursuit is part is in the matrix is true to form for AmaWaterways, which was one of the first river cruise lines to offer complimentary bikes and hiking excursions ashore. My affinity for biking is one of the reasons that I like AmaWaterways so much, but it's not the only reason.

Many of AmaWaterways' innovative staterooms feature unique twin balconies that offer both a French balcony and an actual step-out balcony. Staterooms and suites are spacious and range from 160 square feet to 350 square feet, with most including these signature twin balconies. There are also staterooms with connecting doors to accommodate more than two guests to better cater to families and groups who wish to travel together. Every stateroom features an Entertainment-on-Demand center, with complimentary Internet via an Apple iMac and other onboard amenities such as a sun deck, walking track, a well-equipped fitness room, a spa and hair salon, and a heated pool with swim-up bar.

All AmaWaterways' ships in Europe are also members of the prestigious La Confrérie de la Chaîne des Rôtisseurs, an international gastronomic society dedicated to fine cuisine. A variety of dining venues, including The Chef's Table specialty restaurant, can be enjoyed at no additional charge. If health is front-of-mind, AmaWaterways has some of the best vegetarian menus afloat.

AmaWaterways is a crowd-pleaser. The company's core philosophy is to under-promise and over-deliver, and it does that cruise after cruise. Check out my video, Riverside Chat: AmaWaterways Q&A and Magnificent Europe | https://www.rivercruiseadvisor.com/2017/01/video-amawaterways-qa

AVALON WATERWAYS — VACATION-VARIETY LOVERS
RIVERS: DANUBE, RHINE, MAIN, SEINE, RHÔNE, SAÔNE, MOSELLE (MEKONG, IRRAWADDY, AMAZON, YANGTZE)

Avalon Waterways traces its roots back to 1928, when Antonio Mantegazza used a rowboat to transport goods across Switzerland's Lake Lugano. His business evolved into motorcoach tourism and expanded into an international travel brand: Group Voyagers, Inc.—parent company of Avalon Waterways. This consortium of well-known brands such as Globus, Cosmos, and Brennan Vacations has been a leader in escorted tours of Europe for almost a century, but it wasn't until 2004 that the company launched Avalon Waterways' fleet of royal-blue river cruisers.

The Avalon Waterways' fleet expanded quite rapidly between 2008 and 2012. Avalon Scenery commenced the procession of new vessels in 2008, followed quickly on the heels by Avalon Creativity and Avalon Affinity in 2009. The next year champagne crashed over the bow of Avalon Luminary, with Avalon Felicity and Avalon Panorama continuing this celebration of new berths in 2011. The year 2012 witnessed three new additions to the fleet: Avalon Angkor, Avalon Visionary, and Avalon Vista.

This span of four years reads like a swinging door of river cruisers, introducing newly designed "Suite Ships" while others like Avalon Artistry, Avalon Imagery, Avalon Poetry, Avalon Tapestry, and Avalon Tranquility sailed off into retirement. Today, the Avalon fleet encompasses two dozen vessels. In Europe, Avalon Waterways operates on the Rhine, Main, Danube, Moselle, as well as French wine country cruises on the Saône and Rhône rivers. Avalon also plies the tributaries of Asia's Myanmar, Cambodia and China as well as Egypt's Nile.

Avalon's "Suite Ships" accommodations measure between 200 square feet and 300 square feet apiece and are equipped with Avalon's signature Open Air Balcony—a French-style balcony that opens wall-to-wall, transforming staterooms into a giant veranda. These Open Air Balconies are found in nearly 80 percent of the total accommodations aboard Avalon's Suite Ships in Europe.

Hotel-worthy beds, satellite TV and bathrooms with full-sized showers comprise the interiors and these ships also have complimentary WiFi Internet access, an expansive sun deck and a small fitness center. However, not all of Avalon's ships in Europe are Suite Ships. Aboard the four non-Suite Ships—Avalon Creativity, Avalon Felicity, Avalon Luminary and Avalon Affinity—all staterooms, except for the Royal Suites, measure 172 square feet.

Each ship within the Avalon Waterways' fleet features an intimate dining room, a relaxing Main Lounge with panoramic views, a reception and Internet workstation area, and a small fitness center and hair salon. An expansive sun deck allows guests to stroll and enjoy the fresh air, or relax in a deck chair and take in the ever-changing scenery. And while it's nearly impossible for river cruisers to feature anything more than two dining rooms, Avalon is creative enough to offer guests seven dining options throughout the day.

Continental breakfast is offered through room service—something you don't see a lot on river cruisers. Then there is the early-riser's breakfast, the full main dining room breakfast, and finally a late-riser's breakfast. There are usually two options for lunch (including an outdoor grill), and two for dinner, including the Panorama Bistro, which serves tapas-style, Mediterranean dishes for up to 24 people in a section of the main lounge. Onboard, complimentary regional wines, beer and soft drinks are offered during lunch and dinner.

One differentiating factor for this cruise line is that it boasts the backing of the huge Globus family, which offers some practical value: those who are members of Globus' Journeys Club, for example, receive discounts and other perks for traveling within the family of brands. The brand's large footprint in Europe also helps with operational infrastructure, such as guides and transport, theoretically enhancing the guest experience.

Choices abound for Avalon's passengers even before they embark. Travelers can customize itineraries ranging from 3 nights to 22 nights. Moreover, besides the default included shore excursions, Avalon offers custom options—for a fee. So if you like to have the flexibility to choose whether to head out on a morning excursion and relax in the afternoon or set off on another excursion, Avalon could be just the cruise line for you.

My own "top three" for Avalon Waterways: 1) The large windows that open in the stateroom to create a huge open-air balcony. I called it Europe in HD; 2) Avalon Fresh, a dining program that includes really good Vegetarian and Vegan options, as well as healthy breakfast items; 3) Active Discovery, a program that immerses you into the destinations through active tours, such as walking and bicycling, and cultural immersion. See From Amsterdam To Paris On An Avalon Waterways | https://www.rivercruiseadvisor.com/2017/04/active-discovery-rhine

CRYSTAL RIVER CRUISES - SOPHISTICATED TASTES
RIVERS: DANUBE, RHINE, MAIN AND MOSELLE

Crystal is a name that's been synonymous with cruising for 25 years, but it wasn't until 2016 that the company entered the river cruise market with Crystal Mozart, an older ship refitted to suit the line's exquisite plans. Crystal Mozart made a big splash, boasting a width twice the size of the other river cruise ships and allowing for grander public areas like the Life Spa, fitness center, an indoor pool, plus king-sized beds in every stateroom.

In 2017, Crystal continued to boldly push permissible limits with its brand-new, all-balcony, all-suite, "Rhine Class" river yachts: Crystal Bach and Crystal Mahler. These are more standard river cruisers in size, spanning a length of 443 feet; impressive, but not unmatched by other river cruise companies (it's the maximum size allowed on the Danube, Rhine, Main and Moselle rivers). The major difference between these two ships and Crystal Mozart is the passenger load, with 106 guests and 68 crew. That's a great percentage when it comes to river cruises and results in a better guest-to-staff ratio.

In 2018, Crystal Debussy and Crystal Ravel debuted as sisters to Crystal Bach and Crystal Mahler, replete with many of the same amenities that make Crystal one of the most markedly luxurious cruise lines in the floating market. Among these unique amenities exclusive to Crystal are a pop-up bar on the upper Vista Deck with a vanishing screen for movie nights al fresco.

Crystal River Cruises also unveiled fresh culinary concepts and offerings aboard Crystal Bach. Sailing routes along the Rhine, Danube and Main Rivers, the all-balcony, all-suite vessel offers cuisine inspired by the region, crafted by a team of expert European chefs—from foods favored by local people and nobility for centuries to options showcasing a modern twist. From the elegant Waterside Restaurant—the main dining room aboard Crystal River vessels— to the relaxed Bistro Café and exclusive Vintage Room, guests will find farm-to-table, Michelin-inspired cuisine that complements the cultural discovery. Dine on fresh fish and seafood from Holland, seasonal fruits and vegetables from Germany and the Netherlands, meat and poultry from farmers in Bavaria and the Austrian Alps, along with wine, beer and cheese specific to the region.

Crystal River Cruises aims to redefine river cruising. It is the ideal choice for those who want to explore the rivers of Europe while still getting a splash of ocean-liner-like amenities. Check out Crystal River Cruises: In A Class Apart | https://www.rivercruiseadvisor.com/2017/04/crystal-mozart-class-of-its-own

CROISIEUROPE - FRENCH FLAIR
RIVERS: RHINE, ELBE, SEINE, RHÔNE, SAÔNE, GARONNE, DORDOGNE, LOIRE, DOURO, GUADALQUIVIR, GUADIANA, PO, CANALS OF FRANCE, VOLGA, AND SAVA

Founded by Gérard Schmitter in 1976, CroisiEurope River Cruises is still a family-run business, responsible for the construction, ownership and day-to-day operations of river cruise vessels. The Strasbourg-based cruise line has a lot of ships, more than 50—with 40-plus cruising the rivers of Europe. The all-inclusive cruises impress me with their French flair, inventive itineraries, and innovative ships; including paddlewheelers that can navigate the notoriously shallow Elbe and Loire rivers. The line even offers pseudo river-ocean voyages through the Mediterranean that are wholly unique within the industry. CroisiEurope serves up one of the best values in river cruising - but the line is not for everyone.

Although they have been touring the rivers of Europe for more 40 years, it wasn't until 2013 that CroisiEurope began actively marketing to North American travelers for the first time, so guests are still predominantly European. You may be one of the few North Americans aboard, but I didn't find that to be problematic, as the staff (and often the guests) is multilingual and accommodating.

CroisiEurope is the only river cruise company to feature vessels on every single river in Europe. These include the ones you've likely heard of before, such as Rhine, Main, and the famous Danube. But have you sailed down Spain's Guadiana or Guadalquivir? CroisiEurope does. CroisiEurope is also one of the few cruise lines to offer voyages along Italy's Po River, sailing from the breathtaking city of Venice. You can also elect to take a more intimate voyage through the gorgeous Canals of France aboard a traditional—but modern—barge. CroisiEurope was, and remains, the first river cruise company to take travelers along the Sava River during a 10-day journey to Hungary, Serbia, Bosnia, and Croatia. In addition to continental Europe, CroisiEurope also features voyages along Southeast Asia's Mekong River, and cruises that explore the coasts of Croatia and Montenegro during the summer months, along with Cyprus and Israel coastal cruises during the winter. At the end of 2017, the line welcomed the brand-new 16-passenger, eight-suite African Dream, which offers sailings on the Chobe and Zambezi rivers.

CroisiEurope continues to rebuild existing vessels, too. The 24-guest barge Jeanine was reintroduced to the Canals of France in 2013, completely rebuilt from the ground up, followed on the heels by three new barges in 2014 and another for Portugal's Douro River in 2015.

ms Douce France got a facelift and, in the summer of 2017, began cruising the Rhine on 4- to 7-day journeys in the Moselle, Main and Rhine valleys as ms Douce France II. The 106-passenger vessel has 55 double-occupancy cabins, including four single-occupancy cabins, two suites, and one cabin designed especially for passengers with reduced mobility. All cabins feature air-conditioning, double beds that can be separated into twin beds, private bathrooms, flat-screen televisions, radios, hair dryers and safes. All upper deck cabins feature French balconies. The public spaces include a bar and lounge with dance floor, restaurant, sun deck with chaise lounges and a boutique.

Exceptional French cuisine, excellent service and creative itineraries are the perfect formula for building a steady stream of satisfied customers. The line's newest vessels feature stem-to-stern complimentary Wi-Fi internet access and Samsung Galaxy tablets for guests to use. The rest of the fleet offers complimentary wi-fi access in the ship's Reception and Lounge areas.

Inclusions on CroisiEurope include complimentary beer and wine served with lunch and dinner, and an open bar throughout each voyage. The only items that aren't inclusive are Champagne, wines on the wine list, and fine brandies. The line also includes all onboard entertainment and port taxes.

The main complaint travelers seem to have about CroisiEurope are the relatively small cabins, but consider this: In Bordeaux, Uniworld features cabins that are the same size as CroisiEurope's standard cabins (140 square feet). However, based on double-occupancy, CroisiEurope's eight-day Bordeaux sailing comes in at nearly $4,000 less than Uniworld's eight-day Bordeaux sailing in the same-sized staterooms. One might have to forego on a few luxury extras, like an early-riser's breakfast and late-night snacks, and there are no bicycles on board, but otherwise you'll find it to be a great option for group, family, or just plain affordable river cruising.

See Is CroisiEurope Right For You? | https://www.rivercruiseadvisor.com/2016/11/all-there-is-to-know-about-croisieurope/

EMERALD WATERWAYS - WATERWAY TRAILBLAZERS
RIVERS: DANUBE, RHINE, MAIN, RHÔNE, DOURO (MEKONG)

Emerald Waterways was founded by an Australian-based company, Scenic Tours, which got into business in 1986 as a coach tour company serving Australia. By the early 1990s the company had moved well beyond the borders of Australia and had become a worldwide tour company.

In 2005, Scenic began to charter river cruise ships for its guests traveling in Europe. Then in 2008, the company launched an upscale river cruise line with its own ships, branded as "Scenic Space Ships."

While Scenic's luxury brand catered to travelers who were seeking upscale river cruise experiences, the company also saw a need to serve the less-affluent (and possibly younger) travelers. Thus, the concept of Emerald Waterways was born.

Like the Scenic brand, Emerald Waterways has its own custom-crafted vessels referred to as "Star Ships" that began sailing on a few of the waterways in Europe on April 15, 2014 with two brand-new, 182-passenger ships, Emerald Star and Emerald Sky. Both ships measure 443 feet and hold 182 guests in 92 staterooms—72 of which are suites.

The company followed their modest debut with two more ships in 2015, Emerald Sun and Emerald Dawn, which had the same footprint as the first two. The next two ships built were more diminutive, with 360-foot Emerald Liberté built in 2017 to provide 8-day cruises for 138 guests on France's Rhône & Saône.

The same year Emerald Waterways built their most intimate ship to date, with a capacity of just 112 guests aboard the 292 feet Emerald Radiance, divided into 55 suites. Paired with the crew-to-guest ratio of 1:3, this low capacity provides a heightened level of service. Purpose built for Portugal's warm climate, Emerald Radiance is also sports a bigger sun deck. See my story Douro River Cruises: Six Reasons To Choose Emerald Waterways | https://www.rivercruiseadvisor. com/2017/11/emerald-waterways-douro

Another recent addition to the line is Emerald Mekong, which as the name suggests, explores the waters of Southeast Asia's Vietnam and Cambodia. It's a chartered vessel and though built in 2014, it's one of the newer vessels operating in the region.

Emerald Waterways' eight ships have been referred to as a four-star product operating on five-star hardware, and I think that's apropos. Though there are also some pretty unique features, like a heated pool complete with retractable roof that converts into a cinema. Prepaid gratuities, airport transfer fees and port charges are included in the fare, which can save you a bundle compared to other cruise lines that are less inclusive.

There are a lot of itineraries from which to choose navigating the rivers Rhine, Main, Danube and Moselle on the sister ships, Emerald Star, Sky, Sun, Dawn and Destiny. I particularly enjoyed Emerald Waterways itinerary in Eastern Europe from Budapest to Bucharest. You'll visit less developed ports in places like Serbia, Bulgaria and Romania that are largely untapped by today's river cruisers. I really liked what I saw when I cruised on Emerald Sky in April of 2016. The vessel was modern and sleek, with staterooms and public rooms that were bright, contemporary and inviting. Gratuities are included, and bicycles are on board for those who want to pedal ashore.

Check out my post My Take On Emerald Sky: Five Favorite Things | https://www.rivercruiseadvisor.com/2016/04/23928

RIVIERA RIVER CRUISES — NO NONSENSE PRICING

RIVERS: DANUBE, RHINE, MAIN, RHÔNE, MOSELLE, DOURO

Founded more than 30 years ago in the UK as Riviera Travel, Riviera River Cruises recently started targeting English-speaking guests from the United States and Canada for its value-priced river cruise offerings in Europe.

The company has a fleet of 12 vessels on the rivers of Europe, with more on the way. Unlike other river cruise lines, Riviera offers a price-point that is substantially lower than most of its competitors. It does this by "unbundling" some features, like inclusive drinks. You'll pay extra for things like bottled water and beer, wine and spirits, but Riviera believes the overall cost savings justify the add-on charges by making river cruising accessible to a wider swath of people who might be put off by the multi-thousand-dollar-fares charged by other lines.

For those who want to add a touch of the all-inclusive to their Riviera experience, the company is offering drink packages for its 2018 river cruises that start at roughly $129 per person for an average weeklong voyage (the package will be $159 in 2019, $299 for longer cruises). This adds draft and non-alcoholic beer, red and white house wine, bottled water, soft drinks and juices on a complimentary basis to lunches and dinners served onboard. Spirits, or drinks purchased outside mealtimes, come at an additional but reasonable cost.

For those who don't imbibe – and who don't wish to pay for an inclusion they won't make use of – Riviera's bare-bones pricing structure makes a lot of sense.

What Riviera has going for it is its three decades worth of experience as a tour operator, and the rave accolades its UK-based guests have given its river cruise product. Ships carry between 126 and 169 guests apiece, and are elegantly decorated, with plenty of fine woodworking, brass fixtures, and modern décor.

Riviera also offers some unique extras aboard its ships, including two dining venues aboard most ships, luxury toiletries from Crabtree & Evelyn, L'Occitane or Rituals (depending on the ship), onboard fitness centers, and even steam rooms and saunas aboard select vessels. Other niceties – like the tea and coffee-making facilities included in every cabin – reveal the line's British heritage.

Perhaps one Riviera's strongest features, however, is just how solo-traveler-friendly the line is. Every ship in the fleet offers cabins that can be booked, depending on availability, for little to no solo traveler supplement.

Riviera's river cruises offer plenty of value, with luxurious accommodations and ships operating fascinating and engaging itineraries throughout Europe. With a new office in the United States and bookings available in U.S. dollars, getting onboard a Riviera ship has never been easier.

The Riviera River Cruises fleet is primarily made up of new river cruise vessels, with most of its ships launched in 2017 and 2018. All Riviera River Cruises vessels have a certain number of staterooms that are available to solo travelers with no single supplement, subject to availability. These are usually a lower-category stateroom, but the removal of the single supplement is a huge bonus to travelers wishing to take a solo river cruise journey.

Staterooms and Suites are stocked with luxury toiletries, and all rooms have beds that can be set up as either two twins or one queen. Owing to Riviera's English origins, tea and coffee-making facilities are present in all accommodations across the fleet.

While there are some differences between the ships of the Riviera fleet in terms of size and layout, all feature classic, elegant décor; 24-hour tea and coffee stations; spacious sun decks; and two dining venues: a traditional restaurant and a more casual, stern-facing bistro that serves up light fare throughout the day.

SCENIC — SLEEK BOUTIQUE
RIVERS: DANUBE, RHINE, SEINE, MAIN, RHÔNE, MOSELLE, DOURO, VOLGA (MEKONG, IRRAWADDY)

In 1987, Australian entrepreneur Glen Moroney founded Scenic Tours, a company that got its start offering coach trips to the Australian coast. Initially, Scenic Tours marketed its product to residents of Melbourne but soon realized that its guests would travel further with them. For two decades, Scenic Tours continued to grow and expand, earning accolades from travelers around the world for quality and service, not to mention Scenic's rapidly diversifying array of tour packages.

In 2008, Scenic Tours dove headfirst into the river cruise market with the launch of its purpose-built Scenic "space ships." A fitting name for vessels with interiors that showcase a sleek and minimalist design ethos and technology offerings light years ahead of many of their competitors.

On April 13, 2015, Scenic Tours officially changed its name to simply "Scenic," and like Prince, Madonna and other rock stars, one word is all that's needed to convey its five-star persona. Scenic has a fleet of 16 river cruisers, with two oceangoing expedition ships on order. In addition to the company's itineraries in Europe, Scenic also offers luxury, all-inclusive river cruise voyages along Russia's Volga River;

Myanmar's Irrawaddy; and the mighty Mekong that flows through Cambodia and Vietnam.

Six original "space ships" were built between 2008 and 2012: Scenic Sapphire, Scenic Emerald, Scenic Diamond, Scenic Ruby, Scenic Pearl and the Scenic Crystal. Scenic continued its fleet expansion beyond 2012. In 2013 the Scenic Jewel was christened. Two new "space ships" were added in 2014—Scenic Gem and Scenic Jade. In 2015, Scenic welcomed the Scenic Jasper and Scenic Opal, and 2016 saw the line take delivery of four new ships: Scenic Aura on the Irrawaddy, Scenic Azure on Portugal's Douro River, and Scenic Spirit on the Mekong and Scenic Amber on the waterways of Europe.

Recently, Scenic Diamond and Scenic Pearl were the first recipients of a $10-million investment that has resulted in an extensive refurbishment. All suites received an entirely new look complete with new wallpaper, marble desktops, furniture, soft furnishings and carpeting. In addition, stateroom balconies—all of which are full "step-out" Sun Lounges—have been refitted with retractable windows that allow guests to fully enclose their balconies for use during inclement weather.

Complimentary butler service is offered on all Balcony Suites, along with complimentary shoe shine service and laundry at no charge. Some other notables include Scenic's gym, the Salt Therapy room, the €15,000 coffee machine and more. Apple computers have been linked to HD televisions, providing in-stateroom access to the ship's upgraded Wi-Fi system using Satellite and UMTS Mobile Technology. This represents a considerable speed boost over the previous system.

Ashore, complimentary options like Scenic FreeChoice excursions and Scenic Tailormade, an interactive system that provides GPS-enabled commentary throughout most major cities in Europe, help to personalize the off-ship experience. Scenic is also adding new Scenic Enrich experiences on its France itineraries, including Scenic Rouge—a new on-shore spectacle in Lyon performed under a big-top tent that features a traditional French cabaret experience.

Scenic's refit of Scenic Diamond and Scenic Sapphire coincided with the new Scenic Culinaire program that features an onboard cooking school that uses a new dedicated space in order to offer immersive courses that highlight the culinary delights of France's Rhône, Saône and Bordeaux regions. (See Chapter 5 to read about my participation in the program while in Bordeaux or read the story on my website: In Bordeaux, What Scenic Does Differently | https://www.rivercruiseadvisor.com/2017/06/bordeaux-scenic-differently

Using fresh ingredients sourced from local markets, guests will be able to make regional recipes that will be itinerary-specific, all under the guidance of experienced chefs. Scenic's new Culinaire space will have dedicated cooking stations, a cheese and wine cellar, and cameras linked to video screens to provide detailed instruction to participants. Although class sizes are limited, Scenic schedules ample sessions to ensure all interested guests are able to participate. As with all of Scenic's other programs, Scenic Culinaire is extended to guests free of charge.

Breakfast, lunch and dinner can be ordered in-room, a rarity among river cruise ships, many of which offer no room service of any kind. Though it might be enticing to eat-in, casual meals are available in the River Café, including gourmet pizza made fresh onboard and Table La Rive is dedicated to a full degustation dining experience.

Some of the dishes I had on Scenic Diamond were among the best I have ever had on the rivers – the tortellini in L'Amour comes to mind – while the wines were regional and of some acclaim. Portobellos has undergone a complete redesign, along with The Bar, which now features Eurocave wine dispensers.

Overall, Scenic is for those who appreciate refined elegance with a personal touch. While one might immediately assume stuffiness to go hand-in-hand with white-glove style service, I found Scenic's staff to be professional, personable, and quick to share a laugh.

TAUCK – CULTURE CONNOISSEURS
RIVERS: DANUBE, RHINE, SEINE, RHÔNE

Long-standing American tour operator Tauck distinguishes itself in Europe by offering river cruise tours featuring hallmarks of the company's "Uncommon Access."

Have you ever wanted to have a private tour of Prague Castle or enjoy dinner at the Hungarian Academy of Science? You can do it with Tauck.

Though Tauck was founded in 1925, its river-cruise division is one of the new kids on the block. With its first vessel entering service in 2006, Tauck now operates nine ships in Europe: the 118-passenger Swiss Emerald, Swiss Sapphire and Swiss Jewel, sister ships launched in 2006, 2008 and 2009 respectively. These original 361-foot river cruises already offered outside facing cabins—most with French balconies.

After Tauck got its feet wet in the river cruising world the company started to realize how it could make the onboard experience even better, make the ships bigger. In 2014, Tauck launched two brand-new river cruise ships that represented an entirely new class of ship: ms Inspire and ms Savor. Stretching to the maximum length of 443-feet, these two vessels along with ms Joy and ms Grace that would join the family in 2016, can accommodate 130 guests. These longer vessels extend 22 suites, the most of any riverboat similar in size, each offering 300 square feet of space. In Tauck fashion, the company wondered how it could further outdo itself and it did, by building up, in the stateroom that is. Aboard ms Inspire and ms Savor eight loft cabins offer windows that extend from the first to the second decks, bathing the room in light and a feeling a added spaciousness to the room's footprint.

I left out the description of two vessels, ms Treasures and ms Esprit, which proves a little confusing when visiting the itineraries available. That's because these two 391-foot vessels first came onto the scene in 2011 and were refurbished a few years later. You can still enjoy a 118-person voyage on these ships, but in 2018, the deck will be shuffled and new interiors will emerge. The new layout makes the river cruise experience even more intimate with only 98 passengers. These lucky few have 14, 300-square-foot suites from which to choose, each accommodation boasting brocade upholstery, two French balconies and marble bathrooms with separate showers.

Public spaces feature an aft casual dining area with an opening 180-degree glass wall, a cocktail lounge, piano bar and dining room with panoramic views. The new designs feature an additional dining venue, expanded fitness facilities, bicycles for use by guests on shore and an elevator that stops on all decks (except Sun Deck) if your legs prove too sore after a day of riding. But what I find to be even more memorable about sailing with Tauck is how you benefit from their time-honored relationships. They have an inside edge to craft experiences that you'd be hard-pressed to do otherwise.

Discover the VIP treatment along the Danube, Rhine, Moselle, Main, Rhône and Saône rivers—and during some interesting themed sailings such as a musical tour on the Blue Danube, a culinary voyage from Paris to Provence, and five different family themed sailings. New in 2018 are itineraries between Kraków and Berlin and between Milan and Amsterdam on the only European river cruise that begins with three nights in Milan and explores the Italian Lake District.

On most days, you can join the Tauck Director and local travel experts ashore on well-choreographed day tours that have earned Tauck the distinguished reputation for being the world's top tour operator. Best of all, you have even more reasons to go it alone. This cruise line waives the single-supplement fee and features more dedicated cabins for solo travelers than any European riverboat of a similar size.

UNIWORLD BOUTIQUE RIVER CRUISE COLLECTION – ROYAL TREATMENT
RIVERS: DANUBE, DORDOGNE, DOURO, GARONNE, MAIN, MOSELLE, PO, RHÔNE, RHINE, SAÔNE, SEINE, VOLGA

Uniworld Boutique River Cruises was founded in 1976 by Yugoslavian entrepreneur Serba Illich. Based in California, the company began operating river cruises along the waterways of Europe in 1993 with the 361-foot long River Ambassador. In 1994, her sister ship, the River Baroness, entered service. But don't let their relative ages fool you: both ships underwent dramatic refurbishments in 2011, emerging with the same comfortable, chic look that their newer counterparts boast.

Today Uniworld flaunts a fleet of 18 distinct ships—13 of which are cruising on Europe's rivers. The line sails through some of Europe's most spectacular cities and towns, in addition to offering river cruises that explore the wonders of Russia, the magic of Egypt, and the ancient civilizations of China, Vietnam and Cambodia.

Between 2001 and 2003 Uniworld expanded its offerings by launching the River Princess, River Empress and River Duchess. These highly successful ships were followed in 2006 by the launch of the River Royale. (With space onboard for between 132 and 134 passengers, all four of these ships were remodeled for the 2012 cruising season, with the exception of River Empress, which underwent her refurbishment in 2010.)

In 2009, Uniworld went big—in comparison to its average vessel size limited to 130 passengers, that is—with the addition of 162-passenger River Beatrice, which was completely refitted in 2018.

Along with the new and improved Beatrice, bragging rights are exercised when referring to Uniworld's line of Super Ships: S.S. Antoinette, S.S. Catherine, S.S. Maria Theresa, and S.S. Joie De Vivre, which set out on European waterways, 2011, 2014, 2016 and 2017 respectively. With features like an indoor swimming pools, dedicated cinemas, and yes, even real fireplaces onboard it's easy to see why they bear the S.S. designation, which stands for "Super Ship."

The minute you step aboard any of the Uniworld vessels, you'll sense the line's regal air. The interiors possess classically modern European elegance, designed to resemble baroque opulence, Art Deco chic, or the classic, wood-paneled lounges and public rooms of some of Europe's greatest liners, trains and hotels. Comprising the design DNA is handcrafted furniture commissioned exclusively for Uniworld, carefully curated original artwork and antiques, marble bathrooms, and ultra comfortable beds by London's distinctive Savoir.

In April of 2018, Uniworld launched "U by Uniworld", with ships initially limited to passengers age 21 to 45, but relenting in March of 2018 and opening up reservations to guests of all ages. These all-black-hulled ships revealed a decidedly edgier look complete with hip DJ lounges and trendy onboard features. While this is a departure from a traditionally classic feel, it remains that no two ships in the Uniworld fleet are alike, with each showcasing a singular fit and feel. Thus the "boutique" moniker.

Translating this hotelier ethos to the rivers is really no surprise when one considers the cruise line's long-standing partnership with Red Carnation Hotels—founded in the early 1980s by hotel goddess Beatrice Tollman. Now the family-run business spans four generations—including her husband Stanley and three children. Red Carnation Hotels now owns and operates 17 boutique properties in five countries. The company falls under the banner of The Travel Corporation (TTC), which acquired Uniworld in 2004. Founded by Stanley Tollman, TTC is a travel empire consisting of the like of Trafalgar, Insight Vacations and Contiki. This acquisition brought the Uniworld experience to new levels. This is particularly evident when staying in one of Uniworld's suites. Suite butlers were trained under the tutelage of Zita Langenstein of England's Ivor Spencer Butler School, which trains service staff for Buckingham Palace, among others.

The amenities on board are equally impressive, with restaurants upholding the culinary philosophy of Mrs. Tollman, not only the founder of Red Carnation Hotel Collection but also the author of the highly acclaimed cookbook A Life in Food. Her personal recipes are guest favorites including the Traveling Lite and vegetarian options; and don't order a salad without sampling her favorite dressing. Health is also paramount at The Serenity River Spa and in the onboard fitness centers complete with a wellness coach, and classes incorporation the Five Tibetan Rites, yoga and TRX.

Uniworld offers 26 different itineraries in Europe, ranging from the "Tulips and Windmills tours in Holland and "Gems of Northern Italy" in Europe's famous boot nation to the 13-day Imperial Waterways of Russia tour from Moscow to St. Petersburg. You'll also discover six different itineraries dedicated to France and a gamut of sailings along the Danube, Rhine and Moselle.

I'd be remiss not to mention that Uniworld has my favorite river bar, the Leopard Bar, aft on its Super Ships. Cheers!

Koblenz, where the Rhine and Moselle merge

VIKING RIVER CRUISES - PORT COLLECTORS

RIVERS: RHINE, MAIN, DANUBE, SEINE, RHÔNE, DOURO, MOSELLE, ELBE, DORDOGNE, GARONNE, GIRONDE, RUSSIA'S VOLGA, NEVA AND SVIR (NILE, YANGTZE, MEKONG)

You've probably heard of the company founded by Torstein Hagen in 1997, which earned a Guinness World Record for christening the most ships ever in a single day, a whopping 14. In fact, Viking has more river cruise vessels operating in Europe than any other company, with more than 50 in the fleet.

Established in 1997, Viking River Cruises acquired KD River Cruises in 2000. The California-based company now operates a remarkable fleet of more than 60 river cruise vessels throughout Europe, Russia & the Ukraine, China and Southeast Asia, and Egypt. And, that doesn't include Viking's award-winning ocean-going vessels, which debuted in the spring of 2015 with the launch of Viking Star. Viking's current growth appears to be happening outside of Europe, with a new ship design in Egypt, the all-suite Viking Ra, which will offer new Nile River cruisetours in 2018. But let's get back to Europe.

I could dedicate this entire book to explaining the nuances of ship designs and the fleet's evolution to what it's become today, but what you need to know is that the fleet basically breaks down into categories based on size and the regions they frequent.

The majority of Viking's vessels sailing European rivers are Longships, more than 40, which feature full verandas and boast some of the largest suites on the rivers of Europe. This series of ships was launched in 2012 and quickly became a crowd pleaser. If you're lucky enough to score one of the two Explorer Suites, you'll bask in 445 square-feet of living space. The other 93 staterooms range in size from 150 square feet to 275 square feet. Guest capacity is 190 guests.

The expansive sun deck features an herb garden and walking track. I particularly enjoy the Aquavit Terrace—a sun-filled relaxation area and a second dining alternative to the main restaurant on the middle deck near reception. Even though there are seemingly countless Viking ships cruising Europe's rivers, once you've sailed on one of these Longships you'll immediately have your bearings on future sailings aboard sister ships.

The 189-passenger Prestige Ships, Viking Legend and Viking Prestige, were built in 2009 and 2011 respectively, and though they were constructed before the Longships series was released in 2012 they still feature some innovative "green features," such as a unique hybrid propulsion system that uses less fuel, produces minimal vibrations and offers passengers a smoother river cruise experience.

Five Viking Russia Ships recall the company's start in river cruising more than 20 years ago. Viking is one of the few cruise lines that actually operates purpose-built river cruisers on the Volga.

The Viking Elbe Ships, Viking Astrild and Viking Beyla host just 98 passengers and have customized hulls and engines built specifically to navigate the historic Elbe river, but as I discussed earlier, that doesn't necessarily guarantee transit during low water.

Viking's Douro Ships, Viking Osfrid, Viking Torgil, and Viking Hemming were custom built to sail Portugal's Douro River and are the only ships in Viking's fleet that have pools. Lastly, the Ukraine-based Viking Sineus offers 11-day itineraries between Kiev and Odessa. While the 196-passenger ship was originally constructed in 1979 it was significantly updated in 2014.

All of the Viking itineraries range from 8 to 32 days and Viking has an eager-to-please and-seemingly happy-to-be-there staff. As an active traveler, when I sail with Viking I miss the onboard fitness center and bikes, but the company serves up a satisfying traditional river cruise experience with an impressive geographic reach and eager-to-please staff.

Viking's Longships are some of the most beautiful ships afloat. You'd be hard-pressed, in fact, to find river cruise vessels more appealing to the senses than those in Viking's expansive fleet. The beauty is by and large a product of Viking's Scandinavian heritage and the design aesthetic of the Nordics.

But Viking is not all about beauty. Typically, you will get a great value on Viking. The company nearly always has special offers, including 2-for-1 fares, included or reduced airfare, and often, a combination of both. The value proposition also extends to what the company refers to as "affordable luxury." To give you just one example of what Viking means by "affordable luxury," the bathroom floors in your stateroom are heated. I've not seen this on any other ship, oceans or rivers. There are little touches like the heated bathroom floors all throughout Viking's Longships.

My video shows you all of the fine touches that make for "affordable luxury" on Viking's Longships. Video: Viking River Cruises 'Affordable Luxury' | https://www.rivercruiseadvisor.com/2017/06/viking-hlin-video . Also see What I Learned About Viking River Cruises While Cruising The Rhine | https://www.rivercruiseadvisor.com/2017/05/viking-rhine-cruise

HOW DO THEY STACK UP?

So all of this information is well and good, but you might still be wondering, "How do these lines compare to one another?" I've produced a chart (you'll find it in the appendix) that breaks down each of these items, allowing you to compare which suppliers offer the most inclusive river cruise packages. While I've tried to be as accurate as possible, sometimes the answer required more than a simple yes or no. For example, while all river cruise companies in my table offer complimentary shore excursions in ports of call, some charge for "optional" excursions.

Also, airport transfers are Included when air tickets are purchased with the river cruise company, but may not be included otherwise. I've indicated companies that always include airport transfers, even for guests who have made independent air arrangements.

But the choices don't end there. After you figure out which cruise line you want to sail with you'll need to make one of the most important vacation decision: which ship you'll sail on. After all, this single factor determines what you'll call home for a week or longer during your vacation, and picking the right river cruise ship for you can easily make or break a vacation.

So what is the "right" river cruise ship? The answer lies in your personal preferences.

ASK THE AGE-OLD QUESTION

"Does age really matter?" In practice, the itinerary largely determines the ship you'll sail aboard. But where things get tricky is in choosing between an older vessel on a desirable run, or taking a newer vessel on a more common one.

Newer ships, by definition, are just that: newer. Some are sister-ships to tried-and-true vessels while others are trend-setting new vessels that seek to push the boundaries of the traditional river cruise experience. They tend to have larger accommodations than older vessels built in the 1990's or even the early part of the last decade, but not always: Viking's new Longships have some staterooms that, while beautifully appointed, come in at a much-smaller size: 135 square feet. If you value space, but can't afford to cruise in a higher stateroom category onboard a newer ship, an older ship with more spacious cabins might be the way to go.

Newer ships do have a number of advantages over their predecessors. Most new vessels have more French and full balcony staterooms than older ships, and several new ships are bucking the traditional dining trends by offering more than one restaurant onboard. If you like choice, newer ships can provide that in spades.

But newer vessels aren't always all they're cracked up to be. They tend to command a much higher price than their predecessors, and popular stateroom categories can sell out far earlier. By simply choosing a vessel built three or four years ago, you have the opportunity to potentially get more bang for your buck.

Older river cruise ships also offer something that many ultra-modern vessels may not: a warm and inviting classic cruise atmosphere filled with dark woods, polished brass, and other nautical touches.

ROOM ONBOARD

As diverse as ocean cruising can be, accommodations tend to be fairly standard across all lines: You have your inside staterooms, your oceanview staterooms, your balconies and your suites. But in the world of river cruising, accommodations can vary wildly.

First and foremost, interior (windowless) staterooms on river cruise ships do not exist, at least to my knowledge. In fact, the single most common type of accommodations are French balcony staterooms. These offer a sliding glass veranda window, but lack the space to 'step out' like a more traditional balcony offers.

Full-featured, step-out balconies are becoming more and more common on river cruise ships, as well as "dual balcony" staterooms and suites, pioneered by AmaWaterways. These offer both French and full balconies in a single room, and are exceedingly popular with passengers. Scenic's impressive full-sized balconies convert into glassed-in solariums called "Sun Lounges." With a touch of a button you can still enjoy the view while benefiting from the extra room space.

For the budget-conscious, standard "river view" staterooms typically offer half-height windows positioned at the waterline, but don't worry, unlike the ocean, rivers seldom experience the "washing machine" effect found on the lower decks of deep-ocean cruise ships. And I enjoy these staterooms for couple of reasons: 1) When docked, swans will float by, and I have even had them swim up to my window; and 2) I enjoy being at the water level and watching the flow of the river.

Within these three basic accommodation types lie a whole host of variations, so it's always a good idea to pick up a brochure and familiarize yourself with it before booking anything. Look at what each category offers, and where it is positioned on the deck plan. You may find you can save yourself hundreds of dollars simply by choosing a category that is positioned at the extreme forward or aft ends of a deck, yet still retains all the features of those located amidships.

10

Chapter
TEN

WATER LEVELS

Approaching Paris

WATER LEVELS

As I mentioned in Chapter 7 when discussing the ideal time to take a river cruise in Europe, a lot boils down to personal preference and the rest is in Mother Nature's hands. You'll read about a lot of rules of thumb when to proceed with caution, but that's a bit like predicting winning lottery numbers.

In general, high water occurs in the spring while low water situations develop in heat of the summer, usually August. However, I saw record lows on the Rhine in November of 2015 that made sailing difficult for a number of ships.

First of all, let me explain the fluctuations. High water is usually caused by prolonged periods of heavy, intense rain or runoff from melting snow. The rising river can result in ships being unable to pass under some of the low bridges that span nearly every river in Europe. The horrific floods of 2013 that saw water levels in places like Passau rise to levels that hadn't been seen since the Middle Ages. In April and early May (sometimes into June) the banks of rivers such as the Main, Danube (especially between Vienna and Cologne) and Rhine can overflow to the point of impassibility. This can also be the case in France on the Rhône and Saône rivers; Paris' Seine and Bordeaux's Garonne and Dordogne are less likely to fall prey to high water. To steer clear of rising concerns over high water levels in Spring you could simply head down to Portugal's Douro or Italy's Po, but there's no guarantee there either. The spring of 2018 saw high water levels on the Douro that made navigation impossible.

But even in the cases of high water, cruise lines have developed workarounds, like ship swaps. In particular, Viking River Cruises used its sheer numbers of nearly-identical Viking Longships to continue operations by moving both ships up to the affected area and simply transferring guests and their luggage from one vessel to another. It's a huge process for the crew, but a relatively painless one for the guests. A ship swap is usually the preferred choice over cancellation. Often times it's just a matter of swapping out once, getting on a sister ship that simply returns from the direction which it came.

If things are bad enough (like during the once-in-a-century flooding that occurred along the Danube in 2013), your river cruise might turn into a bus trip as the cruise line attempts to do its best to hit all the major sights and attractions along the way. This usually involves putting guests up in hotels—on the cruise line's dime—and arranging for coach transportation and guides that weren't originally needed. It's a huge logistical nightmare. But on the plus side: You're still in Europe, and can still enjoy nearly all the fantastic things you would have on the river cruise. If information is received that water levels are expected to alleviate in a day or two, you can expect to stay in port for a night or two and then make up the time later. The cruise line may bus you to the next port of call and sail the ship empty to make up time, or a port or two may be dropped in favor of another. Remember: Getting you to your final destination is of utmost importance for the crew, along with seeing as much of the planned itinerary as possible.

A low-water situation is just the opposite: A lack of rainfall can cause water levels to drop to the point where river cruise ships don't have enough under their keels to safely navigate. But water levels can be difficult to predict. When there is low water, rain can raise water levels back to the point where river cruise ships can continue to operate. While disruptions are not all that frequent, when they do occur, they make the news.

The Rhine is perhaps the most dependable river when it comes to being able to continue navigation due to high or low water. I felt the boat scraping the bottom of the Rhine in Rüdesheim in November of 2015, but we made it past. That being said, keep in mind that some waterways are only navigable because of dredging or innovation. And I think it's more important to be aware of what rivers are shallow to begin with; making them more susceptible to low-water woes.

A case in point: the Elbe. The notoriously shallow river has caused headaches for many cruise operators and disappointments for many guests. Some "river cruises" on the Elbe end up being nothing more than bus tours, with the ships tied up along the banks and used as a hotel each night. (A problem more likely to occur in late autumn on small rivers such as Moselle and Elbe after a warm winter with little precipitation.)

In 2016, AmaWaterways made the decision not to begin operations on the Elbe, a painful decision because the company's co-owner, Kristin Karst, hails from Dresden, Germany, and had always dreamed of a river cruiser carrying her company's name through her hometown. "It was a dream to have a ship on the Elbe," Karst told me, "but we decided it would be unfair to offer our guests sailings that may not happen."

So after beginning construction on AmaKristina, the company decided to redeploy the ship to the more reliable Rhine.

AmaKristina's draft was to be just 80 centimeters. The Elbe, however, got as low as 65 centimeters at one point. "We had the plans for the ship; we had a very low draft, but that year, the water level on the Elbe was even lower than the years before," Karst told me. "It was a dream, and we have always gone for our dreams, but if it is not realistic, we should not pursue it."

Nevertheless, AmaWaterways offers its clients a low-water guarantee of sorts. Essentially, for each day that does not go according to what's outlined in the company's brochures or on its website—in other words, if there are deviations—you can count on AmaWaterways to generous, handling each situation as it does everything else it does, case-by-case and with a personal touch.

As you've already read, one company has "conquered" the low waters of the Elbe: CroisiEurope. A paddlewheeler was built to successfully navigate the Elbe between Berlin and the heart of Prague. The Elbe Princesse has met with such success that the company built a sister ship, the Elbe Princesse II. CroisiEurope also has a paddlewheeler similar to Elbe Princesse operating on the Loire River, another notoriously shallow waterway that their ships transit well.

There's no doubt that water levels have thrown a real wrench in river cruise vacations, and have even caused trip cancellation in some instances, but hopefully it's reassuring to know that in my 50-plus river cruises during the past decade, I've never had a serious disruption. I've had small incidents that caused delays in reaching destinations or incidents that required that we embark the ship somewhere other than what was originally planned, 20 miles downriver from Passau, for example, instead of in the heart of Passau on one river cruise in 2015.

Given the unpredictable nature and likelihood that the cruise line will be able to provide a workaround in the event that bad luck strikes, I don't think you should place too much emphasis on booking your cruise based on potential water levels.

The important thing is to manage your expectations. Viking River Cruises' Candi Finkelstein tells me that she worked on the Elbe for entire season when the ship did not move. However, Viking let guest know ahead of time and offered not only compensation but also added in activities that guests would not have experienced otherwise had their ship sailed. An informed traveler is less likely to be a disappointed one.

Most times, you needn't worry about water levels. River cruises are nearly always smooth sailing.

Migratory herons over Hungary's Parliament Building

11

Chapter
ELEVEN

WHERE TO GET HELP

WHERE TO GET HELP

Hopefully this book gave you a feel for each of the ships, rivers and cruises that I've experienced in the past few years. Maybe some of those will appeal to you. Beyond that, I'm here to help. The best way for me to help you is for you to complete my form, Get My River Cruise Recommendations. | https://www.rivercruiseadvisor.com/river-cruise-recommendations

By garnering just a few details, notably where and when you want to cruise, the size of your budget and what you're looking for in a river cruise, I can help match you to a ship and itinerary - at no cost to you, of course. I'm here to help.

Note, while all of my trips were hosted by the river cruise companies and my sites operate with funding from cruise companies and travel agents, I pride myself on arming travelers with honest and comprehensive information. My goal is to help put you on the right cruise, for you. I look forward to hearing from you and possibly seeing you on one of the rivers some day.

Thank you for purchasing my book.

Bon voyage, Ralph Grizzle

Appendix

PRICE COMPARISON CHARTS

2019 EUROPE RIVER CRUISE PEAK SEASON PRICE COMPARISONS

River Cruise Advisor's peak season 2019 lead-in price comparisons should be viewed as general guidelines for comparing prices across the major companies operating on a particular river (or region) in Europe or for a particular itinerary.

The intent of the charts is to provide a baseline for matching a cruise company to your budget. I've calculated what I believe to be the "true per diem" for each cruise company, after factoring in, or out, the various items that are included, or not included, on a particular river cruise.

Pricing is anything but straightforward among the major river cruise companies, as many companies offer two-for-the-price-of-one river cruises, reduced or free air-fare incentives, early-booking discounts and many more pricing tactics that make purchasing a river cruise vacation a complex and confounding exercise. Using a spreadsheet until we were bleary-eyed, my team and I have tried to decipher the various offers and inclusions to arrive at meaningful guidelines for comparisons.

The bottom line, the true per diem, is what you can expect to pay per person for each day of your cruise for a lead-in standard stateroom, or where applicable, a lead-in balcony stateroom.

Price, however, should not be the only consideration when selecting a company for your river cruise. There are a boatload of variables to be considered, not the least of which is what's included in your cruise. If you're someone who prefers everything included, an open bar, for example, and prepaid gratuities, you'll want to look to companies that provide those as part of your cruise fare. For help in figuring out which cruise company includes what, see "Attributes Of The Top River Cruise Companies," a chart that outlines inclusions | https://www.rivercruiseadvisor.com/cruise-companies/viking-river-cruises-vs-uniworld-river-cruises/)

All prices and inclusions were current as of June 2018. I will continue to update the charts at https://www.rivercruiseadvisor.com/handbook/ (password: rivercruise)

As always, I welcome your comments and feedback. While I try to get things right, I do goof now and then, which is why I am extremely grateful to readers who bring errors to my attention so that I can correct them as quickly as possible. And if you run into any bumps along the road (or rapids along the river) while doing your river cruise research, feel free to reach out to me by emailing handbook@rivercruiseadvisor.com

Bon voyage, Ralph Grizzle

ATTRIBUTES OF THE TOP RIVER CRUISE COMPANIES

		AmaWaterways	Avalon WATERWAYS	CroisiEurope	CRYSTAL RIVER CRUISES
	Excursions Included?	✓	✓	✓	✓
	Beer/Wine Lunch & Dinner?	✓	✓	✓	✓
	Drinks Included 24/7?	**	**	✓	✓
	Onboard Bicycles	✓	✓		✓
	Fitness Center	✓	✓		✓
	Exterior Balconies/Veranda	✓	✓		
	Two Room Suites				✓
	Service Guarantee				
	Own & Operate	✓		✓	✓
	Room Service				✓
	Mini Bar		✓		✓
	Dining Venues	3**	2**	1	6
	Personal Butler				✓
	Port Charges Included			✓	✓
	Airport Transfers	**	**		✓
	Prepaid Gratuities	**			✓
	Laundry Included				**

updated 7/1/2018

Comparison Chart Footnotes

While I've tried to be as accurate as possible, sometimes the answer required more than a simple yes or no. For example, while all river cruise companies in the accompanying table offer complimentary shore excursions in ports of call, some charge for "optional" excursions. Also, airport transfers are Included when air tickets are purchased with the river cruise company, but may not be included otherwise. I've indicated companies that always include airport transfers, even for guests who have made independent air arrangements.

AmaWaterways **: Beer, wine and soft drinks included with lunch and dinner; sparkling wine with breakfast; and complimentary cocktails during Happy Hour, introduced in 2018. Complimentary shore excursions included in every port, along with complimentary Special Interest Tours. AmaWaterways features twin balconies, both a French and an outside balcony, in many staterooms. In addition to the main dining room, AmaWaterways features The Chef's Table restaurant, with its excellent multi-course, wine-paired dinners, at no additional charge. Light lunches and breakfast are served in the lounge, along with full lunches and

EMERALD WATERWAYS	RIVIERA TRAVEL	SCENIC	TAUCK	UNIWORLD	VIKING RIVER CRUISES
✓	✓	✓	✓	✓	✓
✓	**	✓	✓	✓	✓
**		✓	✓	✓	**
✓	✓	✓	✓	✓	**
✓	✓	✓	✓	✓	**
✓	✓	✓	✓	✓	✓
		✓			✓
		✓			✓
✓		✓			✓
**	✓	✓		✓	**
**	✓	✓	✓	✓	**
3	2	6	2	1**	2
		✓		✓	
✓	✓	✓	✓		✓
✓		✓	✓	✓	**
✓		✓	✓	✓	**
**		✓		**	**

breakfast served in the main dining room. Nice touches like gluten-free snacks, fruits, Gemstone detox water, 24/7 coffee stations and more. Airport transfers are included when purchasing air through AmaWaterways. Pre-paid gratuities are offered.

Avalon Waterways **: Beer and wine included with lunch and dinner; sparkling wine with breakfast. Coffee, tea and non-alcoholic beverages complimentary 24/7. In addition to the main dining room, Avalon offers small group (30 people) reservations to Panorama Bistro (light menu paired with wine). When weather permits, grilled lunches are available on the Sky Deck. Meals can also served in the Club Lounge and Panorama Lounge. Some optional tours require a fee. Airport transfers included when purchasing air from Avalon. Avalon's beds face floor-to-ceiling sliding glass doors for gorgeous views while your head is propped on the pillow. Stocked in-room mini-bar incurs charges for each item selected.

CroisiEurope **: Extra charge only for high-end champagnes and wines. Wi-Fi internet access with complimentary use of Samsung tablet. Complimentary shore excursions included in every port.

Crystal River Cruises **: All of Crystal's new-builds feature Panoramic Balcony Windows, which function, in essence, like balconies. Crystal Mozart features balconies in about half of its staterooms.

Emerald Waterways **: Complimentary shore excursions in every port. Wine, beer & soda complimentary with lunch and dinner. All staterooms restocked daily with bottled water. Owner's Suites comes with complimentary stocked mini-bars. Room service included for suites. Laundry concierge available for a fee; complimentary for suites.

Riviera **: Riviera's beverage package, which includes wine and beer with lunch and dinner, goes for $129 a week ($159 in 2019).

Scenic **: Inclusions are for all guests, regardless of ship or suite.

Uniworld Boutique River Cruise Collection **: Uniworld charges for at least one optional excursion, the Vienna Evening Concert at 75 euros. Free laundry service in higher-end suites across its fleet. Additionally, most Uniworld ships have complimentary self-service laundry facilities for passengers to use; only River Royale, River Baroness, Douro Spirit, and River Victoria lack this feature in the European-based fleet. Room Service and Butler Service on Uniworld is **at the suite level only.**

Viking River Cruises ** A complimentary shore excursion is included in every port; there are also additional optional shore excursions available on every itinerary. Beer, wine and soft drinks included with lunch and dinner. Specialty coffee & teas available anytime. Optional Silver Spirit beverage packages are available for extra fee & makes drinks all-inclusive. Room service, stocked mini-bars and laundry are included for Explorer Suites. Bicycles and gyms are available ashore and arranged by Viking. Airport transfers included when booking air (or receiving free air) with Europe. Some promotions offered prepaid gratuities or shipboard credits.

PRICING CHARTS EXPLANATION & CLARIFICATION (FOR ALL PRICING CHARTS)

* Nights – A 7-night river cruise spans 7 days, but one of those days is the disembarkation day. Unlike checking out of a hotel, you won't linger until noon (or later) on disembarkation day. Some guests will depart before 6 a.m. for transfers to the airport and their flights home. Others may be able to stay as late as 9 a.m. Either way, you're not getting a full day on your river cruise on that last day. For that reason, the "per diems" are calculated based on the number of "nights" on board. The result is a fairer assessment than calculating the cost per "day."

* Per Diem – The rate divided by the number of nights on board, indicated per person but based on double occupancy. Solo travelers will, in most cases, pay single supplements. Solo travelers can learn more about single supplements by reading this post, Avoiding Single Supplement Fares | https://www.rivercruiseadvisor.com/2017/03/avoiding-single-supplement-fares/

* Port Charges – Not all river cruise companies include port charges. What are port charges? Ports of call, where river cruise ships dock, set their own fees, and these fees are then passed on to the river cruise passengers. See our post on port charges, Port Charges: Which River Cruise Companies Include Them? | https://www.rivercruiseadvisor.com/2015/01/port-charges-river-cruise-companies-include-in-fare/

* Gratuities (on ship) – Some companies include gratuities for crew, others leave it to their guests to take care of gratuities. If your cruise is one of the latter, you may want to have some euro notes handy for stuffing into envelopes (or into the hands of your favorite crew members) on the last night of the cruise. Guidelines of how much to tip also vary by river cruise line. See Prepaid Gratuities: Which River Cruise Companies Include Them? | https://www.rivercruiseadvisor.com/2015/01/prepaid-gratuities-river-cruise-companies-include-fare/

* Gratuities (on shore) – Just as with crew gratuities, some companies take care of on-shore gratuities for guides and drivers; other companies leave it to their guests. If you're traveling with a company that operates by the latter policy, be sure to carry euro coins with you for tipping guides and drivers.

* Beverages – Nearly all river cruise companies offer complimentary soft drinks, specialty coffees, beer and wine during lunch and dinner. In between mealtimes, though, you'll pay for most beverages when traveling with Avalon, Emerald, Riviera and Viking. Beverages are included on CroisiEurope, Crystal, Scenic, Tauck and Uniworld. AmaWaterways introduced a "Sip and Sail" Happy Hour in 2018, which includes complimentary cocktails before dinner. For that reason, I've indicated AmaWaterways as "Beverages Included,"

though you should be aware that you could leave the ship with a balance on your bar tab if you consume beverages outside of Happy Hour or breakfast (sparkling wine is included), lunch or dinner. Riviera does not include wine and beer, even during lunch and dinner. For those who don't imbibe – and who don't wish to pay for an inclusion they won't make use of – Riviera's a la carte pricing structure makes a lot of sense. For those who want to add a touch of the all-inclusive to their Riviera experience, the company offers drink packages for its 2018 river cruises that start at roughly $129 per person for an average weeklong voyage (the package will be $159 in 2019). This adds draft and non-alcoholic beer, red and white house wine, bottled water, soft drinks and juices on a complimentary basis to lunches and dinners served onboard. Spirits, or drinks purchased outside mealtimes, come at an additional cost. Viking River Cruises has a similar package. While Viking includes beer and wine with lunch and dinner, the company also offers a Silver Spirit Beverage Package. At €300 per cabin, double occupancy, the cost of Viking's all-inclusive beverage package may seem steep at first glance, but it can be quite a value when you consider the quality of the beverages offered. Are you a Scotch drinker? Then you may know of Highland Park Ragnvald, which goes for more than $500 a bottle on the internet sites I researched. Yet on Viking, you can enjoy as many glasses as you like of the single malt Scotch whiskey as part of your Silver Spirit Beverage Package. Without the package, a 4 cl shot of Ragnvald goes for €22. Now you know which one to order when you belly up to the bar on Viking.

* Laundry – All-inclusive river cruise companies may provide free laundry service during your cruise. Some companies also provide access to washers and dryers free of charge and even include the soap. Most river cruise companies offer laundry and pressing services for a fee if it's not part of an all-inclusive package. Either way, you'll likely need to do some laundry while traveling, unless you pack like I do. See What I Pack When I river Cruise, What About You? | https://www.rivercruiseadvisor.com/2018/01/pack-river-cruise/ . If you don't pack like me, you'll need laundry services. See Laundry Services: Which Cruise Lines Include Them? | https://www.rivercruiseadvisor.com/2015/02/laundry-services-which-companies-include-them/

* Optional Shore Excursions – All river cruise companies include complimentary excursions in most, if not all, ports of call. However, some companies offer optional shore excursions for a fee. Avalon, Crystal, Emerald, Riviera and Viking are among the companies that offer optional shore excursions. On my April 2017 Rhine cruise on Viking, for example, complimentary excursions were offered at each stop along the way. Viking also offered about a dozen optional tours, ranging in price from €49 per person to €189, the latter being a full-day excursion called Taste the Best of Alsace. Viking Hlin's program director, Candi Finkelstein, told me that this was the number one rated tour on the Rhine Getaway itinerary, so sometimes paying for something you would not otherwise experience is not a bad thing. On Crystal's Danube Dreams & Discoveries, more than two dozen shore excursions are offered, and most of those are complimentary. Crystal's optional shore excursions on that itinerary range from a complimentary Culinary Walking Tour in Bratislava to Michelin-star dining experiences for $249 per person. On Emerald Waterways' Danube Delights itinerary, you can pay extra for its DiscoverMORE excursions for such exclusive events as Tastes of Vienna and a Viennese Concert.

* Current Incentive (per person) – Riviera does not offer booking incentives, CroisiEurope rarely does. The rest offer a range of incentives, ranging from early-booking savings to two-for-ones and reduced or free air. The incentives are always changing so be sure to check with your travel seller or the cruise company about current offers.

* Value of Incentive (per day/pp) –I've divided the amount of the incentive by the number of nights to arrive at a per-diem value. Calculating the value of the incentives was a bit challenging, especially when it comes to air. One challenge: Free air isn't really free air. While Scenic offers free air, for example, the company caps the fare at $1,400 for its lead-in cabins. Emerald Waterways offers free air for all Horizon Deck guests (also capped at $1,400); guests on Vista Deck pay $295 and those on Riviera Deck pay $495. Viking claims its free air is a $1,699 value. When searching peak season air from my home in Asheville, North Carolina to key river cruise destinations, I found that economy air was nearly always above $1,600 per person

* Per Diem/Square Foot – Why provide a square-footage per-diem? Why not? The idea is to provide a guideline of how much space you're getting for the rate you pay for your river cruise. Though I caution that you should not plan to spend heaps of time in your room. There's too much to see and do outside of those four walls.

* Balcony Upgrade – Nearly all of the entry-level staterooms feature fixed windows. The exception is Crystal, where even entry-level staterooms on its new vessels feature "Panoramic Balcony-Windows" that raise and lower, and basically function like a balcony. CroisiEurope does not offer balconies on the majority of its vessels, but it too has windows that open, and though not as elaborate as those on Crystal, CroisiEurope's windows provide fresh air and river views. With other cruise companies, you may want to upgrade to a balcony stateroom. I've provided price differentials for upgrades to entry-level balcony staterooms. Note that some of the entry-level balcony staterooms may be smaller than entry-level fixed window staterooms.

BORDEAUX 2019 PRICE COMPARISONS

Current incentives when I compiled the chart in June of 2018: AmaWaterways, $250 off per person; CroisiEurope, 10 percent off; Scenic, fly free (capped at $1,400); Uniworld, 10 percent off when paid in full; and Viking, two cruise for the price of one and air is offered for $499 per person.

		AmaWaterways	CroisiEurope	SCENIC
	Ship	AmaDolce	Cyrano de Bergerac	Scenic Diamond
	Rate	$3,899	$3,009	$4,695
	Sailing Date	June 13, 2019	June 15, 2019	June 4, 2019
	Nights*	7	7	7
	Itinerary	Taste of Bordeaux	3 Mighty Rivers	Bordeaux Affair
	Cabin Category	Category E	Main Deck Suite	Standard suite E
	Square Footage	160	140	160
	Room With A View?	Window	Window	Window
	Per diem *	$557	$430	$671
	Port Charges *	$22.75	Included	Included
	Gratuities (on ship) *	$18	$11.25	Included
	Gratuities (on shore) *	$2.50	$2.50	Included
	Beverages *	Included	Included	Included
	Laundry *	$3	n/a	Included*
	Optional Shore Excursions *	Included	Included	Included
	Current Incentive *	$250	$310	$1,400
	Value of Incentive *	$36	$44	$200
	True Per Diem	$568	$399	$471
	Per Diem/Square Foot *	$3.55	$2.85	$2.94
	Balcony Upgrade *	$899	$329	$1,145
	Balcony Per Diem	$696	$446	$634

updated 7/1/2018

River Royale	Forseti
$3,499	$6,398
June 2, 2019	June 1, 2019
7	7
Brilliant Bordeaux	Chateaux, Rivers and Wine
Classic	Standard F
151	150
Window	Window
$500	$914
$24	Included
Included	$15.87
Included	$2.50
Included	$10
Included*	$3
Included	$12.50
$349	$4,399
$50	$628
$474	$329
$3.14	$2.20
$1,200	$400
$645	$387

DANUBE (LOWER) 2019 PRICE COMPARISONS

Current incentives when I compiled the chart in June of 2018: Avalon, $500 off per person; CroisiEurope, 10 percent off; Emerald Waterways, free air for all Horizon Deck guests; $295 for Vista Deck and $495 for Riviera Deck; Scenic, fly free (capped at $1,400); Uniworld, 10 percent off when paid in full; and Viking, two cruise for the price of one and air is offered for $500 off per person.

		AMAWATERWAYS	AVALON WATERWAYS	CroisiEurope	EMERALD WATERWAYS
	Ship	AmaCerto	Avalon Passion	Vivaldi	Emerald Dawn
	Rate	$3,599	$3,870	$3,064	$3,145
	Sailing Date	May 26, 2019	June 25, 2019	June 19, 2019	August 3, 2019
	Nights*	7	9	8	7
	Itinerary	Gems of SE Europe	Balkan Discoverer	Balkan Peninsula, Danube Delta	Lower Danube
	Cabin Category	Category E	Category D,E	Main Deck Double bed	Stateroom E
	Square Footage	160	172	140	162
	Room With A View?	Window	Window	Window	Window
	Per diem *	$514	$430	$383	$449
	Port Charges *	$22.75	$17	Included	Included
	Gratuities (on ship) *	$18	$13.44	$11.25	Included
	Gratuities (on shore) *	$2.50	$2.50	$2.50	Included
	Beverages *	Included	$10	Included	$10
	Laundry *	$3	$3	n/a	$3
	Optional Shore Excursions *	Included	$17	Included	$12.50
	Current Incentive *	n/a	$500	$306	$905
	Value of Incentive *	n/a	$56	$38	$129
	True Per Diem	$560	$437	$359	$346
	Per Diem/Square Foot *	$3.50	$2.54	$2.56	$2.13
	Balcony Upgrade *	$899	$814	$365	$650
	Balcony Per Diem	$689	$528	$404	$438

updated 7/1/2018

Riviera Travel	Scenic Luxury Cruises & Tours	Tauck	Uniworld	Viking River Cruises
Thomas Hardy	Scenic Crystal	Treasure	Beatrice	Embla
$4,859	$4,815	$6,990	$3,999	$7,798
June 3, 2019	May 22, 2019	June 25, 2019	June 3, 2019	June 3, 2019
14	8	11	9	10
Budapest to Black Sea	Black Sea Explorer	Budapest to Black Sea	Highlights of Eastern Europe	Passage to Eastern Europe
Emerald lower	Jewel E	Category 1	Classic	Standard F
172	160	150	160	150
Window	Window	Window	Window	Window
$347	$602	$635	$444	$780
Included	Included	Included	$19	Included
$10.00	Included	Included	Included	$15.87
$2.00	Included	Included	Included	$2.50
$21.35	Included	Included	Included	$10
$3	Included	$3	Included*	$3
n/a	Included	Included	Included	$12.50
n/a	$1,400	$0	$399	$4,399
n/a	$175	$0	$44	$440
$383	$427	$638	$419	$384
$2.23	$2.67	$4.25	$2.62	$2.56
$690	$1,000	$400	$900	$600
$433	$552	$674	$544	$444

DANUBE 2019 PRICE COMPARISONS

Current incentives when I compiled the chart in June of 2018: AmaWaterways, Avalon, $250 off per person; Emerald Waterways, free air for all Horizon Deck guests; $295 for Vista Deck and $495 for Riviera Deck; CroisiEurope, 10 percent off; Crystal $1,465 savings; Scenic, fly free (capped at $1,400); Uniworld, 10 percent off when paid in full; and Viking, two cruise for the price of one and air is offered for $499 per person.

		AmaWaterways	Avalon Waterways	CroisiEurope	Crystal River Cruises
	Ship	AmaSonata	Avalon Visionary	ms Beethoven	Crystal Ravel
	Rate	$3,599	$2,209	$2,339	$5,860
	Sailing Date	June 7, 2019	June 4, 2019	July 1, 2019	June 2, 2019
	Nights*	7	7	7	7
	Itinerary	Romantic Danube	A Taste Of The Danube	Danube	Danube Dreams & Discovery
	Cabin Category	Category E	Category D,E	Main Deck Suite	Petite Suite
	Square Footage	160	172	140	188
	Room With A View?	Fixed Window	Window	Window	Pano balcony window
	Per diem *	$514	$316	$334	$837
	Port Charges *	$22.75	$10	Included	$22
	Gratuities (on ship) *	$18	$11.25	$11.25	Included
	Gratuities (on shore) *	$2.50	$2.50	$2.50	Included
	Beverages *	Happy Hour Included	$10	Included	Included
	Laundry *	$3	$3	n/a	Included***
	Optional Shore Excursions *	Included	$19	Included	$37.50
	Current Incentive *	$250	$250	$234	$1,495
	Value of Incentive *	$36	$36	$33	$209
	True Per Diem	$525	$335	$314	$687
	Per Diem/Square Foot *	$3.28	$1.95	$2.25	$3.66
	Balcony Upgrade *	$899	$493	$260	$0
	Balcony Per Diem	$653	$386	$352	$687

updated 7/1/2018

EMERALD WATERWAYS	RIVIERA TRAVEL	SCENIC° LUXURY CRUISES & TOURS	TAUCK	UNIWORLD	VIKING RIVER CRUISES
Emerald Sky	Ms Charles Dickens	Scenic Crystal	ms joy	SS Beatrice	Egil
$3,095	$2,439	$4,745	$7,290	$3,699	$6,598
June 7, 2019	June 2, 2019	June 12, 2019	June 10, 2019	June 12, 2019	June 1, 2019
7	7	7	11	7	7
Danube Delights	Blue Danube	Gems of the Danube	Blue Danube	Delightful Danube	Romantic Danube
Stateroom E	Lower deck standard	Standard suite E	Category 1	Classic	Standard F
162	151	160	150	150	150
Picture window	Fixed window	Picture window	Fixed window	Fixed	Picture window
$442	$348	$678	$663	$528	$943
Included	Included	Included	Included	$24.28	Included
Included	$10	Included	Included	Included	$15.87
Included	$2.50	Included	Included	Included	$2.50
$10	$22.71	Included	Included	Included	$10
$3	$3	Included*	$3	Included*	$3
$12.50	$12.50	Included	Included	Included	$12.50
$905	n/a	$1,400	4 night hotel	$369	$4,499
$119	$0	$200	n/a	$53	$643
$338	$399	$478	$665	$500	$344
$2.09	$2.64	$2.99	$4.43	$3.33	$2.29
$650	$510	$1,000	$400	$900	$500
$431	$472	$621	$701	$629	$415

DOURO 2019 PRICE COMPARISONS

Current incentives when I compiled the chart in June of 2018: AmaWaterways, $250 off per person; Emerald Waterways, free air for all Horizon Deck guests; $295 for Vista Deck and $495 for Riviera Deck; CroisiEurope, 10 percent off; Scenic, fly free (capped at $1,400); Uniworld, 10 percent off when paid in full; and Viking, two cruise for the price of one and air is offered for $1,299 per person.

		AmaWaterways	CroisiEurope	Emerald
	Ship	AmaDouro	Gil Eanes	Emerald Radiance
	Rate	$3,799	$2,982	$3,645
	Sailing Date	June 8, 2019	June 15, 2019	June 8, 2019
	Nights*	7	7	7
	Itinerary	Enticing Douro	From Portugal to Spain	Secrets of the Douro
	Cabin Category	Category E	Middle deck	Stateroom F
	Square Footage	161	129	162
	Room With A View?	Window	Window	Window
	Per diem *	$543	$426	$521
	Port Charges *	$26	Included	Included
	Gratuities (on ship) *	$18	$11.25	Included
	Gratuities (on shore) *	$2.50	$2.50	Included
	Beverages *	Included	Included	$10
	Laundry *	$3	n/a	$3
	Optional Shore Excursions *	Included	Included	$12.50
	Current Incentive *	$250	$298	$905
	Value of Incentive *	$36	$43	$129
	True Per Diem	$557	$397	$417
	Per Diem/Square Foot *	$3.46	$3.08	$2.57
	Balcony Upgrade *	$1,399	$329	$300
	Balcony Per Diem	$756	$444	$460

updated 7/1/2018

RIVIERA TRAVEL	SCENIC° LUXURY CRUISES & TOURS	UNIWORLD.	VIKING RIVER CRUISES
Douro Splendour	Scenic Azure	Queen Isabel	Viking Torgil
$3,119	$4,195	$4,799	$8,398
June 2, 2019	June 4, 2019	June 16, 2019	June 4, 2019
7	7	7	9
Douro, Porto, Salamanca	Delightful Douro	Portugal, Spain, Douro	River of Gold
Lower deck standard	Standard suite E	Classic	Standard F
129	160	161	155
Window	Window	Window	Window
$446	$599	$686	$933
Included	Included	$24	Included
$10.00	Included	Included	$15.87
$2.50	Included	Included	$2.50
$22.71	Included	Included	$10
$3	Included*	Included*	$3
$12.50	Included	Included	$12.50
n/a	$1,400	$479	$4,599
$0	$200	$68	$511
$496	$399	$641	$466
$3.85	$2.50	$3.98	$3.01
$510	sold out	$800	$800
$569	sold out	$755	$555

RHINE 2019 PRICE COMPARISONS

Current incentives when I compiled the chart in June of 2018: AmaWaterways, Avalon, $250 off per person; Emerald Waterways, free air for all Horizon Deck guests; $295 for Vista Deck and $495 for Riviera Deck; CroisiEurope, 10 percent off; Crystal $1,465 savings; Scenic, fly free (capped at $1,400); Uniworld, 10 percent off when paid in full; and Viking, two cruise for the price of one and air is offered for $499 per person.

		AMAWATERWAYS	AVALON WATERWAYS	CroisiEurope	CRYSTAL RIVER CRUISES
	Ship	AmaMora	Avalon Vista	Douce France	Crystal Debussy
	Rate	$3,599	$3,399	$3,265	$5,860
	Sailing Date	June 3, 2019	June 1, 2019	June 15, 2019	June 12, 2019
	Nights*	7	7	8	7
	Itinerary	Captivating Rhine	Romantic Rhine	Basel To Amsterdam	Legendary Rhine
	Cabin Category	Category E	Category D,E	Main Deck Double bed	Petite Suite
	Square Footage	160	172	140	188
	Room With A View?	Window	Window	Window	Balcony window
	Per diem *	$514	$486	$408	$837
	Port Charges *	$22.75	$26	Included	$22
	Gratuities (on ship) *	$18	$12.86	$11.25	Included
	Gratuities (on shore) *	$2.50	$2.50	$2.50	Included
	Beverages *	Included	$10	Included	Included
	Laundry *	$3	$3	n/a	Included***
	Optional Shore Excursions *	Included	$19	Included	$37.50
	Current Incentive *	$250	$250	$327	$1,465
	Value of Incentive *	$36	$36	$41	$209
	True Per Diem	$525	$523	$381	$687
	Per Diem/Square Foot *	$3.28	$3.04	$2.72	$3.66
	Balcony Upgrade *	$599	$1,149	$365	$0
	Balcony Per Diem	$610	$687	$427	$687

updated 7/1/2018

EMERALD WATERWAYS	RIVIERA TRAVEL	SCENIC LUXURY CRUISES & TOURS	TAUCK	UNIWORLD	VIKING RIVER CRUISES
Emerald Sky	Emily Bronte	Scenic Opal	Inspire	Antoinette	Einar
$3,195	$2,929	$4,195	$4,990	$3,999	$6,598
June 28, 2019	June 6, 2019	June 24, 2019	July 8, 2019	June 2, 2019	June 12, 2019
7	7	7	7	7	7
Rhine to Switzerland	Rhine Highlights	Romantic Rhine	Romantic Rhine	Castles Along the Rhine	Rhine Getaway
Emerald Deck Suite	Standard suite E	Category 1	Category 1	Classic	Standard F
172	160	150	150	163	150
Window	Window	Window	Window	Window	Window
$456	$418	$599	$713	$571	$943
Included	Included	Included	Included	$24	Included
Included	$10	Included	Included	Included	$15.87
Included	$2.50	Included	Included	Included	$2.50
$10	$22.71	Included	Included	Included	$10
$3	$3	Included*	$3	Included*	$3
$12.50	Included	Included	Included	Included	$12.50
$905	$0	$1,400	$0	$399	$4,499
$129	$0	$200	$0	$57	$643
$353	$469	$399	$713	$538	$344
$2.18	$2.73	$2.50	$4.75	$3.30	$2.29
$650	$520	$1000	$400	$900	$300
$446	$543	$542	$770	$667	$387

RHINE-MAIN-DANUBE 2019 PRICE COMPARISONS

Current incentives when I compiled the chart in June of 2018: AmaWaterways, $500 per person off; Avalon, $1,000 per person off; CroisiEurope, 10 percent off; Crystal savings of $4,020; Emerald Waterways, free air for all Horizon Deck guests; $295 for Vista Deck and $495 for Riviera Deck; Scenic, fly free (capped at $1,400); Uniworld offers 10 percent off when paid in full; and Viking offers two for one cruises and free air.

	AMAWATERWAYS	AVALON WATERWAYS	CroisiEurope	CRYSTAL RIVER CRUISES
Ship	AmaStella	Imagery II	L'Europe	Crystal Mahler
Rate	$6,899	$6,748	$5,445	$13,400
Sailing Date	June 2, 2019	June 20, 2019	April 9, 2019	June 5, 2019
Nights*	14	14	18	15
Itinerary	Magnificent Europe	Jewels of Central Europe	BUD-AMS	Grand Europe
Cabin Category	Category	Category D,	Main Deck	Petite Suite S
Square Footage	160	172	150	188
Room With A View?	Window	Window	Window	Balcony window
Per diem *	$493	$482	$303	$893
Port Charges *	$22.75	$26	Included	$13
Gratuities (on ship) *	$18	$18	$11.25	Included
Gratuities (on shore) *	$2.50	$2.50	$2.50	Included
Beverages *	Included	$10	Included	Included
Laundry *	$3	$3	n/a	Included
Optional Shore Excursions *	Included	$11	Included	$20.00
Current Incentive *	$500	$1,000	$545	$4,020
Value of Incentive *	$36	$71	$30	$268
True Per Diem	$503	$481	$286	$661
Per Diem/Square Foot *	$3.15	$2.80	$1.91	$3.52
Balcony Upgrade *	$1,198	$2,298	$545	$0
Balcony Per Diem	$589	$645	$316	$661

updated 7/1/2018

EMERALD WATERWAYS	RIVIERA TRAVEL	SCENIC° LUXURY CRUISES & TOURS	TAUCK	UNIWORLD	VIKING RIVER CRUISES
Emerald Star	Charles Dickens	Scenic Jewel	Esprit	River Duchess	Mimir
$5,295	$4,549	$7,495	$8,590	$7,299	$11,598
June 10, 2019	June 23, 2019	June 10, 2019	June 16, 2019	June 14, 2019	June 7, 2019
14	14	14	14	15	14
Splendors of Europe	Heart of Europe	Jewels of Europe	BUD-AMS	European Jewels	Grand European Tour
Stateroom E	Lower Deck	Standard suite E	Category 1	Category 5	Standard
162	151	160	150	151	150
Window	Window	Window	Window	Window	Window
$378	$325	$506	$614	$487	$828
Included	Included	Included	Included	$11	Included
Included	10	Included	Included	Included	$15.87
Included	2.5	Included	Included	Included	$2.50
$10	$23	Included	Included	Included	$10
$3	$3	Included	$3	Included	$3
$12.50	$12.50	Included	Included	Included	$12.50
$905	$0	$1,400	n/a	$730	$7,498
$65	$0	$100	$0	$49	$536
$339	$376	$406	$617	$449	$293
$2.09	$2.49	$2.54	$4.11	$2.98	$1.95
$300	$690	$1,995	$650	$1,710	$1,100
$361	$425	$549	$663	$563	$371

RHONE 2019 PRICE COMPARISONS

Current incentives when I compiled the chart in June of 2018: AmaWaterways, $250 off per person; Avalon, $1,000 off per person; CroisiEurope, 10 percent off; Emerald Waterways, free air for all Horizon Deck guests; $295 for Vista Deck and $495 for Riviera Deck; Scenic, fly free (capped at $1,400); Uniworld, 10 percent off when paid in full; and Viking, two cruise for the price of one and air is offered for $499 per person.

	AmaWaterways	Avalon Waterways	CroisiEurope	Emerald Waterways
Ship	AmaCello	Avalon Poetry II	Camargue	Emerald Liberte
Rate	$3,899	$4,049	$2,733	$3,495
Sailing Date	June 6, 2019	June 25, 2019	July 20, 2019	June 8, 2019
Nights*	7	7	7	7
Itinerary	Colors of Provence	Active Discovery	Burgundy - Camargue	Sensations of Southern France
Cabin Category	Category E	Category D,E	Main Deck Double bed	Stateroom E
Square Footage	170	172	140	162
Room With A View?	Window	Window	Window	Window
Per diem *	$557	$578	$390	$499
Port Charges *	$22.75	$26	Included	Included
Gratuities (on ship) *	$18	$18	$11.25	Included
Gratuities (on shore) *	$2.50	$2.50	$2.50	Included
Beverages *	Included	$10	Included	$10
Laundry *	$3	$3	n/a	$3
Optional Shore Excursions *	Included	$19	Included	$12.50
Current Incentive *	$250	$1,000	$273	$905
Value of Incentive *	$36	$143	$39	$129
True Per Diem	$568	$514	$365	$396
Per Diem/Square Foot *	$3.34	$2.99	$2.61	$2.44
Balcony Upgrade *	$899	$1,149	$322	$500
Balcony Per Diem	$696	$678	$411	$467

updated 7/1/2018

Riviera Travel	Scenic	Tauck	Uniworld	Viking River Cruises
William Shakespeare	Scenic Sapphire	Emerald	Catherine	Heimdal
$2,859	$5,445	$6,990	$4,199	$5,998
June 3, 2019	May 19, 2019	June 2, 2019	June 2, 2019	June 18, 2019
7	8	10	7	7
Burgundy, River Rhone	Enchanting Rhone	Savoring France	Burgundy & Provence	Lyon & Provence
Romeo lower deck	Standard suite E	Category 1	Classic	Standard F
151	160	150	162	150
Window	Window	Window	Window	Window
$408	$681	$699	$600	$857
Included	Included	Included	$24	Included
$10.00	Included	Included	Included	$15.87
$2.00	Included	Included	Included	$2.50
$22.71	Included	Included	Included	$10
$3	Included*	$3	Included*	$3
$12.50	Included	Included	Included	$12.50
n/a	$1,400	2 night Paris hotel inc	$419	$4,199
$0	$175		$60	$600
$459	$506	$702	$564	$301
$3.04	$3.16	$4.68	$3.48	$2.01
$510	$1,145	$400	$900	$400
$462	$649	$742	$693	$358

SEINE 2019 PRICE COMPARISONS

Current incentives when I compiled the chart in June of 2018: AmaWaterways and Avalon, $250 off per person; CroisiEurope, 10 percent off; Scenic, fly free (capped at $1,400); Uniworld, 10 percent off when paid in full; and Viking, two cruise for the price of one and reduced air

		AMAWATERWAYS	AVALON WATERWAYS	CroisiEurope
	Ship	AmaLyra	Tapestry II	Seine Princesse
	Rate	$3,899	$3,699	$2,531
	Sailing Date	June 13, 2019	June 11, 2019	July 27, 2019
	Nights*	7	7	7
	Itinerary	Paris & Normandy	Paris to Normandy	The Seine Valley
	Cabin Category	Category E	Category D,E	Main Deck Double bed
	Square Footage	170	172	118
	Room With A View?	Window	Window	Window
	Per diem *	$557	$528	$362
	Port Charges *	$22.75	$26	Included
	Gratuities (on ship) *	$18	$18.00	$11.25
	Gratuities (on shore) *	$2.50	$2.50	$2.50
	Beverages *	Included	$10	Included
	Laundry *	$3	$3	n/a
	Optional Shore Excursions *	Included	$19	Included
	Current Incentive *	$250	$250	$253
	Value of Incentive *	$36	$36	$36
	True Per Diem	$568	$571	$339
	Per Diem/Square Foot *	$3.34	$3.32	$2.87
	Balcony Upgrade *	$899	$1,149	$329
	Balcony Per Diem	$696	$735	$386

updated 7/1/2018

SCENIC°	TAUCK❀	UNIWORLD.	VIKING RIVER CRUISES
Scenic Gem	Sapphire	Joie du Vivre	Rolf
$4,695	$5,790	$4,499	$6,398
July 31, 2019	May 24, 2019	June 16, 2019	June 8, 2019
7	7	7	7
Highlights of Normandy & Seine	Impressions from the Seine	Paris & Normandy	Paris & Heart of Normandy
Standard suite E	Category 1	Category 5	Standard F
160	150	163	150
Window	Window	Window	Window
$671	$827	$643	$914
Included	Included	$24.28	Included
Included	Included	Included	$15.87
Included	Included	Included	$2.50
Included	Included	Included	$10
Included*	$3	Included*	$3
Included	Included	Included	$12.50
$1,400	$0	$449	$4,498
$200	$0	$64	$643
$471	$830	$603	$315
$2.94	$5.53	$3.70	$2.10
$1,100	$340	$900	$400
$628	$879	$731	$372

83417438R00153

Made in the USA
San Bernardino, CA
24 July 2018